SMUGGLING
in the British Isles

County Council

Libraries, books and more . . .

WML

	2 1 MAR 2022	
~~CONISTON~~		
1 3 DEC 2016		
2 0 NOV 2017		
2 3 FEB 2018		
0 7 MAY 2019		
2 3 JUL 2019		
– 8 AUG 2019		
2 8 AUG 2019		
1 6 MAR 2020		

Cumbria Library Services

cumbria.gov.uk/libraries

CL9

Ask for a CLIC password

SMUGGLING
in the British Isles
A HISTORY

RICHARD PLATT

TEMPUS

First published 2007

Tempus Publishing
Cirencester Road, Chalford
Stroud, Gloucestershire, GL6 8PE
www.tempus-publishing.com

Tempus Publishing is an imprint of NPI Media Group

Portions of the text first appeared in the *Ordnance Survey
Guide to Smugglers' Britain* published by Cassell 1991

British Library Cataloguing in Publication Data.
A catalogue record for this book is available from the British Library.

ISBN 978 0 7524 4249 5

Typesetting and origination by NPI Media Group
Printed and bound in Great Britain

CONTENTS

To Bill. Thanks for keeping Mum.

PREFACE

The explosion of import smuggling that took place in the eighteenth and early nineteenth centuries has been absorbed into the public consciousness leaving only the vaguest of traces. The smugglers gave us phrases such as 'on the spot' and 'the coast is clear', yet they remain, at least in most people's minds, shadowy, romantic figures. I became interested in this period of Britain's history while researching a popular magazine article on the subject, and though I found the story fascinating, I was surprised and disappointed to discover that there were no books in print on smuggling. The book you are reading is an attempt to remedy this situation.

In researching the book, I read many volumes that purported to be histories of smuggling. In reality, most of them were histories of the prevention of smuggling, or of the customs and excise services. This is perfectly understandable: historians prefer to work from primary sources whenever possible, and by the very nature of the game, smugglers left few accurate and detailed records of their activities. Their adversaries in the service of the Crown were, by contrast, prolific correspondents, and in the Public Record Office at Kew there are hundreds of thousands of letters and other documents that deal with the minutiae of life in the country's custom houses. I am not an historian, and early on I came to the conclusion that the story of smuggling is far more interesting than the story of its prevention. I therefore tried whenever possible to write about smuggling from the point of view of those who broke the law, not those who enforced it.

To find this perspective, I left the carefully paved and reliable road of official revenue records. I branched off onto the muddy and rutted paths of traditional yarns, folk tales, and Recollections of the Oldest Inhabitant. I hope the result will please those who are fascinated by tales of smuggling and smugglers. By the same token, this book may well irritate historians. I have shamelessly included a great deal of hearsay and many unverified assertions, and for the sake of clarity, I have used a few revenue terms – such as 'preventive' – in a rather loose way.

This is not to say that I have accepted as fact every yarn I heard and read. On the contrary, I have more often tended towards scepticism. But if a story seemed plausible, I've said so.

SCOPE

In the course of my research, I visited most of the places on the British mainland and the Isle of Wight about which I have written. The exceptions are the most remote areas, and those where I found little evidence of smuggling. Specifically, I stayed south and east of a line drawn between Stranraer and Inverness, and I omitted most of the West Coast between Liverpool and Carlisle.

WEBSITE

This book has a linked website. At www.smuggling.co.uk you can find a comprehensive gazetteer of places assosicated with the history of British smuggling. Interactive maps and directions pinpoint each spot that's worth visiting. Following them will take you to the tunnels, pubs, churches, graves and caves mentioned on the pages that follow. There is also an abbreviated history of smuggling, and many more old engravings and modern photographs. The appendix of this book, on tracing your ancestors, is also on the site, with live links so that you don't have to type in long URLs.

CREDITS

12 'Folkstone' from a watercolour painted 1822 by J.M.W. Turner (1775–1851) and engraved by R. Wallis.

13 'The Smugglers Attacked' by S.J.E. Jones; aquatint by Charles Hunt. Published by J. Moore, London *c*.1830.

14 'Arched Rock, Isle of Wight' by Clarkson Stanfield. Engraved by W. Chevalier for Stanfield's 1836 *Coast Scenery*.

15–23 All these images are from *Smuggling and Smugglers in Sussex*, originally published in 1749. The engraver is not credited.

All other illustrations in the book are by Jack Matthew (b. 1911). They first appeared in J. Jefferson Farejeon's book *The Compleat Smuggler*. With the exception of the image on page 164, which was originally entitled 'Riding officer and dragoons' these pictures appeared as tailpieces without captions. I am indebted to Elaine O'Donoghue at Chambers Harrap Publishers, and to Anne Harvey, for the help they gave me in my (ultimately unsuccessful) attempt to track down Jack Matthew or the present copyright holder.

QUOTATIONS

I am grateful to the following for permission to quote from works for which they hold the copyright:

Page 21 from John William Burrows *Southend-on-Sea and district: historical notes*, 1909. Courtesy of Echo Newspapers (Newsquest Essex).

Page 73 from *Cornish Seafarers by Alfred Jenkins*. Courtesy of J.M. Dent & Sons, a division of the Orion Publishing Group.

ACKNOWLEDGEMENTS

I received an enormous amount of help in writing *Smuggling in the British Isles*, but I am indebted to a few people in particular.

The staff of the British Library, then still at Bloomsbury, helped me track down hundreds of obscure references, and branch librarians all over the country responded to my letters with photocopies of their local archives. The staff of the Customs and Excise Library at King's Beam House helped me in the early stages of my research.

My thanks to the Flat Holm project, and especially the Project Officer, Dr D.H. Worral and the Island Warden, Andrew Gibson, for letting me visit the island and ferrying me out.

Also to Paul Muskett for his permission to quote from his unpublished thesis *English Smuggling in the Eighteenth Century* – even though I didn't.

Robin Wood provided some early encouragement.

Many thanks also to ...

Blue Circle Heritage Trust

Foulkes-Halbard of Filching

Margate Caves

Parham Park

Post Office Postcode Services

The Three Daws Inn, Gravesend

The many people who shared their knowledge of the smuggling trade with me.

The friends who provided meals and beds during my travels, and endured my countless smuggling yarns!

I

INTRODUCTION

A smuggler is …

'a person who, though no doubt highly blamable for violating the laws of his country, is frequently incapable of violating those of natural justice, and would have been, in every respect, an excellent citizen had not the laws of his country made that a crime which nature never meant to be so.'

Adam Smith *An Inquiry into the Nature And Causes of the Wealth of Nations*, 1776, Book Five, Chapter II Article IV

Ask anyone to describe an eighteenth-century smuggler, and they will probably tell you about a Cornishman called Tom dressed in long boots and a striped jersey. He rolls a couple of kegs up a moonlit beach, hides them in a cave, then hawks the brandy round the village. Everybody knows him as Tom the Smuggler, and his neighbours take it in turns to distract the revenue man at the front door while Tom rolls his barrels out the back.

How accurate is this traditional picture of the smuggler? On the one hand it is a romantic impression that doesn't accurately reflect the historical facts about smuggling at any one place or time. However, it might be argued that the substance (though not the letter) of this popular image correctly represents the extraordinary circumstances that supported a vast expansion of illegal imports in the eighteenth and early nineteenth centuries.

But before considering the true story, let's look briefly at the errors: for a start, our real smuggler was just as likely to have been called Jacque or even Hans as Tom; the story would probably have taken place in Kent on a stormy, pitch-black night, rather than on a benign Cornish coast, floodlit by a full moon. There's a good chance that the contraband was tea, not cognac, and the cave is possibly romantic embroidery, too. The revenue man would have received a bump on the head, rather than a discreet diversion. However, as for Tom's (or Jacque's) relationship with his customers, and their attitude towards the revenue man, there's every reason to believe that, for many years and in many places, the picture is an accurate one. Now let's look beyond the myths, at what really happened ...

In the eighteenth century illegal transport of taxable goods across England's coast mushroomed. 'Free-trade' that had previously been mostly small-scale evasion of duty turned into an industry of astonishing proportions, siphoning money abroad, and channelling huge volumes of contraband into the southern counties of England.

Even by modern standards, the quantities of imported goods were extraordinary. It was not unheard of for a smuggling trip to bring in 3,000 gallons of spirits; to picture this in your mind's eye, imagine some 1,500 cases of brandy stacked in your garage. Illegally imported gin was sometimes so plentiful that the inhabitants of some Kentish villages were said to use it for cleaning their windows. And according to some contemporary estimates, four-fifths of all tea drunk in England had not paid duty.

Statistics like this are even more extraordinary when seen in the context of the available transport technology. The first steam-powered ships appeared only in the early years of the nineteenth century, so sailing ships brought the goods from the Continent, and kegs and bales were man-handled – often up sheer cliffs – to waiting files of men. These carriers then transported the goods in carts or caravans of ponies, or lashed the tubs to their own backs for a journey inland.

Whole communities connived in the trade, and profited from it. The Scilly Isles, for example, was totally reliant on smuggling for its survival, and the islanders were brought to the point of starvation when prevention measures were stepped up in the area. A large cargo drained cash from the area where it landed: in Shetland and around Falmouth there were times when residents had spent every coin they had on contraband. And there are numerous instances of whole communities uniting and taking up arms to reclaim cargoes that had been seized by the revenue. For example, in 1801 smugglers had no trouble in enlisting the help of Deal residents when the revenue men forced a smuggling lugger onto the town beach. The mob attacked the luckless preventives, and brought ashore the cargo of tobacco, playing cards and bolts of fine cloth. Sixteen years later, blockademen who were attempting to arrest some local smugglers were set upon by a mob of local people, and had to shelter in a shop. A further insult followed: the Mayor of Deal ordered the arrest of the blockademen, accusing them of assault on the free-traders!

This extraordinary situation was not the result of some plan or a plot hatched in a smugglers' tunnel. Rather, it was a natural and inevitable result of punitive taxation imposed by a succession of governments each more desperate than the last to pay for costly wars in Europe.

Eighteenth-century taxation fell into two categories; each administered and collected by a separate government department. *Customs* duties had a historical precedent in that the English Crown had for centuries claimed a proportion of all cargoes entering the country – or a financial levy in lieu of the fine wine or bolts of fabric. In 1688, the customs duties were streamlined and restructured into a form that would – in theory at least – generate more revenue for the Exchequer.

The other type of duty had its origins in the Civil War: a tax on land took the place of two older taxes – wardship and the parliamentary subsidy – and a new tax, *excise*, was levied specially to pay for the war. Excise was a tax on domestic consumption, and during the years of the Civil War it covered many different items, but its scope was reduced ten years later to cover just chocolate, coffee, tea, beer, cider and spirits. However, after 1688 it was progressively widened again to include other essentials such as salt, leather and soap.

The separation of these two taxes mattered not a jot to the common man, who knew only that he had to pay more for what he bought. As the eighteenth century progressed, the slice taken by the Exchequer increased sometimes steadily and progressively, sometimes by leaps and bounds, as the conflicts with France ebbed and flowed. By the middle of the century, the tax on tea was nearly 70 per cent of its initial cost. Britain's rural population was often close to starvation and resented the double burden of customs and excise duties.

Collection of the customs duties was haphazard and bureaucratic and was largely based on a system, established in the thirteenth century, of *custom houses* at ports around the coast. In the ensuing centuries a creaking and corrupt hierarchy had grown up around the custom houses. The collectors and comptrollers of customs and their multitude of functionaries were primarily concerned with taxation on the export of the wool that made England wealthy. When the dawn of the eighteenth century heralded heavy taxation on *imports*, the system was ill-fitted to combat the spirited efforts of large numbers of Englishmen determined to defraud the King.

We'll return to look in more detail at the historical background to smuggling. But to understand how smugglers operated, it's enough to know that they were opportunists, taking advantage of a demand for heavily taxed luxury goods and the state's almost total inability to collect those taxes. The early chapters of the book explain the mechanics and economics of smuggling, from raising the money to pay for the cargo, through the crossing itself, and concluding with the methods of distribution and sale of the contraband. Subsequent chapters look at how smuggling varied geographically and through time. The book concludes with a comparison of the smuggling stereotype with the reality of the free-trade.

2

WHO WERE THE SMUGGLERS?

If you've ever spent time delving into the local history of a coastal area, you'll sooner or later have come across notes to the effect that 'everybody in these parts is a smuggler' or 'every house is a smuggler's'.

In 1860 the poet Sidney Dobell wrote of Niton, on the Isle of Wight:

> The whole population ... are smugglers. Everyone has an ostensible occupation, but nobody gets his money by it, or cares to work in it. Here are fishermen who never fish, but always have pockets full of money, and farmers whose farming consists in ploughing the deep by night, and whose daily time is spent standing like herons on lookout posts.[1]

Daniel Defoe wrote of Lymington in 1724 that: 'I do not find they have any foreign commerce, except it be what we call smuggling, and roguing, which I may say, is the reigning commerce of all this part of the English coast'.[2]

Twenty-one years later Fanny Burney had a similar opinion of Deal:

> There are said to be in the town of Deal, not less than two hundred young men and sea-faring people, who are known to have no visible way of getting a living, but by the infamous trade of smuggling ... This smuggling has converted those employed in it, first from honest industrious fishermen, to lazy, drunken and profligate smugglers.

If Britain's coastal population couldn't all be branded as smugglers, they at least connived in the trade. John Wesley, for example, noted of St Ives that 'well-night one and all bought and sold uncustomed goods'.

While many such reports were no doubt wildly exaggerated, it's probably true that, at certain times and in certain areas, everybody really was involved in smuggling in one way or another, or at least stood to benefit by its continuing. The menial farm labourer helped carry goods inland; the parson bought cheap tea and wine; the local squire lent his horses for transport; the wealthy merchant obtained cut-price supplies of silks and lace; and at the very pinnacle of society, members of the gentry conducted foreign business through intermediaries involved in smuggling.

When their ships came in, all these people made haste for the beach to look after their interests. So when five luggers unloaded at Arish Mell beach near Lulworth Cove in 1719 there was ... 'A perfect fair on the waterside, some buying of goods, and others loading of horses ... there was an army of people, armed and in disguise, as many in number as ... at Dorchester fair.'

RICH AND INFLUENTIAL

Those in disguise were quite possibly figures of some importance locally, for smuggling was not the monopoly of seamen and those who worked on the land. Though influence provided immunity from prosecution life was much simpler if identification was impossible.

Attempts at disguise were not always effective. When a cargo of fine French wine was seized at Talacre in North Wales, a party of 'Mostyn colliers' attacked the Lletty Gonest inn where the revenue men had taken the cargo. They kidnapped the guards, and rescued the wine, which had been intended for the local gentry. The son of the landlord observed wryly that the 'colliers' wore valuable diamond rings, and fine clothes underneath their dirty rags.

This was not the only place where the wealthy and powerful were widely implicated in the free-trade. In 1770 the Mayor of Penzance was bound over with a large financial surety, to cease smuggling. He clearly lacked influential friends, for farther east the gentry did not fear prosecution:

> Sir William Wyndham patronised the smugglers, the port of Watchet, his town, being used to escape the customs house at Minehead, and growing exceedingly rich from that cause. Col. Luttrell, who owned Minehead, was similarly indisposed to help the preventive officers.[3]

The first Earl of Malmesbury (1746–1820) remarked that around Bournemouth ... All classes contributed to [smuggling] ... the farmers lent their teams and labourers, and the gentry openly connived at the practise and dealt with the smugglers. An incident on the sands at Conwy in 1712 shows how influential friends and customers put smugglers beyond the reach of the law. A smuggled shipment of salt arrived on the beach and the local population turned out en masse to unload it. They arrived with carts to carry off the contraband, and at the head of the procession was a baronet and JP Sir Griffith Williams. A lone customs officer had the misfortune to observe the spectacle, and immediately lay down in the sand in case he should be spotted himself. He was – the smugglers beat him, blindfolded him and tied him up. He was imprisoned in a hen-house for a day and a night. When he reported the incident, the official could get nothing done about his ill-treatment, let alone about the smuggling, because he was accusing people who, if not well-placed themselves, at least enjoyed the protection of the wealthy and famous.

Other Welsh JPs took a more theatrical approach in their support for the free-trade. At Solva:

> a spy informed Mr Raymond, the justice … that a vessel had just come in and that they had salt smuggled aboard. Mr Raymond, who privately sympathised with the poor smugglers and was anxious not to convict the smugglers in this case, came slowly over the hill, roaring like a lion. 'I'll punish the rascals! They shan't thieve from his most gracious majesty, my beloved king. I'll salt the d – ls'. Those in the vessel below heard every word – as he intended. Hailing the men and demanding a boat, he hunted the vessel through. Needless to say, no salt was found. But tradition says that the specific gravity of the salt water in Solva harbour that evening was much heavier than usual.[4]

JP and diarist William Bulkeley, who lived in North Anglesey in the mid-eighteenth century, regularly bought smuggled goods. From a Flintshire man plying between the Isle of Man and Wales, the squire bought white wine, good claret and French brandy at 5s a gallon. In 1750 he mournfully recorded that:

> On account of a very penal law being passed last Session of Parliament against the running of soap and candles, there will soon be no soap to be had, but what comes from Chester at 7d a pound. I bought today of a woman in that business 20lb almost (which I am afraid is the last I shall have of her).[5]

When he sat on the bench at Beaumaris Bulkeley was lenient towards smugglers, and tried to discharge them without punishment at every opportunity. However, there is no evidence in his diaries that pressure was brought to bear to secure lighter sentences.

Another magistrate, John Harriott, was equally candid about his dealings with smugglers. In his 1815 book *Struggles Through Life* he described how he hitched a lift from France to his home at Stambridge. He knew that smugglers from nearby Paglesham plied to Dunkirk, so he went there in search of them:

> … purporting to get home to Essex by the nearest passage, I took my road to this port, being pretty certain of finding smuggling vessels from that part of

England, with whom I made no doubt of obtaining a ready passage to within a
few miles of my house.

Harriott was dropped off less than 2 miles from his home. His account is made
more colourful by his description of the time he spent drinking at the inn before
the Paglesham smugglers arrived. While waiting he handed his pistols – 'my constant travelling companions' – to the landlady, and thus gave a nearby group of
free-traders the impression that he too was a smuggler. They told him that the Essex
men 'Emberson, Bligh or Brown' (see page 176), were expected imminently, and
Harriott sat to drink with them. When he refused to drink a toast to the destruction
of the revenue services, Harriott was assaulted by his fellow drinkers. He wagered
that he could prove that the oath was a false one, and proceeded to argue that without revenue men and laws to prevent or tax imports, there would be no smugglers
and they would all be poorer men. Harriott's eloquence persuaded them and the
smugglers incongruously drank a toast to 'revenue laws and officers for ever'!

GIN UNDER THE PULPIT

When Russell Thorndike created his fictional smuggling vicar Doctor Syn in 1915 he
was simply dramatising a longstanding and mutually beneficial association between
the Church and the free-traders. Though real vicars did not play such an active and
swashbuckling part as 'the Scarecrow of Romney Marsh' many of them bought contraband and – willingly or not – assisted the smugglers. Many, but not all: when the
vicar of Christchurch told his Parish Clerk in 1776 what a grievous sin it was to
smuggle, the clerk replied 'then Lord have mercy on the town of Christchurch, for
who is there here who has not had a tub?'

Other men of the cloth were not so particular. Phillip Meadows, rector of Great
Bealings in Suffolk, was reputed to have cooperated with the smugglers by leaving his
stables unlocked, with the chaise and harness ready. Since the owner of the carriage
was so well respected locally – and effectively above suspicion – the smugglers were
thus able to travel around the district quite freely, and used the chaise to collect cargoes ferried up Martlesham Creek.

In Norfolk, the Reverend Forbes Phillips wrote in *The Romance of Smuggling* of
his predecessors at Gorleston vicarage. One tale tells how, in the course of a landing, a newcomer to the parish arrived, and was horrified to find that goods were
being illegally landed: 'Smuggling! Oh, the shame of it! Is there no magistrate to hand,
no justice of the peace? … Is there no clergyman, no minister?' The innocent man's
enquiries were silenced when one of the locals points out the vicar holding a lantern.

More often, the involvement of the clergy in smuggling ventures was a pas-
sive one: turning a blind eye, for instance, to the use of the church for storage.
Contraband in pews, tombs and crypts is a theme that runs through countless

smuggling yarns, set everywhere in Britain. One writer from Rochford, for example, commented in 1909 that 'The whole district is honeycombed with traditions concerning smuggling … The tower of Rochford Church was used to store gin, Hollands and tea – the cavity under the pulpit was known as The Magazine.'[6]

There are first-person accounts, too. James Woodforde was the parson at Weston Longville at the very height of the smuggling era, and he kept a careful diary in which he noted every detail of life in a rural community in the mid-eighteenth century. Today it makes fascinating reading, if only for the matter-of-fact way in which he deals with aspects of life that are now remote and almost forgotten. This approach extends even to smuggling and smuggled goods. Like the clergy elsewhere in Britain, Parson Woodforde was not averse to a little smuggled tea, though as far as we know he was simply a customer of the smugglers, and did not provide any sort of help and assistance to them. We read that in March 1777:

Andrews the smuggler brought me this night about 11 o'clock a bag of Hyson Tea 6 Pd weight. He frightened us a little by whistling under the parlour window just as we were going to bed. I gave him some Geneva and paid for the tea at 10/6 a Pd.

The parson regularly bought smuggled gin, brandy and tea, not only from Richard Andrews, but also from Clerk Hewitt of Mattishall Burgh, and from the blacksmith at Honingham, Robert 'Moonshine' Buck. Not all of Woodforde's suppliers of brandy and gin were as happy to show their faces as those that he names in his diaries. On at least one occasion the parson describes how a knock took him to the door, and he discovered a couple of kegs waiting for bottling: by the time he peered out into the night, whoever delivered them had melted away.

Nobody would have accused Woodforde of actually being a smuggler himself, but his reference to 'Andrews the Smuggler' makes it clear that the meaning of 'smuggler' is elusive. Though the term stops short of the customer, it embraces not only the mariner whose boat actually transported the goods across the water, but also the wealthy landowner who supplied the capital for the operation, and the thug who protected the cargo as it came inland. 'Smuggler', in fact, is about as specific as crook, villain or blackguard, and the profession could potentially be minutely split up into numerous specialists.

SEA SMUGGLERS

If we confine ourselves to the men who actually made the trips abroad, answering the question 'who were the smugglers?' becomes simpler. The stereotyped sea smuggler, of course, is easy to picture. He wears enormous seaman's boots, perhaps a smock or a striped jersey, baggy trousers, a heavy overcoat, a sou'-wester, and maybe a handkerchief round his neck. In fact, this was the traditional garb of the sailor of the eighteenth and nineteenth centuries, so while the outfit looks distinctive today, it was hardly exceptional 200 years ago.

Most sea smugglers were seafaring men who had a sense of adventure or an eye for a quick profit. They were fishermen, or they crewed colliers, coasters and river vessels. When times were tough, they'd look for a novel way to use their knowledge of navigation and sailing. At Shoreham, for instance, a writer noted in 1785 that local boats no longer went to the Yarmouth fishery, because they had taken up the more profitable pursuit of smuggling.

From what little verifiable information we have about the lives of sea smugglers, it seems that they slipped in and out of the trade. Jack Rattenbury, for example (see page 190), started life learning fishing, but got bored and joined a privateer. This semi-piratical pursuit perhaps pushed him towards smuggling, but he plied an honest trade from time to time too, running a pub, and working as a pilot. This last employment is particularly telling, since it highlights the extraordinarily detailed knowledge of the sea that smugglers possessed, especially of localised coastal conditions.

It's simplistic to imagine that sailors like Rattenbury were either honest, hard working seamen or else roguish smugglers. More often, they just slipped from one trade to the other, even in the course of a single voyage. This is made clear by following the course of a trip made by the Shetland ship *Catharine*, in 1814. The crew first sailed her to Orkney, and loaded up with an illegal cargo of meal, which was landed at Bergen, where a load of hides and tallow (legal) was waiting. This travelled to London, and from there it was just a short cross-Channel journey, loaded with coils of rope (legitimate) to pick up a cargo of 600 ankers of gin from Rotterdam. This was then run in Shetland, and the coils of rope were bound for Orkney. The process would have continued had the smugglers not been caught and the vessel seized at Kirkwall.

Surprisingly, perhaps, the smuggler had a good chance of being a foreigner. After all, smuggling was only an illegal form of the import/export business, and wasn't restricted to English citizens. In times of peace, the market-places of coastal towns rang with many different foreign accents, and a French or Dutch smuggler taking orders for his next trip could easily merge with the crew of a legitimate vessel out getting drunk on the local strong ale. In times of war (and these were frequent) a little more caution was in order, but it wasn't usually difficult to arrange for a school of small English boats to meet a larger vessel from the (nominally) enemy power, a few miles off-shore.

Daniel Defoe highlighted the role of the foreigners in the smuggling trade in his 1825 *Tour through the Whole Island of Great Britain*. Of Faversham he wrote:

> … I know nothing else this town is remarkable for, except the most notorious smuggling trade, carried on partly by the assistance of the Dutch, in their oyster

boats … the people hereabouts are arrived to such proficiency, that they are grown monstrous rich by that wicked trade.

LAND SMUGGLERS

The sea-going men were just the beginning of the story, though. Face away from the sea, and the land party comes into view: a group of shadowy figures who skulk around the coast waiting to land the cargo, and protect it on its onward journey inland. These people were usually labourers who would supplement their paltry agricultural wages with a little fetching and carrying, to make ends meet. Only 20 per cent of the eighteenth-century population lived in towns and cities, and a quarter of the rural population was made up of landless labourers, many of whom lived in a condition that we would today describe as grinding poverty. According to one estimate, a fifth of the population occasionally received parish relief – the equivalent of today's social security benefit.

For those who had jobs, working hours were long – typically twelve or thirteen hours a day, Saturdays included, and though wages may have been sufficient to buy food, they often didn't pay for cooking it: vast tracts of woodland had been cut to build ships, and as fuel for the industries of glass and steel manufacture. As a result, firewood was scarce, and transport – except by water – was very costly, so coal was not yet an economical substitute for wood. The poor commonly ate food such as cheese, that did not require cooking.

For these people, acting as tub carriers and batmen – the thugs who made sure that the King's men didn't interfere – must have seemed like an easy way to cook the beans. For those who could get it, a week's work on the fields paid 7 or 8s (35–40p), but a successful 'run' of a smuggled cargo could bring between 5s and 7/6 (25p–38p) for a night's exertion. For those turned out of work – for example by the contraction of iron-smelting in the Kentish Weald – smuggling may have been the only source of income besides the parish.

The definition of smuggling, though, extended even to people who distributed the contraband inland, and these included not only landless labourers, but a broader section of the working classes, including skilled trades-people. A roll-call of unfortunate Dorset land smugglers whose cases came up in Lyme Regis court makes revealing reading:

Anthony, John	quarryman
Bagwell, Maria	dressmaker
Charles, Emmanuel	tin-plate worker
Dowall, George	ferryman
Etchcock, Richard	labourer
Ford, James	cooper

Gummer, Ann	needlewoman
Hatton, Robert	butcher
Jerrard, John	flax dresser
Kearley, George	innkeeper
Lumb, Martha	chairwoman
March, David	pig jobber
Oxford, William	miller
Powell, William	shoemaker
Rutledge, Levia	twine spinner
Sceard, James	fell-monger
Trim, William	bricklayer
Vivian, Martha	labourer
Way, Mercy	twine spinner
Zeally, Thomas	labourer

Women *do* appear in the list, though, challenging the widespread assumption that all smugglers were men. Women were universally land smugglers, and commonly played a peripheral role in smuggling ventures. They sold, transported or hid contraband; they provided protection, alibis and assistance to smugglers who played a more central part in runs; and sometimes they fought off the revenue men.

Scots women mounted the best defence. In 1777 when a tide-waiter from Ruthwell on the Solway tried to seize a cargo of smuggled tobacco, a multitude of women pounced, making off with the contraband. To make matters worse, the revenue man was imprisoned in the house where he had found the tobacco. When he escaped and returned to his headquarters, he received little reward for his bruised body and ego, and was sent back to the scene with ten men. This time they had more success, and located one pack of tobacco in a ditch. Nevertheless, they still had to run the gauntlet of 'A monstrous regiment' of women armed with clubs and pitchforks. Some of the women were tried at the circuit court, but revealingly were discharged because witnesses for the prosecution pretended to 'entertain malice against the prisoners'. A similar attack also took place at Glenhowan, near Glencaple, the following month.

Women rarely played quite such an aggressive role. More often, they provided a distribution service, hiding contraband under their clothes with the knowledge that no customs officer would dare search them. At Whitby, housewives would go to market wearing loose-fitting garments, and return with buttons bursting, having stuffed their clothes with contraband goods. Mrs Gaskell, who lived in Whitby for some time, commented on 'The clever way in which certain [Whitby] women managed to bring in prohibited goods; how in fact when a woman did give her mind to smuggling, she was more full of resources, and tricks, and impudence, and energy than any man'.

She also observes that even a couple of Quaker brothers in the town bought smuggled goods, and that 'Everybody in Monkshaven smuggled who could, and everyone wore smuggled goods who could.'[7]

At Boulmer on the Scottish border, the contraband salt trade relied on women for distribution. Salt was heavily taxed, and in the days before refrigeration it was the staple preservative for pork or fish. It was regularly smuggled both across the border, and from the coast inland. One author wrote in 1909 that a friend recalled childhood memories of a woman of the village appearing at the door, to announce simply 'He has come' before hurrying on to tell others that the salt man had arrived in town.

Salt was retailed by the local women who would carry it round in sacks on their backs: if the excise man caught them, a deft slash with a knife would spill the cargo. The contraband goods travelled as discreetly as possible, and a path among the hills near Newton Tors was known locally as Salters' Path. Green lanes in the region still appear as Salters' Road on local Ordnance Survey maps.

Exceptionally, women had a controlling interest in smuggling operations – even if this stopped short of actually going to sea. The Neath area provides the best example of this: the local smugglers were led by Catherine Lloyd, who was the landlady of the Ferry Inn at Briton Ferry. They were by all accounts success-ful, and quick to defend their interests when threatened.

When in 1726 a 'sitter in ye boat at Briton Ferry' seized some brandy and wine, four of the smugglers rescued their contraband, and 'abused' the revenue man. Eight years later Catherine Lloyd was still running the pub (now called the Bretton Ferry) and still smuggling. She made the mistake of offering contraband India cotton to an off-duty customs collector from Llanelly:

> Edward Dalton … Stop'd at the publick house to drink a Pint of ale, the woman of ye house, one CATHERINE LLOYD a widdow not suspecting him to be an officer bro't out the s'd goods & offer'd the same to sale as India Goods, moreover told they were RUN GOODS she had secured the night before … Said Widdow is very well to pass in ye world & Suppos'd to have All Her Riches by Running of Goods for SHE is an old offender and NOTED SMUGGLER

The trade continued through the century, still under the control of women. An anonymous informer wrote from Gower to the tidesman at Briton Ferry in 1758, giving the names of four women who had gone from Neath to Bridgewater to buy uncustomed tea. What is not clear from any of these accounts is the exact role of the women involved. Most probably, Catherine Lloyd would have been financing the operation and storing the contraband in the pub.

NOTES

1   Sidney Dobell's letters, 1860, published in the *Isle of Wight County Press*, 22 October 1960

2   *Tour of England*

3   Chadwyck Healey, Sir Bart *The History of the part of West Somerset comprising the parishes of Luccombe, Selworthy, Stoke Pero, Porlock, Culbone and Oare.* (H. Sotheran & Co., 1901.)

4   Unattributed source, Haverfordwest library clippings file, 7 March 1924.

5   Roberts, B. Dew, 1936

6   Burrows, John William, *Southend-on-Sea and district: historical notes*, 1909

7   Chadwick, Esther Alice, 1913

3

RAISING FINANCE AND BUYING CONTRABAND

Every business requires capital, and illegal enterprises were no exception. However, the first English smugglers needed no funding, for they worked through barter. The Kentish and East Coast smugglers would ship out bales of wool to destinations in Normandy, and return packed to the gunwales with tubs of wine or bales of silks and lace. No money changed hands – it was a simple and direct arrangement.

The smugglers might themselves have bought the wool in England, but this would obviously have involved a considerable capital investment, beyond the means of a rough-and-ready fisherman/smuggler. More likely, the amateurs and dabblers in the free-trade acted as haulage contractors, taking cargoes of wool on trust, returning with other contraband, and either paying off the farmer when the incoming cargo had been sold, or just paying in kind, and keeping a share of the contraband as a fee for the trip.

When import smuggling began to replace exports, it's likely that this sort of petty smuggling continued with goods shipped across the Channel on small fishing vessels. When profits in the business were high, and preventive measures unsuccessful, finance was little problem. A menial deck-hand on a smuggling ship might be paid in contraband and could amass a tidy sum from a few trips – enough, perhaps, to buy his own boat, and start trading on his own account.

But as the trade developed, new patterns of finance started to emerge. In the West Country, smugglers operated a sort of club scheme in the neighbourhood: everybody bought a share in the trip, each according to their means, and probably paying the organiser in cash. This system had much to recommend it: if the trip went badly wrong, no one person was ruined; and since the whole community had a stake, the risks of the game being spoilt by an informer were slight.

This sort of arrangement continued throughout the history of British smuggling, in parallel with more sophisticated and centralised finance schemes.

A smuggling trip made in 1726 by a couple of Medway men illustrates how it worked. It was a very small-scale operation, since in all the men brought back just

400lb of tea, plus a few yards of calico and some silk handkerchiefs. There were seven men on the ship *The Sloweley*, and everyone bought tea in Ostend, paying for their passage in tea, too.

The mastermind of this voyage, and many other similar trips, was one Edward Roots of Chatham. Though this excursion was organised on a cooperative basis, most of the others followed more conventional business lines, with a London financier, and a 'fence' in Blackheath who had organised an efficient distribution system through the pubs of Deptford.

Similar 'co-ops' were still operating at the end of the century. On Anglesea island in 1798, fourteen people from Amlwch had shares in a 25-ton sloop, including the doctor – and the custom house officer! They made a trip to the Isle of Man – supposedly a holiday – and on their return, a search of the ship revealed seven dozen bottles of wine and 4 gallons of rum. The crew excused themselves by saying that they'd bought the contraband for personal consumption on the trip, but that the weather had been too bad to open the hold.

HOW SMUGGLING DRAINED AREAS OF CASH

When communities paid for contraband in cash, the effect on the local economy was considerable. Between 1796 and 1798 there was a shortage of money on the Shetland Islands because so much had been paid out on contraband gin; and the minister of Unst at one stage reported that gin imports were worth half the rent of the island. One writer complained that illegally imported gin had 'drained the poor of this country … of every shilling they could spare or raise'.

An incident in 1762 from the other end of Britain shows that this problem was not confined to the Scottish Islands.

Three East Indiamen returning from China anchored in Falmouth bay, and for a fortnight held a regular on-board bazaar, selling silk, muslin, dimityes, porcelain, tea, arrack, handkerchiefs and other goods. The town was filled with people of every rank from a 20-mile radius, and the ships drained the area of cash: a writer estimated that through the private adventures of the East Indiaman's crew £20,000 worth of business was concluded and complained that 'a week after ye ships sailed I could not get a bill of exchange from any merchant in town'. He added 'The captains and officers are allowed large priveleges, and there are ways and means of dealing with Custom-house officers … '

Clearly such ways and means were not universally effective, for when a similar incident happened three years later, an excise vessel came down from London, and carried out several seizures.

WEALTHY SOUTH EAST FINANCIERS

In the South East of England the arrangements were somewhat different. Kent and Sussex smugglers had access to London, and the wealthy home counties. Here trips were more likely to be financed by individuals or by smaller numbers of merchants. A London draper, for example, might stock his shop from smuggled silks and gloves, and a publican with substantial cellars would be able to dispose of a cargo of wines and spirits across the bar.

These are examples, though, of natural business arrangements in which the financier was also the retailer. There is additionally a suspicion that in the later years of the eighteenth century smuggling was bankrolled by highly placed figures who never actually saw the contraband – any more than one of today's speculators on the futures market ever expects to physically take delivery of 18-tons of pork-bellies.

The method of payment that regular smugglers used also points to the involvement of city financiers in the trade. In the early years of the eighteenth century smugglers paid in cash only, but as the trade assumed greater proportions and the transactions became almost routine, the merchants began to settle their accounts by cheque or bank draft. It was even possible to insure a smuggling ship at Lloyds. This suggests a sophistication not popularly associated with rough, rude smugglers, and confirms that a well-oiled organisation backed up the men who got their hands dirty. Indeed, tea trader Richard Twining complained that the smuggling was financed by 'the most extensive dealers ... who possessed the fairest reputation.'[1]

Another approach was for the suppliers of the contraband on the Continent to finance the venture by organising smuggling trips 'on spec'. French brandy distillers, for example, and Dutch gin manufacturers bought their own ships, and transported goods to within a few miles of the English coast, where they traded with small boats that flocked out from the fishing communities dotted along the shore.

But the most common pattern of venture finance for smuggling was probably a small consortium of home counties land smugglers, often well-placed on the route from the coast to London. These individuals had sufficient capital between them to front the money for the purchase of contraband abroad, and would receive payment when the goods had been sold on the informal wholesale market that thrived on the outskirts of London. The Hawkhurst and Hadleigh gangs (see pages 165 and 174 respectively), are examples of this method of capitalisation in practice.

Some indication of the profits to be made can be gleaned from the will of William Baldock. He was a member of the North Kent-based Seasalter company which flourished for over a century from 1740. When he died in 1812, he left over a million pounds – the equivalent of nearly £50 million today.

BUYING CONTRABAND

With finance found, a representative appointed by the entrepreneur of the smuggling trip often travelled with the outgoing ship to the Continent to purchase the contraband. However, this was not always considered necessary, and the purchase might have been entrusted to the ship's master. A common arrangement was to have agents abroad, who could strike a bargain with the suppliers, and have a cargo stacked ready for loading on the quayside when the tide brought the vessel into port. Another option was for a representative to cross the Channel alone by some legitimate vessel such as a postal packet, and then on arrival to charter a French or Dutch boat and crew.

This wasn't difficult: at the height of the smuggling era, in the middle and late eighteenth century, continental ports reaped vast profits from the smuggling trade, and an enormous industry grew up in supplying the goods demanded by the British market, and shipping them over. The most important suppliers were based in Flushing (Vlissingen) in the Netherlands, and Calais, Boulogne, Dieppe, Dunkirk, Nantes, Lorient and Le Havre in France.

It's no coincidence that some of these are now familiar destinations for cross-Channel travellers – then as now, the ports were conveniently situated for a short crossing, and had fine harbours. To a certain extent, each served a different part of England: Calais and Boulogne, for example, supplied Kent and Sussex, and Cherbourg stocked the West Country.

It's possible to judge the financial value of the free-trade to continental ports from the transformation of Roscoff after the British government imposed restrictions on the free-trade through the Channel Islands in 1767. The French response was to develop Roscoff into a major depot for the supply of the Devon and Cornwall, and …

Roscoff, till then an unknown and unfrequented port, the resort only of a few fishermen, rapidly grew into importance, so that from small hovels it soon possessed commodious houses and large stores, occupied by English, Scots, Irish and Guernsey merchants. These on the one hand gave every incentive to the British smugglers to resort there, and on the other hand, the French government afforded encouragement to the merchants.[2]

KINDS OF CONTRABAND

What sort of goods came into Britain from Roscoff and the other smuggling ports? The stereotypical smuggler brought 'brandy for the parson, baccy for the clerk' to Britain. Certainly there were advantages to smuggling high-value, low-volume goods, so tobacco and spirits were always popular, but cargoes were far more varied than this cliché suggests. Tea smuggling, for instance, was widespread, but is perhaps too mundane to make it into Kipling's famous poem or fictional smuggling stories.

In fact, smugglers were prepared to run practically anything that would turn a profit. When pepper was taxed heavily, it became a popular item for the Cornwall smugglers, and tiny Pepper Cove a little way north of Porthcothan takes its name from the boatloads of spice that were landed there.

Not all smuggled goods were expensive luxuries. Salt – essential for food preservation – was smuggled in many parts of Britain and at Solva in Pembrokeshire, the Baptist chapel was lit by candles made from smuggled tallow:

' … One evening, the chapel being lighted with those candles, by some means or other, the excise officer became aware of it, and he suddenly appeared and commandeered all the candles, leaving the congregation in the dark.'

The custom house books recording seizures at Aberdeen in November 1721 point to a fascinating diversity of other goods:

80	ankers containing 672 gallons of brandy
5½	hogsheads and 11 ankers containing 446 gallons brandy
35	matts containing 3059 lbs leaf tobacco
10	small casks containing prunes
4	small casks containing raisins
2	small casks containing figs
1	small cask of currants
2	small casks of sweet liquorice
3	small casks of white soap
2	hampers of earthenware
2	casks containing molasses
1	anker of coarse oil
1	cask black pepper
1	small matt of twine
32	firkins and 10 half firkins of soap
6	casks of aniseed
22	reams of writing paper
7	casks of white starch
111	bars of Swedish iron.

SPECIAL PACKAGING

When it came to packing and loading contraband, smugglers' needs were quite different from those of legitimate traders. An honest importer required goods in the largest possible containers, so as to make economies of scale at the dockside:

the hogshead was one standard packaging, and could hold up to 140 gallons (640 litres), though 52½ gallons (238 litres) was more usual. A hogshead packed with tobacco weighed more than half a ton.

Large packages like these were hard to hide, and required a quay and winches to unload, so contraband was packed in much smaller quantities. Tobacco came in bales of 22–45kg – a convenient size for a one-man lift – and was wrapped in oilskin to make a virtually watertight bundle. This approach was highly effective, and bales of tobacco tossed overboard by smuggling ships in an attempt to destroy the evidence stayed afloat in the sea for hours.

In 1736 the tide in the Bristol Channel washed up hundreds of such bales. News of recent legislation to prevent smuggling had reached the incoming vessels as they approached the coast, and the seamen, fearful of stiff penalties when they arrived, threw the goods overboard. Though the bales penetrated by sea water were of course worthless, dry bales were eagerly picked up by the local population, and sold off.

Tea was protected in a similar way, and spirits were packaged in small barrels or 'tubs' called half-ankers, which contained a little over 4 gallons. Ankers, holding 8⅓ gallons, were less commonly used. The coopers made both sizes of barrel with flattened sides for easier carrying, and usually supplied them slung together in pairs on ropes. This arrangement meant that 'tubmen' on the English side of the Channel could easily carry a pair of half-ankers across their shoulders, one at the front and one at the back. When pony transport was available, the rope slings on ankers fitted neatly across the beast's back.

Thomas Hardy described the tubs in his notebooks:

… my grandfather used to do a little smuggling, his house being a lonely one, none of the others in Higher, or Upper, Bockhampton being then built … He sometimes had as many as eighty tubs in a dark closet (afterwards destroyed in altering the staircase) – each containing four gallons. The spirits often smelt all over the house, being proof, and had to be lowered for drinking. The tubs, or little elongated barrels, were of thin staves with wooden hoops. (I remember one of them which had been turned into a bucket by knocking out one head and putting in a handle.) They were brought at night by men on horseback, 'slung' or in carts. A whiplash across the window-pane would wake my grandfather at two or three in the morning, and he would dress and go down. Not a soul was there, but a heap of tubs loomed up in front of the door. He would set to work and stow them in the dark closet aforesaid, and nothing more would happen till dusk the following evening, when groups of dark, long-bearded fellows would arrive, and carry off the tubs in twos and fours slung over their shoulders.[3]

To save tubs, and space in the ships, spirits were supplied just as they came out of the still: over-proof, and virtually colourless. Dilution prior to sale was – at least theoretically – a simple matter, but who would buy crystal-clear brandy? To solve this problem, the French distillers offered caramel, to be added to the kegs along with the water.

Over-proof spirits as they came out of the keg were just about drinkable, but lethal in any quantity. In 1811, for example, a smuggling ship ran aground in the shallows off Harwich's Landguard fort, and the crew threw overboard 600 tubs of spirits in order that the ship would draw less water. The soldiers from the fort took full advantage of the situation, and four of them died of the drink.

There had been a similar incident seventeen years before, when customs officers who seized 4–500 tubs of gin on Brighton beach carried them to Shoreham custom house with the help of troops stationed nearby. En route, two of the soldiers broached a barrel. They drunk themselves insensible, and were found comatose on the beach the following morning. One, who was due to be married that day, was quite literally dead drunk – he never recovered from his over-indulgence.

QUANTITIES AND MARGINS

The illicit nature of smuggling means that it is impossible to know exactly how much contraband entered the country, but it's clear from the size of seizures, and from anecdotal evidence, that the scale was enormous:

In a single week of 1813 free-traders were known to have landed 12,000 gallons (54,500 litres) of brandy at Dungeness.

One day in 1766 an enterprising smuggler bought at a Nantes warehouse 229,282 litres of tea – that's nearly 110 tons.

In a single run in 1743 smugglers brought 2,000lbs (900kg) of tea across the coast at West Wittering.

At Ludgvan, near Penzance, customs officers could not find a buyer for seized liquor in 1748, because of the vast quantity smuggled in. Smugglers were asking 3*s* 3*d* (16p) a gallon for the illegally imported liquor: the reserve price on the seized goods was 5*s* 6*d* (27.5p).

Similarly, when 1,100 gallons (5,000 litres) of spirits were found in a house at Nash, on the South Wales coast, local merchants were appalled that the sale of the seizure might cause prices of drink in the area to plummet, so the brandy was sold in London.

There have been a few attempts to make more methodical estimates of contraband volume. William Goodwin, a surgeon who lived at Earl Soham, Suffolk in the second half of the eighteenth century, counted smugglers' carts passing through the town from Sizewell Bay. In summer of 1785, he noted that, in less than a week, twenty carts had passed by carrying 2,500 gallons (11,350 litres) of spirits. In February of the same year, five carts carrying 600 gallons (2,725 litres) passed in the course of just one morning. On 23 February, though, the smugglers were not so lucky, and they lost six carts loaded with spirits to the preventive services.

There have been occasional glimpses of a bigger picture. In Aberdeen in 1788, for example, there were three luggers and two small sloops smuggling goods into the city – totalling 350 tons. Each made six trips a year, employing 100 men, smuggling spirits and tobacco – 200 hogsheads (about 47,500 litres) a year. The annual overheads were judged to be £10,000 or more: a little under a million at today's prices: a building worker of the time earned less than 19*d* (8p) a day.

A smuggler on a shopping trip was as keen as a modern day-tripper to save money, but eighteenth-century bargains make our duty-free savings look stingy. The profit margin varied with the prevailing rates of duty, but typically tea cost 7*d* (3p) a pound on the Continent, and could be sold in England for 5*s* (25p). Tobacco cost the same, and fetched 2*s* 6*d* (12½p) at home. A tub of gin or brandy cost £1, and found English customers at £4 even before 'letting down' to a drinkable strength. Diluted, the profit would have been even greater.

NOTES

1　Mui & Mui, 1968, p.59
2　Duncan, Jonathan, 1841
3　Hardy, Thomas, 1955

4
CROSSING AND LANDFALL

With contraband safely stowed, the smugglers awaited the tide for the return trip. In the harbour, the ship would rub shoulders with all manner of other smuggling vessels, from tiny deckless boats with small sails, right up to large, well-armed cutters. Smuggling ships recorded at Nantes and Lorient harbours ranged from 2 to 200 tonnes.

These smuggling craft had one thing in common: they were all fore-and-aft rigged. That's to say, they had sails like today's yachts, aligned *along* the ship from bows to stern. This form of rigging first appeared in Holland in the sixteenth century, though arguably it can be traced to the much older lateen sails of Southern European vessels. In the next three centuries coastal traffic all over Europe gradually adopted it in place of the square rig – roughly rectangular sails hung from yardarms aligned *across* the hull from port to starboard.

The difference between the two forms of rigging is not just of academic interest to naval historians: without the development of the fore-and-aft rig, it's fair to say that smuggling could never have developed on the scale that it did.

A vessel with square sails has to have the wind coming from behind to make any progress – it cannot move across the wind or into it. By contrast, a fore-and-aft-rigged vessel travels most quickly across the wind, and can move into the wind by *tacking*. This is a process of sailing across and slightly up-wind, then turning and heading diagonally in the opposite direction, but again slightly upwind. The ship thus progresses in a zig-zag manner.

A fore-and-aft-rigged vessel can sail nimbly up the same creek, discharge the cargo, and then scoot away on the same tide. A square-rigged vessel that enters the same creek with the breeze behind it cannot get out until the wind changes; trapped in the falling tide, such a vessel would be easily seized. Because of these limitations smugglers sailing square-rigged ships chose their landfalls with special care. Headlands, capes and necks such as the Lleyn peninsula at the north of Cardigan Bay were especially popular. Their double coasts made running feasible whatever the direction of the wind.

VESSEL SIZES AND TYPES

In the early eighteenth century when prevention was mainly land-based, small smuggling vessels were popular because they were highly manoeuvrable, and because losing one of several small ships was less damaging than losing a solitary large one. The vessels were commonly less than 50 tons, and were simple luggers, or gaff-rigged luggers. A lugger had the mast positioned close to the bows, and a sail hung from a diagonal spar fixed about to the mast about a third of the way along the spar's length. The gaff rig adds a second triangular sail in front of the mast, and the spar that supports the lug sail is joined at one end to the mast.

Later in the century smugglers began to use larger vessels, which could travel faster and carry greater burdens. They chose wherries and cutters; the latter were introduced around 1740. They were gaff-rigged but with additional sails: typically three square ones in front of the gaff-sail, on a taller mast, and another one or two at the bows, attached to a spar that extended straight forward from the bows – the bowsprit. A long bowsprit gave a cutter great speed, and smugglers had some of their vessels built with a *running bowsprit*. This had a second movable spar mounted above the main bowsprit. Sliding it forward spread even more canvas to the wind. Because of the speed it gave a cutter, private vessels were not permitted to use a running bowsprit, but the measure was ineffective since the customs services hired in cutters from private owners – who clearly also operated such vessels for their own purposes.

As prevention developed, ships were custom-made for the smuggling trade. The cost was roughly £2,000 for a large ship; a ship-owner could earn this back by making just four smuggling voyages. In Scotland, the economics were even more favourable. It cost half as much to build a ship as it did in southern Britain, and profits per trip were higher. After just two trips, a Scottish smuggling ship had paid for itself, and made £600 profit.

To get maximum possible speed, they were carvel-built: each board of the hull was lapped up against the adjacent one, giving very smooth lines that slipped easily through the water. By contrast, the revenue men more often had slower, clinker-built vessels constructed with each board overlapping the one below. This form of construction increased the ship's resistance and slowed it down.

Ship-building centres on the coast became expert at supplying vessels to the smugglers' specifications. Cawsand in Cornwall, for instance was famous for its luggers. They drew very little water – handy for trips up shallow estuaries with muffled oars. The larger vessels built at nearby Mevagissey were capable of tremendous speeds, making the crossing from Roscoff in a day or less.

These purpose-built smuggling vessels were cheap to manufacture, and were made from fir. Compared to building in traditional English oak this not only saved money, but weight as well, which gave the vessels that much more of a competitive edge in eluding the King's men. To stack the odds still further in their favour, the smugglers armed the ships to the teeth, with carriage guns and smaller swivel guns.

Crossing the Channel in these large sea-going vessels was not exactly routine, but at least relatively safe. The same could not be said of sailing for England in one of the smaller ships in use in the early part of the century. The smugglers performed amazing feats of seamanship in bringing deckless ships as small as 2 tons across from France in atrocious weather, and in every season of the year. If anything, smugglers favoured bad weather, since it reduced the risk of detection, and in winter vessels sometimes arrived with the rigging festooned with and partly disabled by ice.

The use of small vessels continued in a few places, such as the Solway Firth. There smugglers traded with the Isle of Man, and the shortest crossing was less than 30 miles. The smugglers of South West Scotland often sailed from the island in fleets of ten or more small ships and boats, in order to saturate the coast with landings, and outwit the over-stretched customs and excise services.

There were other dangers besides the weather and the sea. As the century progressed, and preventive service developed, more and more customs and excise cutters appeared on the scene. Small unarmed smuggling ships could do little when approached by a speeding revenue sloop, which by 1760 averaged around 50 tons, and had a modest complement of carriage guns. For the larger smugglers, though, such a challenge could be, and was, dismissed with a wave of the arm.

Military superiority partly accounted for this casual attitude. Smuggling ships of 80 tons were commonplace late in the century, and they easily out-sailed and out-gunned their opponents. However, there were other reasons why the smugglers often made light of the customs and excise ships. The King's crews were frequently second rate in every respect: the commanders were timid and often poor seamen, and the other crew-members may have been the dregs of the navy, or serving the King against their will. By contrast, the smugglers were highly motivated, very skilled at handling their vessels, and spoiling for a fight. It's therefore not surprising that there were many instances of the hound turning tail and being chased by the hare.

In all fairness to the revenue sloops, there were, it's true, some fearless crews who terrorised the smugglers they pursued and caught; and when pay was good and the ships well equipped, the government had no difficulty in securing a better class of sailor. However, until the end of the Napoleonic wars, the smugglers ruled the waves more often than the revenue vessels.

Smugglers were proud of their sailing skills and quick to counter suggestions that their calling was unpatriotic. Deal men, for instance, never let anyone forget that they served as pilots for Nelson. Smugglers positively revelled in tales that celebrated their seamanship. A favourite yarn from Scotland concerned a narrow escape on the Solway Firth. A smuggling ship was sighted off the Mull of Galloway, and a revenue cutter gave chase. The two ships sped around Burrow Head and the smugglers made for the harbour under the Isle of Whithorn – effectively a cul-de-sac. Seeing this, the revenue men shortened sail, and made a leisurely entrance to the harbour. When they had tied up, they were astonished to find no trace of the ship of which they had minutes before been in hot pursuit. The smugglers had skilfully piloted their vessel out of the harbour through a channel so narrow that it was normally passable only to small boats. They had the full tide on their side, it's true, but low water revealed what a tight squeeze it had been: the ship's keel had cut a deep furrow in the shingle lining the channel.

OFFSHORE ENTREPÔTS

Smuggling crossings were not always straightforward point-to-point journeys. Some were indirect, or even circuitous, either because such routes were safer, or because the most direct route did not make economic sense.

The risk of capture could be reduced by sailing first to an island close to the British mainland destination. The most notorious of these entrepôts was the Isle of Man. For 300 years the island was a private domain, outside of the control of the Crown, and even today the island maintains a degree of financial autonomy that is unparalleled on the British mainland.

Henry IV granted trade freedom for the island to Sir John Stanley in 1405, and the status of the Isle of Man was theoretically that of a kingdom quite separate from the rest of England (or Britain, after the Act of Union incorporated Scotland in 1707). The monarch of the island was for centuries known as King of Man.

The Isle of Man operated a free-trade policy, and regarded the English customs duties as protectionist. Smuggling on the island did not begin with illegal imports from continental Europe. In the early eighteenth century it instead took the form of merchants exporting goods to the Isle of Man from mainland Britain, and claiming the 'drawback' – a refund of import duty paid. The now-uncustomed goods were shipped back to England. This system grew rapidly, and eventually ocean-going ships began to sell direct to the Manx – a simple drawback fraud had become wholesale smuggling.

A major industry of the island was brewing: the brewers on the Isle of Man bought barley in England, and brewed strong beer for sale to ships sailing to the New World. Much of their production, of course, found its way back to the English and Scottish mainland. Scots customs officials complained about the loss of revenue this caused: since the Manx brewers bought raw barley, they didn't pay malting duty – neither did they pay duty on the beer they brewed. At one stage it was estimated that 40 per cent of all British beer was brewed on the Isle of Man. Though this estimate is probably exaggerated, it gives some indication of the scale of the problem.

By 1751 Manxmen had become expert importers of highly taxed continental luxuries. A letter in the *Gentleman's Magazine* that year denounced the island as '*the great STOREHOUSE or MAGAZINE for the French*'. In the same letter the correspondent helpfully lists as the principal contraband wine, brandy, coffee, tea and 'other India goods' and the sources as Denmark, Holland and France.

Goods from the Isle of Man were destined for the Solway, Cumbria and North Wales, and in 1763 the master of a revenue cutter from Anglesey outlined how the Manx trade worked. Welsh smugglers travelled as passengers on the first available boat to the Isle of Man, often independently. After a rendezvous on the island, they hired an Irish wherry to take the cargo back to Anglesey. The wherries had crews of nine or ten, and the smugglers added a further six to eleven crew. They scheduled a landfall in the early hours of the morning, and simply enlisted local help with unloading, which took an hour or less. Farmers were in league with the smugglers, and had carts and other transport waiting; they also served as lookouts, with tinder-dry warning beacons at the ready.

Manx apologists for the trade point to the fact that the local parliament, the Tynwald, took steps to stop illegal trading, and that it was not Manx themselves who were guilty of the accusations – it was bad folks from the mainland, especially Liverpool merchants, and 'Irish bankrupts and fugitives' who were the bad apples.

If the smugglers who used the island as a depot did not enjoy local support (and it's hard to avoid the suspicion that in actual fact they were made quite welcome by the locals), then they certainly got a warm reception on the mainland. The Scottish customs authorities complained that:

> their correspondence with the common people of these coasts … on the South and North sides of the Solway Firth is so well established, that the least appearance of danger from thence is conveyed to them by signals which, at the same time, inform them to what parts they may with safety steer.

The Manxmen continued to take advantage of unrestricted (and uncustomed) trade through until 1765. In that year the Crown finally regained control. The sale of the island back to the English Crown was not a popular move, and was carried out in some secrecy. In the short term it led to a rise in the cost, and a fall in the standard of living for the islanders, to considerable emigration, and a drop in land values.

SMALLER ISLANDS

Even if they fell under the jurisdiction of the English Crown, smaller islands made fine bases, because they were inaccessible to land patrols and often all but deserted.

In particular, smugglers made good use of the Scottish islands. In Wigtown Bay on the Solway Firth, they made Ardwall Island their depot, despite the fact that it was just 100 metres or so from the mainland. Off-shore to the north, Ailsa Craig was a smuggling base, and McNall's Cave there was used by a smuggler as a home and for storage. The Campbeltown smugglers used Sanda Island as a stronghold, and imported such quantities of foreign spirits that Scots distillers complained that their trade was being damaged.

Elsewhere in Britain Looe Island, Hayling Island, Lundy Island and especially the Scillies all played similar roles. So too did Canvey Island in the Thames estuary. Until the Dutch were invited to build a sea wall there, Canvey was little more than a glorified mud-flat – unhealthy for living on, and poor grazing land, so smugglers could go about their business watched only by sheep. It was convenient, too, within easy reach of both Kent and Essex coasts, and close to the mouth of the Thames. Dickens wrote in 1880 in *Dictionary of the Thames from Oxford to the Nore* that ' ... this part of the Essex coast has a history of runs carried out by "gentlemen."'

LANDFALL

Though an ocean voyage might be fraught with danger, it was the end of the crossing that brought with it the greatest risk of arrest and the loss of a valuable cargo. To make a safe landfall, the skipper of a smuggling ship had to bring his vessel within sight of the shore to a tight schedule; he had to communicate with his conspirators on land; he needed to bring the vessel safely to the landing point they indicated; he needed a small army of labourers to unload the cargo; and throughout all of this he had to evade or distract customs men who were intent on his capture.

Here's how he did it ...

CHOOSING A LANDING SPOT

Before even leaving British shores, smugglers picked a general area for their landing. Often they just chose the bays or coves they knew best, but some regions had special advantages.

For example the Gower peninsula is conveniently close to the huge marketplace of Swansea, yet is amply supplied with secluded bays and sandy inlets where it was a simple matter to bring contraband ashore unobserved. Swansea coal ships found it convenient in the late eighteenth century to be 'blown off course' to Ireland, where they could load up with salt and soap. On the return trip, Gower made a handy stopping-off point.

Remoteness was an advantage, too: Orford, for instance, was controlled by a customer and searcher from Aldeburgh, and these officials visited Orford just a couple of times a week. As late as 1856 one local ship's master observed that by timing the visit carefully, any would-be smuggler could spend two undisturbed days in Orford harbour unloading an incoming cargo – perhaps wine – and loading a new one for export to the Continent.

Where the sea ebbs far from the land, almost any spot would do. At low tide a beached smuggling vessel would appear in toy-like scale on the horizon and kegs of brandy and parcels of tea could be tossed overboard with impunity, to be carried back to the shore hidden under cart-loads of kelp. An approaching customs man could be spotted long before he reached the rendezvous.

Other landing sites offered singular advantages. Weymouth smugglers had the unique advantage of Chesil Beach. This extraordinary bank of shingle stretches unbroken nearly 17 miles, from Burton Bradstock to Portland. Smugglers landing on the beach in the pitch black of a moonless night were able to judge their position to within a mile or two by simply picking up a handful of shingle, and gauging the average size of the stones. At the Portland end, the pebbles are the size of potatoes, and then progressively slim down to pea-shingle on the beach at Burton Bradstock. Tubs landed here on the beach were humped over it, and sunk in the quiet waters of the Fleet for collection at a more convenient time.

Responsibility for bringing the ship in to the right section of coast lay with the spotsman. He had an intimate knowledge of every creek and beach on his patch of the coast, and could instinctively make out features inland on even the darkest night. The spotsman would guide the vessel into a position from where all the pre-arranged landing points – or a signal from some high-point – could be seen.

The choice of the exact spot was not made until the last possible moment, when collaborators on shore had identified a beach or creek where opposition from the authorities was weakest. This wasn't always easy. Careful observation could establish the routine movements of land-based preventive men, and bribery or threats could sometimes ensure that a particular spot was safe. But there was always a chance that an eager young officer would appear on the scene at an inconvenient moment. So the land party made last-minute checks before guiding the smuggling ship ashore.

SIGNALLING AND COMMUNICATIONS

As the vessel approached the shore, communication with the land party became vital. Smuggling ships were frequently painted black, with dark sails to hinder identification at night, and without a moon they were all but invisible. To indicate that they were off-shore, the spotsman showed a light. On a clear night, a spark from a tinder-box would be enough to alert the men on the beach. An answering

flash from the land party showed that the coast was clear (a phrase that significantly is still used in a wider context), and indicated which beach or cove had
been chosen for the landing. A Salcombe man recalled that: 'We used to strike a
match and hold it in our hands a moment to call the boats in.'

Another popular signalling method was a 'flash' – a flint-lock pistol without
a barrel. Charging the pan with powder and the pulling the trigger produced a
distinctive blue light that was unmistakeable on shore.

Today, the coastline is so brilliantly lit that it is easy to forget just how conspicuous such flashes would have been two centuries ago. Before electricity made
bright lights ubiquitous, even candles were used sparingly in all but the most
wealthy households, and on a moonless night the shore would have appeared as a
dim silhouette against which a lantern, a fire or even a spark was obvious.

Where the land was low and flat a moderately high point allowed a smugglers'
light to be seen a great distance away. At Leigh in Essex the ruins of thirteenth-
century castle made an ideal vantage point for a shore party equipped with a flash.
From this commanding position overlooking the river, a lantern was capable of
sending messages to ships in the Thames estuary, and as far as Cliffe marshes in
Kent on a dark night. Some local high points still carry names that point to their
former function: Beacon Hill at Saint Lawrence in Essex was used by smugglers
for signalling to Salcott-cum-Virley.

SIGNALLING IN PRACTICE

A riding officer's journal from Bournemouth gives a practical example of how
smugglers used the signals to lure their foes away:

October 4th 1803
... set out with Mr Bacon to the west coast on discoveries ... In the Heath at
Bourn we saw a fire lighted up, and immediately went to the spot, by the time we
got there the fire was out, the smugglers flashing and striking up light with flint
and steel all night in different parts of the heath and on the cliffs.

October 5th
Early in the morning Mr Williams, mate of the *Batt* cutter, called to inform me
that smugglers were working to the east, so I set out with Mr Bacon and party and
examined the cross roads through the forest leading from Highcliffe and Barton.

October 6th
Mr Williams ... informed me that there had been a run of goods, about three
or four hundred casks ... Traced the smugglers into the country and at Hinton
searched several suspected places. No success.

E. Russell Oakley, in his book *The Smugglers of Christchurch*, explains that the lugger had probably being hovering off Hengistbury Head while the unhappy riding officer was patrolling near East Cliff. On seeing the flashes, fires and sparks, the ship would have landed the cargo between Highcliffe and Barton. To make an interception, the customs officers would have had to ride across the heath, following winding country lanes and crossing narrow bridges to Christchurch, via Iford, then to Somerford and on to the coast. The lighting of fires on the heath was probably a diversion to attract the officers to Boskum (Boscombe).

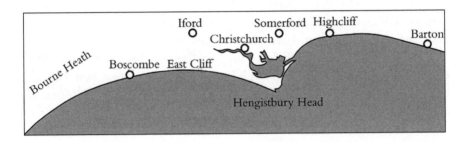

When stiff penalties were imposed for signalling to ships at sea, waving a lantern on a beach became too risky. Smugglers hid their lights in the depths of a sea cave, or hung them in windows that faced out to sea. These were often specially constructed so as to be all but invisible to those on land.

Norfolk Old Mill House, Overstrand, for example, had a squint placed so as to provide a view of the sea in the direction of Holland. Outside the house, it was at head height, but indoors it would have been inconspicuously at floor level, perhaps concealed by a flap in the skirting board.

These purpose-made signalling points were sometimes some distance inland. At Herne in North Kent, nearly 3km from the sea, you can still see a small triangular spy-hole that looks out to the coast. An oil lamp in this window today would be unnoticeable against the bright background of street and car lights, but in the eighteenth century it would have been very conspicuous.

When background lights swamped a smuggler's flash, technology came to the rescue, in the form of the spout lantern. As the name suggests, this had a long spout in front of the flame, sometimes with a bull's-eye of glass to focus the beam. An even more distinctive lantern used a primitive rotating shutter to produce a regularly flashing light.

If there was a risk of discovery, the land party might fire a furze beacon to warn the vessel off. This too was forbidden by law, and because such fires were so conspicuous, lighting them quickly attracted the attention of the authorities. At Branscombe, Devon, a table tomb implicitly records one of the clashes that inevitably followed:

John Hurley, Custom House Officer ... was endeavouring to extinguish some
Fire made between Beer and Seaton as a Signal to a Smuggling Boat then off at
Sea He Fell by some means or other from the Top of the Cliff to the bottom by
which He was unfortunately killed.

Daylight landings were not unknown, especially in remote areas, and by day,
smoke replaced fire: wet gorse or bracken thrown on a beacon formed conspicuous plumes. In some parts of the country a bed-sheet stretched over a hay or peat
stack or across a thatched roof confirmed plans for the landing.

At Seasalter on the North Kent coast smugglers were more original: they sent
messages along a chain of safe houses using rods running up their chimneys or the
trees outside. Pushing the rod from the grate end pushed up a broom fixed to the
end, and the signal was copied down the line. The signalling points were Moat
House in Blean, Frogs Hall, Honey Hill Farm in Blean, a house at Pean Hill built
by the company, Clapham Hill Farm, Martin Down Mill, and on to Borstal and
eventually to Whitstable.

DEVIOUS SIGNALS

Other signalling methods were equally subtle or ingenious: smugglers on Looe
Island knew the coast was clear by watching the behaviour of a cooperative
farmer on the mainland. When he was able to divert the customs authorities, or
when they posed no threat to a landing, he would ride his white horse along the
coast. This acted as a signal to the islanders who would then use a lamp to tell a
ship waiting off-shore that the coast was clear. If there was danger, the farmer
would walk the horse home.

Warden Manor on Sheppey was once the home of Sir John Sawbridge, a
respectable magistrate who dabbled in smuggling in the late eighteenth century.
He cleverly incorporated into his house a novel signalling mechanism that innocently alerted him to the arrival of his kegs of spirits: a pigeon loft in the house
could be observed from the smoking room, and the smuggling vessel released a
bird as the contraband was dumped overboard at the mouth of a nearby creek.
The tide swept the barrels in, and the cooing messenger warned the magistrate to
collect the goods before anyone else found them.

The wherrymen who plied the Norfolk Broads evolved an equally ingenious
semaphore system to warn of the approach of the customs authorities:

If a search was suspected by those on the watch ... warning was sent by a run-
ner to the nearest marshman. If his mill was turning he would stop it at the St
Andrew's (diagonal) cross, then wait until those at the next mill had seen him
and done the same. Then he would let the mill turn again. If there was no wind

the boy would be sent up to climb on the sail, and his weight used to turn the mill to the required position … The clear signal would be telegraphed using the St George (square) cross on the mill sail.[1]

Horsey Mill was reputedly used in this way: a message could travel from Yarmouth to Horsey in a quarter of an hour – much faster than a customs man could ride.

Smugglers also used the mill at Langstone county: it was worked by both tide and wind, so the sails were easily positioned to form a pre-arranged code without interruption to the miller's work.

As long as the preventive forces were stationed on land, smugglers' simple signals worked well. A smuggling vessel could travel very much faster along the coast than a mounted officer could on shore, and by taking advantage of any coastal feature, smugglers made sure that it was a very uneven match. A typical trick was to bring the ship into the mouth of an estuary, establish which side was most heavily protected, then land on the other side. Since the lowest bridging point was usually a long way upstream, the contraband was nowhere to be seen by the time the hapless custom house officer arrived on the spot.

At Pagham Harbour, for instance, smugglers in 1830 used a decoy light to lure revenue officers to Sidlesham, then landed landing 700 tubs from a galley at Pagham. Saling across the ¾-mile-wide harbour took minutes, and the contraband was well clear of the beach once the revenue men had negotiated the 5-mile circumference on horseback.

Smugglers regularly used a similar ruse at Barry Island, where the customs officers complained that:

… if [smugglers] find the officer on the Iseland [sic] they land the other Side of the harbour. If [they find the officer on] the other Side of the harbour, they'll land on the Iseland, and the officer can't get over till the tide is out, wch may be five or six hours; and there is so much Cover on the Iseland, and such conveniencys for hiding of goods on the other side, that an officer has but poor chance to meet with em after they have landed.[2]

This subterfuge didn't work if officers could use a ferry to cross a stretch of water, as on the Exe estuary, where there was a ferry at the river mouth. To solve the problem smugglers bribed the ferry-man to ensure that his vessel was mysteriously unavailable when the customs men needed it. Ferry-men were also frequently and lavishly entertained in the Mount Pleasant Inn at Dawlish Warren, so that they were in no fit state to ply their trade when a run was due.

Bad navigation could put paid to even the best-planned landing: a smuggling cutter dropped anchor off Oxwich Sands on the Gower Peninsula, and two of the crew rowed to the beach to ask directions to Highway Farm, the local smuggling headquarters (see page 196). The two men walking on the beach gave the mariners detailed directions, and as the helpful locals ambled away the run began. By midnight most of the contraband had been carried to Highway, and hidden in cellars. A skin of earth concealed the entrance to the cellars. Unfortunately the apparently casual passers-by were actually members of the preventive authorities, and in the early hours of the morning they raided the farm. Early searches were fruitless, but eventually the customs men discovered the hidden chambers, and seized 420 casks of spirits.

GETTING GOODS ASHORE

Once the crew of the vessel knew they were 'on the spot' they put on all sail, and headed for the coast. When they reached the shore, responsibility passed to the waiting *lander*. He had the job of mustering the muscle to get the goods out of the hold, and inland as far as a place of safety. The lander organised ponies, horses and carts for transport, or in particularly difficult areas, 'tub carriers' or 'tubmen' to hump the barrels and bales quickly away from the sea.

The size of the vessel and the characteristics of the chosen spot dictated the nature of the landing. Small ships could be just run against the beach, and the contraband thrown overboard onto the shingle. In other places the tubmen might have to wade through the surf to reach the ship. Larger vessels moored a little way off-shore, and an army of tub-boats shuttled to and fro to pick up the cargo.

At Poole, for example, smugglers unloaded the contraband into 'dragger' boats with a shallow draught designed for use on the oyster beds. The draggers then took the contraband to stores on Brownsea Island, and from there to Poole and farther inland.

In very isolated spots, all this urgency would have seemed out of place. At some locations on the East Coast the sea ebbs for miles, and smugglers simply moored in the shallow water, and waited until the flat-bottomed ship settled into the sand. Then kelp carts came out from the villages nearby, loaded up with tubs, and concealed them under a superficial layer of seaweed.

In most places on the South Coast, though, time was of the essence, and no sooner was the contraband on the beach than it was whisked away into the hinterland. The real beasts of burden were the tubmen, who carried two kegs, each weighing about 45lbs, one on the chest, and one on the back. This was no simple task, and the combined pressure of the two tubs apparently made breathing difficult and caused permanent injury to some of the tubmen. Nevertheless, these athletic figures were capable of moving their 90lb burden at a pace described as 'a very brisk walk' for 10 miles or more.

If the landing took place at the foot of a cliff, the tubmen might additionally have to negotiate a hundred feet of swaying rope ladder before making off into the dark – a challenge that most of us would decline even in daylight without a load.

Sussex smugglers used winches to avoid detection and capture. By 'derricking' they could bring goods up a cliff from an inaccessible beach far below.

The contraband was landed on the beach, and stacked in baskets or on some sort of pallet. Using a horse-driven winch or windlass on the cliff top, the smugglers then hauled the contraband up the face, and unloaded at the top. The derrick itself was purpose-built, and could be trundled quickly into position, or wheeled off equally rapidly at the sign of danger. There are records of this happening at numerous spots, but notably Rottingdean, Newhaven and Birling Gap.

The same method was used in Devon: a descendant of one of the Offwell smugglers described in 1953 how his grandfather had helped land cargoes. Tubs were offloaded to a particularly inaccessible beach at the foot of a 400ft cliff close to Branscombe and Salcombe Regis. The tubmen then appeared at the top of the cliff with a long rope, and tied a farm gate to one end. One of their number was then lowered to the beach, where he loaded the gate with tubs, and was hoisted up again. This system was not foolproof – on at least one run, the rope broke, and the smuggler dashed his brains on the rocks below. The recollections were in this case particularly vivid, and only third hand, since the father and grandfather of the old man relating the story both lived into their nineties.

There were no such hazards when a landing took place on a gently sloping beach, but there was still the risk of discovery. A hundred burly men waiting on the coast on a dark night were hard to explain to an inquisitive customs man, so tubmen hid themselves as best they could. On Weybourne beach, Norfolk, there was so little cover for the waiting land party that the men were reputed to bury themselves neck-deep in the shingle until the smuggling vessel appeared on the horizon. This story perhaps stretches the credulity to the limits, but the fact that it is also told of Suffolk locations adds at least a little weight:

> A boy going down to a lonely part of the beach one evening was asked by a man if he would like to earn a sovereign ... the latter forthwith dug a hole in the beach and making the boy lie down in it, covered him up to the chin with beach. 'There' said he 'You lie there and don't move till you hear a whistle blow and then do you get up and do the same as others do'. By and bye the whistle blew, and jumping up the boy saw ... hundreds of men unseen before coming up out of the beach all round. Then a boat ran ashore and her cargo was unloaded and carried away inland.[3]

HOVERING AND ESTUARY LANDINGS

When the risk of an open landing was too great – or when the coast was unsuitable – smuggling ships waited offshore, and a string of smaller boats came out to ferry the goods ashore. For example, at Cambletown, custom house officials complained that:

'When the vessels employed in [smuggling] appear in the channel there are boats … waiting towards the said Mull as if fishing, but with a view of receiving their illegal importations.'

The same method was used at Aberdeen – the small boats that ferried the contraband ashore stopped at several points on the coast to make deliveries – and at Elgin, where a merchant sent these highly specific instructions regarding signalling to hovering vessels in 1710:

> I have ventured to order Skipper Watt … to call at Caussie, and cruise betwixt that and Burgh Head, until you order boats to waite [for] him. He is to give the half of what I have of the same sort with his last cargo, to any having your order … The signal he makes will be all sails furled, except his main topsaile; and the boats you order to him are to lower their saile when within muskett shott, and then hoist it again; this, lease he should be surprised with catch-poles … [4]

Estuaries and saltings also provided opportunities for landing goods unobserved. Ships making their way through treacherous channels and numerous mud-banks to find a safe harbour often made unscheduled stops in the sticky mud. Sometimes these halts were the legitimate result of bad navigation. Frequently, though, the overnight wait for the tide was simply an excuse to unload half the cargo into a necklace of small boats that appeared from the reedy margins of the river as soon as the ship grounded. Throwing parcels of tea from the deck of a large ship to a passing rowing boat was a simple matter; in the unlikely event that the preventive forces were watching from the shore, the ship's master could always excuse himself by claiming that the off-loading was necessary in order to float the ship off the mud. Once ashore, pursuit was virtually impossible, since the low-lying land was studded with brackish pools, and broad drainage dykes, and safe routes to dry land were known only to the locals.

DEFENDING THE CARGO

Such subterfuge was inconvenient compared to a regular landing, and smugglers generally preferred an open beach, relying on force of numbers to avoid capture. Unloading a large cargo required an army of helpers and when smuggling reached its zenith in the middle of the eighteenth century, some gangs were indeed capable of mustering hundreds of labourers in a couple of hours. For example, at Cuckmere Haven in Sussex, on 18 September 1783:

> … between two and three hundred smugglers on horseback came to Cookmere and received various kinds of goods from the boats, 'till at last the whole number were laden, when, in defiance of the King's officers, they went their way in

great triumph. About a week before this, upwards of three hundred attended at the same place; and though the sea ran mountains high, the daring men in the cutters made good the landing ...[5]

Men laden with barrels, bundles and bales could not also protect themselves, so 'batmen' usually defended the tub carriers. These hired thugs equipped themselves with a variety of weapons – typically a stout oak club, a flail, or handguns, and when called upon didn't hesitate to use them. When opposition was expected, two rows of batmen stood back-to-back a couple of yards apart to form a corridor stretching inland away from the beach, so that the tubmen could run unhindered for safety.

The customs men were most of the time greatly outnumbered, and when a patrol of two or three chanced upon a smuggling run in full flow, there was little they could do except signal for assistance and then watch and wait.

Knowing this, smugglers could be quite brazen. For example, when troops stationed close to Luce Bay heard about a landing, they lined up on the beach, while the two smugglers' luggers, armed with a total of thirty-six guns, and with a complement of 100 men, hovered offshore. The smugglers shouted to the troops that they should retire a little, as a run was about to take place, and they did not care to be observed too closely. The alternative – a fight against far superior forces – was declined, and the dragoons retreated. When the excisemen returned, there was a reward waiting for them – a row of barrels on the shoreline.

And at Arish Mell, Dorset a local newspaper reported that:

A Dunkirk schooner landed ... upwards of twenty tons of tea, in sight of and in defiance of the Custom House officers as they were mounted twenty four-pounders, which they brought to bear on the beach. The smugglers on shore carried it off in three waggons and on horses, except twelve hundredweight, which the officers seized, and carried to a public house at West Lulworth ... but thirty or forty of the schooner's people, well armed, followed after, and broke into the house, beating and cutting the people they found there in a cruel manner, and carried off the tea.

Smugglers constantly threatened revenue men with physical violence and death, and this theme is explored at length in the chapter 'Deconstructing Kipling'. However, some of the pluckiest preventives refused to be intimidated, and took on gangs of smugglers against quite overwhelming odds. Frequently these brave (some would say foolhardy) young men paid a high price – read on page 173 how Sydenham Snow died opposing a run at Herne Bay.

Harsh laws against smuggling, if anything, made the batmen more violent and murderous; until the late seventeenth century the penalty for smuggling – as for many petty crimes – was death, so a smuggler caught in the act tended to deal out violence on a wholesale basis. Whether or not he killed his opponent hardly mattered, since if convicted of either smuggling or murder the sentence would be the same.

Smugglers' attempts to defend their cargoes were not simply skirmishes with revenue men. When the stakes were high they escalated into full-scale military combat. Indeed, one of the most famous incidents, remembered as the Battle of Mudeford, amounted to trench warfare.

BATTLE ON THE BEACH

In 1784 two smuggling luggers had shipped across from the Channel Islands a huge cargo of tea and brandy, and on 15 July a crowd of some 300 people were busy unloading at Mudeford beach, at the entrance to Christchurch harbour. The goods were being loaded into about 50 carts, drawn by 300 horses, when a navy sloop, HMS *Orestes*, rounded Hengistbury Head, with two escorting revenue cruisers.

This setback led to pandemonium. John Streeter, a Christchurch man who had crewed on one of the two luggers, rode to the nearby Haven House, and herded the customers out of the pub and down to the beach. The luggers had by this time been beached on the shingle, and the patrons of the Haven House helped to strip them of all their lines and rigging. Meanwhile, the cartloads of contraband were moving away from the shore.

At sea, activity was just as frenetic. Seeing what was happening ashore, the captain of the *Orestes* resolved that he would seize the cargo if possible. Failing that, he would destroy the luggers. The sloop-of-war and the escorts lowered six rowing boats filled with heavily armed sailors, and the boats closed in rapidly on the beach. As they neared the shore, William Allen, the master of the *Orestes,* shouted to the smugglers remaining on the decks of the ships to surrender. The reply was a deafening fusillade, and Allen fell back in the boat, mortally wounded. Still some 200 yards from the shore, the naval and revenue men returned fire. A running battle ensued, but it was hardly a fair fight: the smugglers were firing from trenches that they had dug along the beach, whereas the preventive forces had to take aim from rocking open boats, with no cover.

When the boats landed, the smugglers retreated to the Haven House, and continued firing from there. The fighting continued for some three hours (some accounts say for fifteen hours) during which the guns of the *Orestes* were trained on the *Haven House.* Somewhat inaccurately, it would seem: stray canon balls actually struck the Christchurch Priory 2 miles away. Eventually the revenue and navy men captured the two luggers and a number of small boats that the smugglers had scuttled in shallow water.

The price of the seizure was high: while the preventive forces were pinned down on the beach, they suffered many casualties – quite apart from the death of one of their number. By contrast, the smugglers had secured their cargo, esti-mated (probably generously) at 120,000 gallons of spirits and 25 tons of tea, and had for the most part melted away into the surrounding countryside. It's not known whether any of them were injured.

Three men were eventually arrested on a murder charge, but two were released for a technicality. Eventually the might of the British legal system descended on the shoulders of one George Coombes, who was hanged at Execution Dock. His body hung in chains at Haven House Point until sympathisers cut it down and gave him a decent burial.

John Streeter escaped punishment, and continued to operate as a smuggler, using as a cover a tobacco processing plant adjacent to the Ship in Distress. The authorities hounded him, though, and 1787, William Arnold, the collector of cus-toms at Cowes, commented that Streeter was 'Supposed to be now in the Island of Guernsey or Alderney, but occasionally [returns] to the neighbourhood of Christchurch, where Streeter narrowly escaped from being retaken by disguising himself in woman's clothes.'[6]

The Mudeford battle focused public attention on the Christchurch smugglers, but the incident was exceptional only because of the violent resistance the smug-glers put up. There's little evidence to suggest that the cargo was anything out of the ordinary. One local writer described how on another occasion he saw:

> a procession of twenty or thirty wagons, loaded with kegs of spirits, an armed man sitting at the front and tail of each, and surrounded by a troop of two or three hundred horsemen, every one carrying on his enormous saddle from two to four tubs of spirits, winding ... along the skirts of Hengistbury Head, on their way towards the wild country to the northwest of Christchurch ... [7]

TREATING CASUALTIES

Those smugglers who were injured in clashes like these could hardly call an ambu-lance, but their wounds were not left untreated. The largest and most powerful smuggling gangs retained the services of a surgeon: the Aldington gang of Kent used a physician from Brookland. More often, though, smugglers recruited medi-cal help as best they could when the need arose. Doctors were usually wise enough to ask no questions, and scared enough to keep their duties secret. A surgeon from Christchurch, Dr Quartley, described an incident that must have been typical. Soon after setting up in the town he was woken by a loud rapping on the door in the mid-dle of the night. On opening it, he was greeted by a pair of horsemen, who told him his skills were needed urgently, and that he should saddle a horse and follow them.

The surgeon wasn't really given any choice, so he did as he was told, and fol-lowed the horsemen (who were soon joined by others) out of the town, and to

Bransgore. There he was shown into a small cottage where lay a smuggler, severely wounded. The doctor quickly removed a musket ball from the man's shoulder, and told companions of the injured man that he should not be moved, but should get some rest. At this news, one of the uninjured smugglers turned to their groaning colleague and asked 'Well, Tom! Whilst thee stay here and be hanged, or shall we tip thee into a cart?' The lad preferred to die of his wound than at the end of the rope, and was duly carted off into the forest (where he later recovered) as the learned doctor was escorted back to Christchurch. Dr Quartley's reward was a keg of brandy left anonymously on the doorstep, chalked with the legend 'Left there for the doctor's fee.'[8] Dr Quartley's doorstep can still be seen on Castle Street at the end of one of Christchurch's bridges.

NOTES

1   *Eastern Daily Press*, 18/10/1963
2   Cardiff custom house letters to board
3   *Eastern Daily Press* 29/12/1926; *Smuggling in Norfolk* by 'Suffolk Coast'
4   Dunbar, Edward, 1865
5   Parry John Docrwa, 1833
6   Foster, D. Arnold, 1936
7   Warner, Rev. Richard, *Literary Reflections*, quoted by Short, Bernard Charles, 1969
8   Third Earl of Malmesbury, *Memoirs of an Ex-minister*, quoted by Short, 1969

5
TEMPORARY HIDING PLACES

To a land smuggler, the eventuality to be avoided at all costs was to be caught in possession of incriminating tubs, so hides and dumps for contraband near the coast were of great value. Caves and tunnels were certainly useful, though probably not to the extent that legend might suggest see pages 59-64).

Probably the most often used hiding places were also the most obvious: pubs and inns. They had enormous cellars which were used for legitimate barrels. They were also an outlet for contraband spirits – either by selling it openly to trusted customers, or by mixing with duty-paid goods.

However, contraband liquor in a pub cellar was inviting discovery. Among duty-paid goods, the tiny barrels favoured for smuggled spirits were obvious. Landlords could conceal contraband behind walls of bigger barrels, but some pubs also had hidden storage areas. The sixteenth-century Spread Eagle pub in Witham town centre still retains a reminder of the cunning of the smugglers who would have been innocently refreshing themselves at the bar when the revenue man walked through the door. A concealed well, once accessible only from the roof, pierces the pub from attic to cellar. Climbing on the tiles, the smugglers would lower their goods down the shaft on ropes. To make the shaft visible to present-day drinkers, a small window has been installed in the bar.

When customs men came banging on the door of an inn where contraband goods were stored, landlords had to be resourceful to escape suspicion. This embarrassing situation has spawned a whole genre of smuggling yarns. In the most common plot, the landlord's wife, daughter or mother sits on an incriminating keg, and spreads her voluminous skirts around it. The customs men and dragoons then search the pub and leave empty handed.

A few such yarns have a more original twist, such as this one from Mother Redcap's pub in Wallasey:

... on one occasion ... the smugglers were desirous of getting a cask of rum or some other merchandise away from one of the hiding places, but were prevented by the unwelcome presence of the officer. So it was arranged that one of the smugglers was to creep down to the shore from the Moor, and lie down in his clothes in the water, at the edge of the receding tide. The attention of the solitary officer at Mother Redcap's was called to the supposed body which had been washed ashore, and he made his way to it as quickly as possible. He had removed the watch, and was going through the pockets when the corpse came to life, sprang up, and laid out the surprised officer. By the time he had come to, the rum had been removed from Redcap's, and started its journey to the moss. No blame could be attached to the 'drowned man' who said he was walking along the shore, when he must have had a fit, for the next thing that he became aware of was that he was lying in the sand with his pockets being rifled.[1]

CRYPT AND CHANCEL

Churches were popular hiding places, too. At Ivychurch on Romney Marsh a vault under the nave was used for storage, and cargoes of tobacco stored at nearby Snargate Church smelt so strongly that in the marsh mists the vicar was able to locate it with his nose. The vicar was R.H. Barham who wrote the smuggling poem that appears in the *Ingoldsby Legends* (see page 142). Snargate Church is particularly interesting to visit today, since the wall of the nave is decorated with a painting of a ship – an early smugglers' coded symbol marking a place of safety.

Storage of contraband in churches has often been the subject of light-hearted anecdote that pokes harmless fun at clergy who connived with smugglers. It shouldn't all be dismissed as worthless hearsay, though. At Hove, for example, there is a yarn about St Andrew's Church, which shared a vicar with Preston Church. Since services alternated between the two, it was perhaps only a matter of time before a confused vicar got his preaching timetable wrong, and arrived at Hove to find a congregation of bales and barrels. It may never have happened, but this doesn't change the fact that the church was used as a store for tobacco and brandy.

In the church at Langton Matravers, on the isle of Purbeck, tubs were stored in a void above the ceiling in the church roof. A local story tells that on one memorable Sunday the choir were singing from a psalm the words 'And Thy paths drop fatness', when the roof collapsed, bombarding the congregation with kegs.

Smugglers also used graveyards for storage, sliding aside the slabs of table tombs at Boldre, near Lymington, at Herstmonceux, and in many other places. At Mottistone on the Isle of Wight their cache was stored in a large tomb, originally excavated for the bodies of seven sailors washed ashore from a wreck.

HEARTH AND STABLE

Smugglers were inventive and ingenious in their choice of hiding places, and concealed contraband beneath natural obstacles that they knew would deter close investigation. An aphorism from Fordingbridge – 'keystone under the hearth, keystone under the horse's belly' – identified the two favourite places for hiding contraband: under the stable floor, and under the fire-place, with a fire burning innocently on top.

These hiding places were used far from the New Forest. On Scotland's west coast at Clome Farm, there was a 'brandy-hole' covered by a fireproof trapdoor – the farmer lit a fire in the kiln above it when he expected a visit from the revenue men. The trick didn't work forever though, and a 1777 raid yielded 80 chests of tea, 140 ankers of brandy, and 200 bales of tobacco.

And at Saltburn the local 'King of the Smugglers', John Andrew, used the stables of the White House to conceal contraband in a chamber under one of the stalls. When the place was to be searched, the stable lad had strict instructions to put in that stall a mare that could be counted upon to kick viciously at any stranger.

CONCEALMENT AND BETRAYAL

These brief tales of concealment fail to convey the frantic measures that smugglers used to evade the law, but exploring at greater length a true story of hidden contraband shows that, for smugglers, hide-and-seek was far from a game.

The story is set in the summer of 1778, when a group of smugglers brought in a cargo of gin to the Suffolk shore. They landed the 300 tubs undetected, shipped them a couple of miles inland in six carts, and hid the contraband in a barn at Leiston Common Farm, under the watchful eye of Crocky Fellowes, a trustworthy accomplice.

All would have been well had the cache not been found by another local of Leiston, the club-footed 'Clumpy' Bowles. Either Bowles did not have the same sympathy for the local smugglers, or he smelled a reward, because he reported the find to the local revenue man, Read. Realising that he'd need some support if he was going to separate the spirits from their owners, Read tried to summon a pair of dragoons who were billeted at the White Horse in the village. The dragoons were drunk, so Read looked elsewhere for reinforcements. He sent for two dragoons from the inn at Eastbridge, but the landlady there plied the two men with spirits before they left, so their assistance was equally useless.

Read eventually got together some help, and the party was met at the locked door of the barn by Crocky Fellowes, and two chums – Sam Newson and Quids Thornton. The three men kept Read and his party occupied while twenty of the smugglers moved the tubs through an adjoining hay-loft and onto waiting carts.

When the work was complete, the three men guarding the barn unlocked the door, admitted the revenue officers … then locked them inside. The carts trundled off to Coldfair Green, a mile south-west of Leiston.

Here the smugglers had another hiding-place waiting. A dung-heap concealed a trap-door, which led to a sizeable underground vault. The tubs were bundled in and the dung moved back into position; the finishing touch was to eliminate all the cart tracks and footprints by driving a herd of sheep over them. This subterfuge seems to have been sufficient to outwit the revenue men, but the tale is not yet over.

Some time later, the gang returned to recover their cache. They shovelled the manure away from the door and opened the vault. Despite warnings from Crocky Fellowes, they didn't wait for the foul air from the dung to disperse before descending, and three of the gang were overcome by the fumes; two of them died as a result.

News of the deaths travelled fast, and eventually reached the ears of a revenue officer at Saxmundham. He guessed that the smugglers would move the tubs to Aldringham, probably to the Parrot and Punchbowl. He was right. He rode to the pub with two dragoons, and caught the smugglers red-handed.

However, while their gin was in hiding, the gang had not been idle. They soon found out who had informed on them, and at nine o' clock one night two of them arrived at the crippled breech-maker's house on the Yoxford Road close to Leiston High Street. They dragged Clumpy from the house and took him on horseback to somewhere a little less public. There they gagged him with the bung from a beer barrel and savagely whipped him. They threw the apparently lifeless body over a hedge, but Clumpy was clearly a man of some stamina. A farm labourer found him, and took him to the Green Man at Tunstall, where a servant recognised the bung with which Clumpy's assailants had gagged him; she had lent it to a man called Tom Tippenham. Clumpy's testimony, and this corroborative evidence, earned Tippenham and his accomplice to a two-year stretch in Ipswich Prison.

BURYING CONTRABAND

When smugglers couldn't find a convenient cellar, crypt or tomb, they excavated their own hides, often in the shifting dunes that fringe so many beaches. The preventive forces used long probes to search for hidden contraband in soft sand, but there were ways to avoid detection by this method, and also to conceal tell-tale traces left by armies of men with shovels.

The smugglers at Slains took elaborate precautions to hide the elaborate pits they dug deep in the sand, each big enough to hold up to 300 tubs of gin. An account written in 1858 describes how the barrels were taken from a lugger to a temporary resting place while the pit was dug. Sand from the pit would be turned onto two sails – dry sand from the surface on one, and the damper sand from below onto the other, so that the completed hiding place would not be betrayed by a change in the colour of the dunes. The pit was lined with bricks or timber, and the roof was always at least 6ft underground, because the probes used to locate hidden caches on the beach were 6ft long. Once the labourers had been paid off, the 'partners' in the run themselves transferred the barrels to the pit, sealed the entrance, and took bearings to landmarks so that they could locate the hoard. Within hours, wind-blown sand would cover all traces of activity.

Smugglers used the dunes of Mablethorpe, Lincolnshire, in a similar way, and early in the twentieth century a partly decayed barrel of tobacco was unearthed there. The owner had clearly been unable to return to claim his cargo, or perhaps had failed to take accurate bearings to locate the hiding place among the drifting sand-dunes.

On Hayling Island, too, sand and shovels were as essential as the sea itself for a successful run. The island was approached along a causeway before Victorian times, and until contraband landed on the island could be inconspicuously moved along this link to the mainland, the kegs and bundles of tobacco were stored in vast depots dug in the sandy soil. A writer commented in 1826 that 'When this nefarious and demoralizing system was at its height … Many subterraneous caverns were known to exist along the south beach, for the reception of contraband goods.'[2]

By 1826 most of the caverns had disappeared, with the exception of one 'not far from the new buildings' – about one-third of the way along the south shore travelling west to east.

Occasionally smuggling caches were buried inland, though heavy soil made this much more difficult than on the beach. The Branscombe, Devon smugglers buried contraband in a novel way that apparently has no parallel elsewhere in Britain. They dug a sloping tunnel leading to the centre of a field, then at its end hollowed out a circular pit, some 12ft underground. The entrance to the chamber was concealed using earth and turf. These storage places have been repeatedly uncovered during farming, and in 1953 an estate map showed the location of no fewer than six of them, found between 1909 and 1939.

SUNKEN CONTRABAND

Why dig a hole, though, when an ideal hiding place was so close at hand? The sea surrenders its secrets reluctantly, and smugglers were quick to recognise that the highway that brought them over from France and Holland could also conceal their cargoes. If the revenue man appeared on the scene, tubs of spirits were tipped into the sea for later recovery. Adding a weight anchored the barrel in shallow water. Much of the contraband destined for Yarmouth came ashore like this:

smuggling vessels would sink tubs in the treacherous Yarmouth roads for local fishermen to collect.

If the sea bed was covered in soft silt, tubs sunken in this way were difficult to recover. Instead they were attached to a plank, which was weighted so that it floated some 6ft off the muddy bottom. To mark the position of the tubs, smugglers at Durlstone Bay, Purbeck used bottle-corks tied to pieces of cord – pulling on the cord would bring to the surface a stouter line attached to the string of tubs. Lobster-fishing provided the cover for recovering tubs, and the smugglers took care that their floats were indistinguishable from the markers used for lobster pots.

This habit had on occasion dire consequences: a local yarn tells how a well-bred lady was travelling to Poole in the market boat, and noticed the bobbing corks. She asked the captain what they were for, and on learning that they marked lobster pots, She exclaimed that, although she had eaten lobster, she'd be fascinated to see how they were caught. When the obliging captain hauled in the pot to satisfy the woman's curiosity, he was dismayed (but perhaps not surprised) to find a couple of kegs attached. As ill-fortune would have it, one of the other passengers was a custom house officer from Swanage, who promptly chalked a broad arrow on each keg, and resolved the following morning to keep an eye on the lobster fishermen. He was not disappointed, and had the pleasure of seeing the astonishment on one man's face as he hauled in tubs marked as seized by HM government. On returning to the shore, a reception committee was waiting for the unfortunate fisherman.

Isle of Wight smugglers also sunk tubs off-shore, though this was practical only in the Solent, since surf on the south of the island would soon set tubs adrift. Recovering sunken barrels was unlikely to arouse suspicion: as at Purbeck, crabbing and lobster fishing were major industries on the Isle of Wight, and 'creeping' for tubs could easily be passed off as the baiting of pots, or checking the catch.

Sunken tubs could not be left floating indefinitely: the sea-water eventually seeped through the cheaply made barrels, rendering the spirit undrinkable. In the West Country, spoiled French brandy earned the nick-name *stinkibus* or *stinky-booze*.

RAFTING TUBS

What started as a convenient way of concealing incriminating evidence developed with time into a systematic smuggling technique. Barrels were lashed together to form a raft, and weighted so that it floated just below the surface of the water; pushing the tubs into the sea was known as 'sowing a crop'. The tubs could either be collected later, or floated together to some convenient landing point. In Essex, Goldhanger smugglers floated rafts of tubs down the Blackwater, landing them at Mill Beach opposite Northey Island.

At natural harbours which filled with the tide, such as Christchurch, the flowing current would tow the raft along. There, the sole entrance from the sea is a narrow channel, the Run, and the tide flows through it at alarming speed. A raft of sunken tubs could be swept into the harbour right under the noses of the unsuspecting preventive men. The weighted tubs were released just off-shore, and often guided into the run by a strong swimmer. Abe Coates (or Coakes) was possibly the last of the Mudeford smugglers to make a living as a human tug-boat: he would ferry the tubs into Mother Sillers' Channel, or even to Bergman's Mill on Christchurch quay, a distance of 6 miles.

Tubs were also concealed under fresh water: at Fordingbridge in the New Forest smugglers sank tubs in the river Avon, but the still waters of a pond provided a more reliable hiding place.

At Peldon in Essex, a pool outside the Rose Inn hid a large well. Weighted tubs of spirits could be lowered down this on ropes until the revenue men had completed their searches. At Bishops Cannings in Wiltshire smugglers caught in the act of raking the village pond to haul out tubs feigned stupidity to make their activities seem innocent. When excisemen demanded to know what was going on the smugglers pointed at the moon's reflection in the water, and said they were raking the pond to recover the 'big yellow cheese' that was floating in it. The trick earned them the nickname 'Moonrakers'. (Revelling in their reputation, they also put it about that they spread manure around the church tower to make it grow taller, and told strangers that every inhabitant of the village had once walked to Devizes to watch an eclipse of the moon.)

On the Norfolk Broads wherryman sunk their tubs in the still waters, marking the spot with a float made of reeds. The marshman at a nearby mill would pick up the contraband later, and share in the proceeds. There was a risk attached to this procedure – sometimes the kegs would drift free and be lost. This possibility was avoided by lobbing the tubs into a drainage ditch: the mill gradually pumped the water along the ditch, so that the tubs were delivered directly to the marshman.

Wells hid barrels, too, though few compared with the well at the ancient manor house at Sully, South Wales:

> the flow of water could be stopped, and what remained pumped out. Underneath the false bottom was a vault in which a horse and cart could easily have been turned. It was evident that smuggling had been carried on here extensively, but so secretly that it was not even suspected.

CAVES

Where coastal erosion created caverns, some of these were used for short-term storage. However, few caves around the coast of Britain make really suitable warehouses:

many are very shallow; others are so easily accessible that they offered inadequate security; and most fill with water at high tides, precluding their use for the storage of dry goods. Even spirits would not be completely secure in a tide-washed cave: a heavy surf could dash stored tubs against the rock walls, smashing them in minutes.

Where a cave exists, its use for smuggling is not always plausible. For example, according to tradition, a small cave in the east cliff of Flat Holm in the Bristol Channel was used for the storage of contraband, but the writer who commented in 1902 that '… men are still living who claimed to have seen (the cave) filled with kegs of brandy that had never paid the Queen's dues …' had clearly not visited the island himself. The entrance to the cave is hardly large enough to squeeze into, and just a couple of barrels would have filled the chamber. Elsewhere on the island, though, there is circumstantial evidence that points to smuggling activity. An old mine shaft on the north side connects with a series of natural tunnels, and a sea-facing exit to the system has been cleverly filled with masonry and disguised as solid rock. These concealed chambers are well-hidden, and even on close inspection would pass for a derelict tin mine. However, an old mine shaft does not quite have the romance of a cave.

Flamborough Head is dotted with caves that were associated with smuggling, and one of them – Rudston Church Garth – is reputedly connected by a tunnel to the church mentioned in its name. Another cave is simply called the 'Smugglers' Cave', though an elderly local comments that, 'We called it that when I was a lad to amuse the visitors. The cave that was really used was "Dovecote" (now called "Pigeon-Hole".)' In *The Book of the West*, the vicar of Morwenstow describes a cave – though not a sea-cave – used for concealing contraband, a little way up the valley from Porthcothan Bay, just west of Padstow.

> At Porth Cothan the cliffs fall away and form a lap of shore, into which flows a little stream … About a mile up the glen, is a tiny lateral combe. Rather more than halfway down the steep slope is a hole just large enough to admit a man entering in a stooping posture …

The cave is still in existence, though there is no trace of the extensive tunnel that the writer goes on to describe. Some of the details he wrote about over a century ago can still be seen. There are notches near the mouth, into which smugglers lodged a beam of timber; they then heaped earth against the beam and covered the pile with furze to hide the entrance. The tunnel supposedly led to a farm half a mile away.

There are a few examples of smuggling caves that really seem credible. Smugglers certainly used caves in Margate to store their goods, and the earthworks remained a closely guarded secret until they were revealed by sheer fluke: a gardener working at Trinity Square disappeared in a fatal fall when his spade penetrated the roof of the long-forgotten cavern. There is also a tradition that Sampson's Cave near Barnstaple was used by smugglers, and exploration of it suggests that it ticks all the boxes for a practical hiding place.

SMUGGLING TUNNELS – MYTH OR METHOD?

No smuggling story would be complete without a secret tunnel, yet this most persistent of all legends of smuggling concealment is also the one least founded on fact. Virtually every village within 5 miles of the southern coast of England is supposed to have a smugglers' tunnel, the location of which the locals will divulge after several stiff drinks an hour after closing time. Almost always, though, the entrances to the tunnels have been lost or bricked up.

Legendary smuggling tunnels usually start or end at the church, the pub or the rectory, or (better still) link two of these places:.

At Church Norton, on the west of Pagham Harbour, a tunnel connected the eponymous church and the Old Rectory.

At Selsey Bill a passageway led from the Old Rectory to the Mound. The course of the tunnel was marked by a depression on the surface of the ground as late as 1911.

At Langstone, a tunnel linked the Red Lion pub to the nearby tide- and windmill. Such a passage would have been so close to sea level that keeping it dry would have presented formidable problems – though perhaps the mill was used for pumping out when the tide filled the tunnel?

At Maningtree, the White Hart had a tunnel that led underground from the cellar to the Stour estuary.

At St Austins near Lymington there are stories of a tunnel leading down from the ruined monastery chapel to the waterside. In dry summer weather, the meadow grass changes colour in a strip that marks the route of the tunnel. (Sceptics suggest that the line shows where the monks spread gravel to form a path.)

At Clome Farm on Luce Bay, Scotland, the farmer can still point out evidence of a tunnel: a combine harvester parked over an underground chamber began to sink into the ground, and a puddle in the farmyard bubbles as water seeps into the tunnel below. The entrances to the tunnel have long been lost, though.

The list goes on. If every one of these yarns, and the hundreds of others, was true, the coast of Britain would resemble Swiss cheese, and most cliffs would collapse into the sea.

Many of the hypothetical tunnels cut through unsuitable rock, or they burrow along beneath the water table. Some such tunnels would be prodigious feats of engineering: one of Isaac Gulliver's shafts (see page 184) was rumoured to run from Kinson, now a Bournemouth suburb, to the coast some 4 miles away!

However, the smuggling tunnel capital of Britain is not on the South Coast, but in Scotland. Eyemouth, it is said, was riddled with passages, and there was more of the town below ground than above. The centre of this labyrinth was a house that is now the library: passages ran underground to the adjacent premises. Just around the corner in Chapel Street there were underground windings leading from the shop on the corner opposite the butchers. Gunsgreen Mansion – now the golf club – was reputed to have an opening in its walls that formed a slipway giving direct access to the sea, and from the opening a passage led to the house. Beneath the lawn there was a vast cellar and according to tradition, tunnels led to a cottage on Gunsgreen Hill above the mansion, and on to Burnmouth. Indoors, there were tales of concealed passageways, and ' ... a massive grate or fire-place, which, by moving some knob or lever, could swing out of its place like a gate being opened. This strange contrivance was the door-way into a secret passage'.

But why shouldn't this tale, and all the others, be true? Simply because the purpose of a tunnel was to conceal a smuggler's activities, and its construction would have exactly the opposite effect. Tunnelling is dangerous, exhausting, labour intensive, but most of all, conspicuous. Rock doubles in volume when excavated, and even a short tunnel would yield vast quantities of rubble. Where the tunnel ends at a quarry, a cliff, or on a beach, the story is perhaps plausible, because spoil would be inconspicuous. Elsewhere, though, digging a tunnel would attract attention more often than it would aid concealment.

Looking closely at just one story illustrates just how impractical most of the tunnels it describes would be.

In the Gravesend area smugglers' tunnels were supposed to have linked several local landmarks:

> ... there are good reasons for believing that an extensive system of underground roads existed at one time or another for more or less illicit purposes. Some sections of these have been supported by proof of a reasonably reliable kind during excavations ...

... writes one local historian. He goes on to say that there were tracks cut in the chalk ...

> from Cobham Hall in the South-East to Wombwell Hall; to Swanscombe Wood, where Clapperknapper's Hole is regarded as the exit in the extreme southwest: to Parrock Manor, or Parrock, or both; to the river bank at the old sulphur mill, near the Ship and Lobster; and to an unknown destination from an unknown source at Pelham Road – Old Road – Perry Street.

Clapperknapper's Hole, which has now been removed by quarry working for the cement industry, was a small indentation in the ground in Swanscombe Woods. However, at that point at least 50ft of sand lay over the chalk. Digging a vertical shaft in such soft ground would have been virtually impossible – a local geologist commented: 'You'd need to cut down all of Swanscombe woods to make pit-props'. The other tunnels are supposed to have run for several miles through hard chalk, crossing a water-course. Digging such tunnels would have required a phenomenal amount of labour, and a string of windmills to drain them.

The account contains a germ of truth, though. The *Ship and Lobster* pub (which still stands) has an impeccable smuggling pedigree, and Dickens used it as the model for an inn he described in *Great Expectations*: 'It was a dirty place enough, and I dare say not unknown to smuggling adventures.' In the eighteenth century, the pub stood in an industrial area, sandwiched between a windmill and a sulphur mill. The sulphur mill was probably a blind for smuggling operations: contraband was reputedly unloaded from ships at Folkestone and carried overland to Denton, to be hidden in tunnels under the mill. Some credence was added to this story when the Strood Canal was being built: workers fell into one of the tunnels as they were digging.

A few other tunnel stories turn out to be plausible. At Hayle, for instance, in the garden of a house that was formerly the local youth hostel, there is a remarkable tunnel. A sloping trench leads down from ground level to the arched entrance, where the hinges for a gate or door can still be seen. The tunnel is still open, and runs due north for hundreds of yards. It is possible to walk along it only in a stooping posture, though in the last two centuries, the average stature has risen considerably, so possibly seventeenth-century smugglers could have walked upright. Many smugglers' tunnels prove disappointing, or just non-existent, but this one seems authentic as any: it is the right shape; it runs towards the coast; it even has a drainage gulley along its length to keep the flat floor dry.

There are other examples: on Thanet not only did preventive officers discover a 300-yard-long tunnel that started at a Ramsgate house in 1822, but they actually caught the 'mole' red-handed. Significantly, the tunnel ended at the beach, thus neatly solving the problem of disposing of the spoil: it could be tipped in the sea. Contemporary estimates put the cost of the digging at £200.

And in East Budleigh rumours of a tunnel that led from the fifteenth-century rectory (since named Vicar's Mead) to the church were corroborated when twentieth-century rebuilding work revealed two secret passages, eighteen inches wide, concealed within the thick north and south walls of a bedroom formerly known as the Parish Room. It was here, according to tradition, that the village's vicars planned landing of cargoes at the mouth of the Otter between 1741 and 1852. But even here, where there is some supporting evidence, there is still no trace of the legendary tunnel.

If real tunnels are so extremely rare, why do they feature so prominently in smuggling histories? Romanticism alone can't account for their ubiquity. One possible explanation is that smuggling tunnels were actually built for some other purpose, such as drainage.

At Lymington, for instance, a tunnel from the shore reputedly led up the hill to the Angel Inn, and from there to the Nag's Head. The course of the tunnel would have been a logical one for a rainwater or flood drain, so perhaps the smugglers simply made enterprising use of existing facilities. Drains did not need to be big enough to walk through: Poole smugglers made good use of the town drains, dragging contraband from the quay directly into the cellars of the town pubs. When there was a good flow of water through the pipes, after a rainstorm, the task was made considerably easier, because the smugglers could stand high up in the town, and let the water wash a rope down the channel to their colleagues at the quay. Contraband was then tied on, and the rope hauled up against the flow of water. It's said that when the customs men got wise to this trick, they waited at the harbour end for the rope, tied on a tub chalked with the legend 'The end is nigh', then gave a tug to signal that the load was ready. The tub was hauled into a cellar of one of the town pubs, and the smugglers read the message at the very instant their adversaries burst in upstairs.

But there is perhaps another explanation for the tunnel story. Possibly 'tunnel' was used metaphorically to describe a sunken road. Smugglers certainly used these: on the Isle of Wight the chines such as Blackgang Chine were valuable points of entry, because most featured a safe beach on the coast, and a secure path inland, hidden from view by dense brushwood and small trees. Sunken lanes are a fairly common feature in the South West, particularly on routes leading down to coves from the cliff top. Embankments on either side conceal from view anyone passing down to the sea. There is a fine example at Wilmington: though it has now been developed for much of its length, a section of the sunken road remains and is known locally as Featherbed Lane.

And maybe tunnels provided local people with a convenient excuse when the customs man asked if they saw a caravan of wagons pass through the village loaded with tubs: 'Why, sir, I saw nowt! Perhaps them cunning smugglers dug 'emselves a tunnel, and trundled their wagons down that.'

QUARRIES

There is one place in Britain where stories of smuggling tunnels are demonstrably true. On the Isle of Purbeck the marble quarries were a gift for the local free-trading population: much of the marble was extracted by sea, so there was constant activity all along the coast, and an extra ship or two berthing alongside the stone ships passed almost unnoticed. The workings themselves formed a maze of passages and trenches, and a smuggler pursued could dart down a tunnel and soon be hidden behind a pile of rubble, or a slab waiting to be dressed.

The quarry at Durlstone Bay was particularly useful because of its size: from about 1700 stone was worked from shafts or lanes that sloped steeply downwards, and at Durlstone the lanes continued a long way inland. Many of the passages were interconnected, so that the knowledgeable smuggler could disappear down one shaft, and emerge some distance away. At times there were fourteen gangs of quarrymen working there, and with the crews of the stone boats milling around, it was impossible for the customs officers to keep an eye on what was happening, as they frequently complained:

> One mile from Swanage Bay is Durlstone. Here goods are very frequently landed and immediately concealed in the stone quarries where from their great number and extent it is wholly impossible to discover them.

Small quantities of contraband could be removed in the rush baskets which the quarrymen carried to work and back each day. Larger cargoes were frequently stored at the quarry until the coast was clear. A particularly effective hiding place was inside a hollowed-out block of stone: the small entrance was concealed by a pile of loose rocks. Customs men, ignorant of the intricacies of quarrying, were told that the rock was unsaleable, because there was no longer any demand for that kind of marble. Other hiding places included a small cave near Durlstone Head, concealed with a thin block that could be slid aside. This hiding place was unfortunately sniffed out by a coastguard's dog.

DISCOURAGING UNWANTED ATTENTION

Wherever contraband was concealed awaiting onward shipment, its owners were keen to discourage anyone from taking an interest in the cache. After all, few premises had locks, and guarding a pile of tubs was impractical or incriminating. Threats of violence were usually sufficient to keep away the inquisitive and nosey, but smugglers also took advantage of superstition and fear of the supernatural.

For example, an eighteenth-century vicar of Talland, Cornwall, the Rev. Richard Dodge, was reputed to be able to raise and lay ghosts at will. Parishioners dreaded meeting him at night for fear of his devilish accomplices. It seems likely, however, that he fostered these stories to keep people out of the way while a smuggling run went on.

Not far away at Clovelly smugglers may have encouraged stories about the contents of their hidden tubs, for according to locals, cannibals stored barrels of salted human flesh in caves along the coast. The origin of the story can be traced to a late eighteenth-century chap-book called *The history of John Gregg, and his family of robbers and murderers*. So the smugglers were simply taking advantage of a local legend and using it for their own ends. Norfolk smugglers did the same. Old Shuck the ghost dog is a persistent Norfolk legend: Shuck is an enormous black dog with one glowing eye, and fiery breath. Anyone who sees Old Shuck is sure to die within a twelve-month. Norfolk smugglers exploited the gullibility of the villagers and tied a lantern round the neck of a black ram, sending it running off to frighten nosey locals when a run was due.

But for an inventive and original smuggler, an existing legend wasn't necessary: hauntings in the Sampford Peverel area in the early years of the nineteenth century were probably staged by the Beer smugglers. They were known to pass through the area, and would have been anxious to draw attention away from their activities. The Old Haunted House, as it was called, was at the extreme north-west end of the village, and at the turn of the century was used as a bakery and grocer. The house was reputed to have double walls, which made it a fine place to store contraband: however, rolling barrels would have caused some considerable amount of noise, which – so the story goes – was concealed by the ghostly howls and thumps …

The chambers of the house were filled, even in day-time, with thunderous noises, and upon any persons stamping several times on the floors of the upstairs rooms, they would find themselves imitated – only much louder – by this mysterious agency.

One owner of the house, in seeking to explain the noises, said that the sound was made by 'a cooper banging tubs with a broomstick'. For 'cooper' read 'smuggler' perhaps – a man equally likely to have a tub handy.

Similarly, at Beaulieu smugglers used Palace House as a warehouse, since it was frequently unoccupied. To discourage unnecessary interest, and ensure that the premises remained vacant, they laid on a variety of stage ghost effects – clanking chains, hair-raising screams in the night, and mysterious apparitions.

NOTES

1   Woods, Edward Cuthbert, *Smuggling in Wirral* from *Transactions*, Historical Society of Lancashire and Cheshire, lxxix (1927), p. 119

2   Scott, Richard, 1826

6

TRANSPORT, DISTRIBUTION AND SALE

Once their contraband was ashore and safe, smugglers had to get it to market. Where they could, they used boats: transport on rivers and estuaries was quick and cheap.

On the Thames, free-traders would 'break bulk' near the mouth of the estuary, and transfer their stocks to smaller boats, such as coasters and colliers, for transport up the river. In London, these small boats could lose themselves among the hundreds of masts in the port and unload surreptitiously at illegal quays; or openly, with a payment to ensure that the customs officials turned a blind eye.

Many other rivers were transport arteries: in Wales ships could move contraband directly inland as far as Dolgellau up Mawddach estuary; and on the Beaulieu river contraband landed in many places along the thickly wooded banks. According to one account '… all the farms along the river were more or less concerned in the traffic it.'[1]

In Norfolk, the Broads provided an elaborate and intricate system of distribution. Barges plying a perfectly legitimate trade were happy to take on board a little extra cargo that provided a higher return than a hold full of coals.

Land transport was much more labour-intensive than moving goods by water: a cutter with a crew of six or eight could land enough cargo to load up a hundred ponies and fifty men. It was more expensive, too. Moving a box of tea or a bale of tobacco from Galloway to Edinburgh in the early eighteenth century cost 15s – a craftsman's wages for a fortnight.

The hazard of moving smuggled goods from the coast to the customers inland varied with the vigilance of the revenue men. If there was little opposition, a chain of armed horsemen – sometimes 150 men and twice as many horses – carried the cargo quite openly. However, in the early nineteenth century when the tide turned against the free-traders, more caution was called for. Then distribution took place in the dead of night, and consignments might be split up to spread the risk.

TRANSPORT LOGISTICS

Tubmen could and did manhandle cargoes over considerable distances, and this method of transport was considered the safest. In Lincolnshire, for example, the villagers of Louth and Horncastle were especially adept at carrying illegal tobacco to Lincoln for manufacture into cigars or snuff.

Transport by cart or packhorse was less energetic and cheaper, but required more care: convoys usually travelled by night, wrapping hooves and cartwheels in rags to muffle their noise. Contraband was stored in safe houses during the day.

The convoys often followed green lanes and ancient trackways, out of sight of the main thoroughfares. In Norfolk the *Peddar's Way*, which runs south-east from Hunstanton, was widely used, and the section north of Massingham used to be known as *Smugglers' Way* for this reason. The same label was attached to other local routes:

> Across the barren wastes of Bodney there is a sandy trackway known as the 'Smugglers' Road' which appears originally to have been ... connected with the road from Swaffham to Hillborough, with a junction about a mile north of the above-named place ... A Smuggler's Way ... left Peddar's Way at Pettigards, but is lost before crossing the Necton-Hale Road ... it reappears as a grass lane to the Hale Fox Cover ... is again lost, but continues as a lane which runs into West End, West Bradenham, where it turns sharply north east, follows the highway to the cross-roads, and runs for some distance as a sunken lane ... it starts again inside the edge of Bradenham [Great] Wood, whence it runs to Fransham and Litsham.[2]

Some Scottish tracks are still called *Smugglers' Way* or, like *Salt Path*, named after the contraband moved along them.

The use of these old roads was not just for secrecy, but also because of the state of Britain's other highways. Their condition was generally appalling, and at their worst during the winter. Until major road-building programmes began in the 1790s, the Roman roads that criss-crossed the country would have been the only reliable way of transporting heavy wagons. On other roads carts often foundered in the mud.

CARTS AND HORSES

Obtaining enough beasts of burden to move contraband was a constant headache for smugglers, because possession of a herd of horses which apparently did no productive work was itself incriminating. Smuggling gangs that maintained large numbers of horses specifically for the purposes of transport used legitimate trade as a cover. For example, the North Kent Seasalter company loaded contraband onto horses that were legally used by day for shifting timber in the nearby Forest of Blean – probably to supply oak bark to the many tanneries in the area. On Romney Marsh gangs dispersed horses and ponies across misty saltings; grazing in twos and threes, the beasts attracted little attention, but mustered together, they formed a caravan sometimes 200 strong.

Extra transport could also be 'borrowed' from farmers and landowners. Sometimes carts and horses were willingly loaned. A farmer close to the coast knew that a meaningful wink from one of his fisherman friends indicated that the stable doors should be left unlocked, or the key under a milk-churn. In the morning, the horses would be back in the stall, muddy and exhausted, but there would be a keg of the best brandy in the corn bin.

At Clacton, for example, smugglers seem to have enjoyed genuine partnership and cooperation with the farmers and labourers along the coast. A story from Great Holland illustrates the way the relationship worked: the farmer was fond of a drop of gin, and a party of London smugglers who worked the area were happy to supply his tipple. He simply asked them to 'leave the lane gate locked' as a signal that his barrel was running low. In return for this kindness, the farmer provided stabling and feed for the smugglers' fifteen horses.

This mutually beneficial relationship is widely romanticised, not least in the famous Kipling poem. This is another typical example, from Wales:

> Cargoes (generally French Brandy) were run into every southern bay from Tenby to Dale … The story goes that when a cargo was in, and the revenue men alert, or the weather squally, teams were requisitioned right and left, not infrequently the squire's carriage-horses were found in the morning sweating and exhausted; but a mysterious keg of excellent eau-de-vie stood in the hall, so no questions were asked.[3]

The arrangement sounds like a cosy bargain, but this was not always the case. A winded horse was worthless for ploughing, and an exhausted farmhand of little more value. Farmers who rebelled against the smugglers using their horses and labourers for transport, and their barns for storage, were kept in line by systematic intimidation resembling today's protection rackets. Sheep could fall unaccountably ill; a hayrick might catch fire; or, returning late from the market, the farmer might ride at speed into a strong black cord stretched between two trees. Before long, the free-traders extracted the grudging cooperation they needed to operate. When labourers were hard to find, as at harvest, farmers faced a double handicap because wages were driven up by the demand for carriers and bat-men.

They were not always paid in cash. Often they took a small share of the goods they were carrying, which they could then sell on, or keep for themselves. This arrangement occasionally had tragic consequences. Labourers working on the sea wall near Clacton one Christmas received gin as a reward for helping smugglers land a cargo. The payment was clearly more than sufficient, because one of their number fell off a plank bridge into Holland Brook, and his colleagues were so drunk that they had difficulty fishing him out. Unable to carry the poor man home, they simply propped him up against a hay-stack and covered him up: he froze to death in the cold December night.

FOUR-LEGGED SMUGGLERS

Where the free-traders relied on horse-power, rather than human muscle, to shift their cargoes, legends grew up around these four-legged helpers. They were intelligent, superbly trained, and ingenious. They were as brave as their masters were cunning. Smugglers, we're told, shaved their nags, and soaped them or oiled them to make capture more difficult; they muffled their hooves with rags for silent progress through the dark. Many a smuggler trained his horse to stop on the command 'Gee-up', and to bolt when told 'Whoah'. Under instruction from a suspicious revenue man, the smugglers could then pull in the reins and innocently call 'Whoah' to provoke a headlong and apparently spontaneous dash into the night.

At Dumfries the local smugglers employed horses as well-trained as any circus animal:

> Individuals … had frequently seen one famous troop of these quadrupeds, heavily laden, at day-dawn, with contraband goods, unattended by any human being, and preceded by a white horse of surpassing sagacity, scouring along the Old Bridge, down the White Sands, and through the streets of Dumfries, without any one daring to interrupt their progress … on one or two occasions, when some individual more officious than the rest rashly attempted to intercept the leader of the troop, the wily animal either suddenly reared and struck its opposer to the ground, or by a peculiar motion swung the kegs with which it was loaded with so much violence that no one durst approach within its reach.'[4]

Like yarns of smuggling tunnels, equestrian stories throughout Britain share some themes. In the most common plot a caravan of ponies is ambushed, and the nags with their burden of tubs are released and whipped away into the darkness. When the exhausted owner arrives home at dawn, he finds his four-legged friend standing dutifully by the door. For example, according to a St Erth legend, a Redruth man was being pursued by the excisemen, when he decided at St Erth Bridge that his exhausted nag could no longer carry both himself and the tubs. He dismounted, and hid under the bridge, whipping the horse off at a gallop. Once he had heard the officer's horse pass overhead, the man emerged and walked back home – the horse arrived a good deal earlier.

While this story is widely repeated with only superficial changes, there are occasionally interesting and amusing variations. According to a story from Purbeck, a smuggling quarryman had an old and faithful nag that had been trained to find its own way home, with a cargo of tubs across its broad back. On reaching the smuggler's house, the horse would wait patiently in the porch until the door was opened, and some kind soul unloaded the night's goods. However, the quarryman had the misfortune to have for a neighbour 'a zealous custom house officer' – not an unusual situation in a small town. One particular night, the horse was perhaps affected by the rich aroma wafting up from the tubs, and turned into the wrong porch. Hearing a clatter of hooves, the customs officer got up from his chair and discovered a windfall seizure waiting on the doorstep. The horse, relieved of his burden and doubtless horrified by the mistake he'd made, crept back to the correct house hanging his head.

RUMOURS OF MY DEATH ...

If a smuggler and his cunning horse could not always escape the customs man, he might sometimes at least outwit him. In the numerous (and usually self-serving) tales of smuggling smartness, one theme stands out conspicuously: funerals. Every corner of Britain has a yarn about a smuggler feigning death, or a coffin full of brandy. These stories may have been passed on around the coast, and adopted with little more than a change of name and location. On the other hand, it's possible that funerals *really did* provide smugglers with good alibis: after all, death was more familiar and less of a taboo in the eighteenth and nineteenth centuries; and perhaps superstition might help deter suspicion. Compare these stories, and draw your own conclusion ...

A ship moored at Lymington. Weeping passengers and downcast crew came ashore with the sad news that the captain had expired during the voyage. A doctor was called, and he duly certified the death, and called the undertakers. Soon a sombre procession (including the local customs men) headed up the main street. To drown their sorrows, the mourners called at the Angel Inn, where the King's men were especially well treated. The cortège continued, in a slightly less dignified manner, but as soon as there was a clear road, the hearse sped off at a pace that was far from funereal, and the coffin and its contents of contraband were spirited away to a safer spot, no doubt to the benefit of undertakers, doctor and all of the mourners. There's good reason to believe that this ruse would have been successful even if the customs men had not had their brains fuddled by drink: the vicar was in league with the smugglers, and allowed the tower of St Thomas' Church to be used for storage.

A similar story from Lowestoft was set in 1910 – long after smuggling had been effectively stamped out. This time the boat was French, and a British passenger on the ship. The coffin, which contained contraband, was actually buried, only to be secretly disinterred.

A Brixham smuggler earned his nickname – 'Resurrection' Jackman – from the same funeral ruse. When revenue men appeared at the door of his house with incontrovertible evidence that he was a smuggler, keening women met them at the door. Jackman, they wailed, was dead, and was to be buried in Totnes: the corpse was to be taken there the following night. The customs men were suspicious, because the coffin seemed unnaturally large, so they decided to keep watch on the funeral cortège. The two officers assigned to the duty had difficulty making out the procession in the pitch black, but to their horror, they were soon met by Jackman himself – pale as death, and riding a spectral horse.

> … The nag cocked his tale
> like a harpooned whale
> and snorted a crimson flame

Screaming with fear, they fled. In reality, of course, the coffin contained brandy, which made its way safely on to Totnes – possibly to the Bay Horse Inn, which was a notorious watering hole for smugglers. This legend crops up again with small changes of detail nearby. The 'dead' man is Bob Elliot, who stored contraband in a cave at Berry Head

At Helston, Cornwall, the funeral is a little less central to the story. There George Michell drove a cart-load of silk up to the Angel Inn, but was met by the landlady, who warned him of a party of searchers, awaiting his arrival. Michell sent his son round to the yard with the cart, walked brazenly into the bar, and bought the crowd of searchers a drink. Relieved that they had their quarry in sight, they accepted, and Michell managed to spin out the conversation for a good while, lacing the talk with flattery about the preventives' skill and insight. Eventually, they heard a rumble of cart wheels, and, rushing to the window, the searchers saw an old horse-drawn hearse driving off – which they dismissed as a pauper's funeral. Needless to say, when the officers eventually got round to searching Michell's cart, they found only innocent provisions.

When there was no handy coffin, smugglers made the most of whatever distraction they could find to lure the revenue man away from their activities. When George IV's Coronation in 1821 set the whole of Brighton celebrating, the free-traders took advantage of the empty streets and moved tubs of spirits out of the stables of the Old Ship Inn completely unobserved.

When a circus and wild-beast show visited nearby Shoreham in August 1855 complimentary tickets were handed out to important local folk, and also to the valiant preventives stationed in the town. As the proceedings reached a climax, few noticed a suspicious-looking ship tie up at the town quay. Before the tide had even begun to ebb, a cargo of tobacco had been unloaded into barges and was on its way up the river to Beeding. Though the plan was discovered, little of the cargo was ever found, and as a result of their negligence, virtually all of the Shoreham coast guards were replaced.

PREPARING FOR SALE

Smugglers who succeeded in escaping or tricking the excisemen had not quite completed their work. The contraband might be close to its final consumers, but it was not necessarily ready to sell. It usually had to be repacked in smaller quantities – and this provided an opportunity for further increasing the profits of the enterprise. Tea, for instance, was often adulterated with rose leaves to bulk it up.

Spirits were usually smuggled over-proof, and were diluted to bring them to a strength that was both profitable, and would not sear the throats of drinkers. One writer who was peripherally involved in the free-trade described how as a boy he learned his 'first lesson in hydrostatics' by doing just this:

> I can well recollect large quantities [of over-proof spirits] being put into an earthenware pan, and diluted with water till reduced to the proper strength which was shown by floating glass beads properly numbered; it was my part to watch them and see when the properly numbered one came to the surface.[5]

This process of 'letting down' to drinking strength could be fraught with difficulties. The smugglers themselves generally spurned the extra profit to be made in dilution, on the grounds that they would have to collect extra tubs to hold the increased volume, so the spirit arrived at its destination in concentrated form. The water added to reduce the strength came from wells, and frequently all manner of unpleasant substances flowed into the brandy along with the water. Some drinkers were permanently sick as a result.

Spirits had to be coloured, too, as a man from Madron, Cornwall described:

> to vary the monotony of the work [as shoe-maker's apprentices] they often turned out ... to Gorran or Portloe, ten miles away, to fetch home smuggled goods – chiefly brandy. ... On arriving home, the liquor was coloured the right shade with burnt sugar, after which it was returned to the kegs and sold to trusty customers.[6]

Smuggled goods were also disguised so that they could not be distinguished from the legitimate article. For example, the sea salt factory on Salt Island in the centre of Holyhead mixed in smuggled rock salt to improve the quality of their product, and then passed the salt off as wholly of local origin. With tobacco it was usually a matter of mixing in leaf from a legitimate source.

Canny smugglers disguised the illicit origin of their products in other ways. In the early years of the eighteenth century a smuggler called Charles Weeks, who worked out of Lulworth, would buy seized goods at legitimate auctions, and mix in the smuggled article for onward shipment, often to London. When an officer challenged Weeks to produce receipts showing that duty had been paid, Weeks could often do so. When he couldn't, he would threaten the officer with litigation; on the pittance paid by the government, no customs officer could afford a legal action, so the smuggler escaped.

WHOLESALE MARKETS

With their products finally in a saleable form, smugglers arranged rendezvous with trusted merchants. Around London they met in outlying villages or held what amounted to open-air wholesale markets. In the south, Stockwell was the base, and elsewhere, the heaths and woodlands which are now part of, or hemmed in by, the greater London sprawl provided effective cover: Hounslow Heath and Epping Forest were depots to the west and east. In the home counties, similar markets took place on land that still retains much of its eighteenth-century character, such as Tiptree Heath, and Daws Heath near Hadleigh in Essex. These areas were notorious as the haunts of vagabonds and villains, and smugglers were able to melt easily into the general criminal milieu. On Tiptree Heath gypsies and squatters held auctions of smuggled goods. For storage, they dug shallow holes in the sandy soil, and covered the packages with turf and brushwood.

RETAIL

In cities, final retail and distribution of the smuggled goods was sometimes via apparently reputable dealers who, through offering smuggled goods, were able to undercut the competition. At other times, the contraband would be hawked round the public bars, or sold through the many gin houses. There were even smuggling 'brands': Crowlink Gap in East Sussex gave its name to the illicit brandy that entered England there: 'Genuine Crowlink' was a guarantee of a good drink. During a period when illegally imported goods could be legally sold over the bar, some landlords even chalked this slogan on the brandy barrels. Usually, though, sales were more discrete. The Hastings Arms in George Street still has a barrel concealed under a window ledge on the first floor (not in a public area, unfortunately) which was once linked by pipes to a tap above the bar so that brandy could be dispensed from the wood without attracting undue attention.

In rural areas tradesmen who visited big houses could use their business as a cover for retailing smuggled goods. Near Sidmouth, for example, Abraham Mutter cut wood and turf at Peak Hill and carried the fuel into nearby towns for sale.

This innocent activity acted as a convenient cover for the transport and sale of contraband. Since the biggest houses would consume large quantities of both fuel and brandy, frequent visits by Mutter's carts and donkeys aroused no suspicion. This lucrative business ended when the railway brought cheap coal to the area.

Final distribution of spirits was sometimes carried out by concealing a pig's bladder or skin full of the stuff under clothing. In Devon one man at least escaped conviction by puncturing the skins, thus destroying the evidence, when he saw a revenue man approaching. Women with a 'skin-full' of spirits about themselves had a particular advantage, for they could not be legally searched, and could use pregnancy to explain a particularly large swelling. In the last years of the eighteenth century a visitor to Cawsand described how:

> … we met several females, whose appearance was so grotesque and extraordinary, that I could not imagine in what manner they had contrived to alter their natural shapes so completely; till, upon enquiry, we found that they were smugglers of spiritous liquors; which they were at that time conveying from cutters at Plymouth, by means of bladders fastened under their petticoats; and, indeed, they were so heavily laden, that it was with great apparent difficulty that they waddled along.

The main hazard of this trade, it appears, was not the customs authorities, but drunken sailors who delighted in puncturing the bladders.

NOTES

1   *Hampshire Notes and Queries* v9, p. 104–5
2   Unattributed press cutting (*Eastern Daily Press* or *Norwich Mercury*) 14/4/1970
3   Laws, Edward, 1888
4   McDowall, William, 1873
5   Banks, John, 1873
6   Jenkin, Alfred Kenneth Hamilton, 1932

7

CORRUPTION AND COLLUSION

The extended description of a 'typical' smuggling run in the previous chapters is of course a fiction, for no two trips were completely alike. Chapters that follow outline how smuggling practices varied in different parts of Britain, and how they were adapted chronologically as patterns of prevention changed. However, some aspects of smuggling that are independent of both time and geography also merit closer examination.

The most important of these is corruption of public officials and their collusion with the free traders. Landing a cargo on a deserted beach at midnight was hardly a pleasant prospect. But if port officials could be persuaded to turn a blind eye, then a smuggling ship could instead unload openly on a town quay. It was a Faustian bargain, for once a venal official had taken a bribe he could hardly say no to another without the risk that his dishonesty would be exposed.

Collusion was a problem from the very earliest days of the customs service. For example, in the sixteenth century officials at Weymouth sided with the smugglers when the ironically named George Whelplay tried to stamp out the free-trade. Whelplay wasn't acting out of altruism: a London haberdasher, he had already made considerable sums of money by becoming a public informer. As such he was entitled to half of the fine levied on people caught as a result of his actions. Since smuggling amounted almost to a national pastime, this did not make him a popular man. Whelplay overstepped the mark in 1538, incurring the wrath not only of the crooked merchants, but also of the customs officials themselves. He had uncovered a plan to illegally export horses to France, and had intercepted the cargo. However, he was also aware that three French ships were at anchor in Weymouth harbour, ready to set sail with contraband on board. Whelplay tried to enlist the help of local officials in rounding up the three French boats, but far from assisting, the controller, searcher and deputy customer joined a gang of merchants to rough up the informer. It appears that Whelplay didn't learn his lessons easily – soon afterwards he tried again to intercept 200 horses bound for France.

This time he was beaten with bills, swords and staves, again by customs officials among others.

The alliance of the hare and hound at Weymouth is perhaps not surprising, since had Whelplay's intervention been successful, both smugglers and officials stood to lose tidy sums of money. The mechanics of this shared interest were exposed later in the century at Bristol. Then Britain's second port, Bristol was famous for wine smuggling from France and the Mediterranean. According to some reports only half the wine landed there paid duty, and the customs officers pocketed a £30 bribe (worth perhaps £5,500 in today's money) for each ship that tied up.

In the seventeenth century the principal contraband smuggled through Bristol had switched to tobacco from Bermuda and Virginia, but the Bristol customs authorities were still taking a cut. When Revenue official William Culliford investigated the port in the 1680s, he found arrat's nest of fraudulent officers. The only Bristol tide-waiter considered to be honest was blind!

The Bristol smugglers were carrying out a familiar fraud. The ship's master kept two sets of accounts. One showed the true cargo: this was for the benefit of its owners. A second set of books was presented to the customs authorities with a nod and a wink. One example was a ship called the *Bristol Merchant*, which docked with 9½ tons of tobacco on board. It cost the crew £80 to get the customs officials to turn a blind eye, but this was less than half what they saved in duty.

This trick worked well far beyond Bristol: in Shetland it was almost an expected part of everyday trade. A cargo from Hamburg in the mid-eighteenth century was declared as consisting of 'Salt, lines, iron and tar' – all commodities that attracted little or no duty at that time. The cargo invoices tells a different story: half the cargo was made up of corn brandy, cognac, claret and other wines. The ruse was stamped out there by sending the land-surveyor along to supervise the unloading.

Bristol smugglers paid off their uniformed collaborators at Mother Grindham's Coffee House on Bristol quayside. The money that changed hands there was not fairly divided, for when a clerk threatened to inform on his superiors he spent eighteen months in prison on a trumped-up charge of debt, and even when he reported the illicit dealings, no action was taken.

It wasn't just at Bristol that senior customs officials were implicated. Culliford's report found corruption everywhere in Wales and the West Country, and many government employees lost their jobs as a result. It was a rare example of a new broom, but any resulting improvement in the integrity of the customs service in the region was short-lived, as examples from Cornwall in the next century illustrate. At St Ives the collector of customs John Knill was himself a smuggler. While he was also mayor of the town in 1767 he paid for the fitting out of a privateer, which was used to ferry contraband. Knill's involvement in smuggling was nearly exposed when a boat loaded with china ran aground. Before the customs men arrived to seize the ship, the crew fled – taking with them the ship's papers, which implicated Knill and a squire of Trevetho. The steeple Knill built – both as a mausoleum and as a landmark for his vessels – still stands above the town.

Knill clearly could see little contradiction between breaking the law and enforcing it, but he was far from unique in this respect. Around the same time the Penzance Collector of Customs described Richard 'Doga' Pentreath of Mousehole as 'an honest man in all his dealings though a notorious smuggler.'

The dishonesty of West Country officials was so thorough and complete that it became part of the folklore of the region. When Reverend Hawker, nineteenth-century vicar of Morwenstow, wrote his famous tales of smuggling folk in the area, he couldn't resist a swipe at the bent exciseman in his yarn about 'The Gauger's Pocket' or the Witan-Stone (rock of wisdom) at Tidnacombe Cross. It is on the edge of the moor, near the sea ' ... grown over with moss and lichen, with a moveable slice of rock to conceal its mouth ... a dry and secret crevice, about an arm's length deep. Smuggler Tristram Pentire, who tells the tale to the vicar adds ...

'There, sir have I dropped a little bag of gold, many and many a time, when our people wanted to have the shore quiet and to keep the exciseman out of the way of trouble; and there he would go if so be he was a reasonable officer, and the bye-word used to be, when t'was all right, one of us would go and meet him, and then say, 'Sir, your pocket is unbuttoned'; and he would smile and answer, 'Ay! ay! but never mind, my man, my money's safe enough'; and thereby we knew that he was a just man, and satisfied, and that the boats could take the roller in peace ... '

It would be unfair, though, to suggest that West Country officials were more corrupt than their counterparts elsewhere in the country. Indeed, the venality of officials was largely taken for granted, as a customs man in Sussex discovered in the nineteenth century. He wrote that:

I was posted as sentinel on duty at the point near the mouth of Cuckmere Haven when two men came up to me. One of them, who has since called himself John Clare, laid money on the beach, desiring me to pick it up. I told him I did not want it. The two men then sat down for some time underneath the cliff when John Clare put on a lump of chalk £20 and pointing to it said there should be twenty pounds for me and a cart in readiness to carry me to what part of the country I pleased admitting them to work tubs, asking me at the same time which was the most convenient place for that purpose. [1]

Such accommodations between smugglers and their 'foes' were commonplace, though more often they are less explicit than this in the historical record. For example, the 1726 smuggling trip from the Medway, mentioned briefly on page 27, probably ended with a bribe that secured the freedom of those taking part.

Once the smugglers had landed the contraband they carried it to Northward Hill near Strood, and concealed it in woodland. By the time the tea and fabric had been hidden it was three in the morning, and two of the group departed, leaving some of their fellows on guard – perhaps the plan was to rendezvous the following day to divide up the profits. After a long night in the cold, the three men who were left behind went into the village to get food, and when they returned to the hiding place, two more of their fellows joined them. By this time, though, the silk and calico had disappeared, and since the tea was in six bags, it proved impossible to give each man his exact share.

The delay in distribution provided the preventive forces with an opportunity – there is a suggestion that one of the smugglers was an informer – and at five o'clock four customs men arrived. We'll never know what sort of a deal took place in the gathering dusk on Northward Hill, but whatever happened, it wasn't entirely to the benefit of the customs authorities. They took three-quarters of the tea, but the smuggling conspirators retained the remainder, and were never prosecuted. The most likely explanation is that the customs men were 'squared', and simply sold the tea they had seized in order to line their own pockets.

Collaboration between customs officers and smugglers was occasionally more pantomine than crime. The Seasalter company from North Kent, for example, had rehearsed a cosy ritual which ensured the safety of their cargoes. One of the company would stand close to the coastguards' cottages at Seasalter, and bellow 'The coast is clear' at the top of his voice. This was the cue for a 'suspicious' coastguard, to pursue the 'smuggler', who would of course head away from the true landing point. In order to make pursuit more difficult, the decoy carried a long plank, which he used to bridge the numerous dykes. The panting coastguard had to take the long way round, and the cat-and-mouse game kept suspicious eyes off the truly dubious activities on the coast.

Even the most senior officials turned a blind eye when it suited them. An eighteenth-century Dorset commissioner of customs, Edward Hooper, Squire of Hurn, lived directly alongside one of the major routes used by smugglers to bring contraband spirits inland. Interfering with this thriving trade would have lost him the goodwill of his neighbours, so when entertaining Lord Shaftesbury, the Chairman of the Customs and Excise, Hooper shrewdly sat with his back to the window during dinner. He did not turn round when six or seven wagons noisily rolled past, loaded with tubs. Shaftesbury sprang from his seat to look at the spectacle, staggered by his host's complacency. When the meal was interrupted again, by a party of dragoons in hot pursuit of the smugglers, the old squire could truthfully assert that he had seen nothing. His guest followed his example.

WARSHIPS, EAST INDIAMEN AND POSTAL PACKETS

Customs men – whether great or humble – were not the only public servants to benefit from the contraband trade. Sailors on international voyages had the opportunity to buy dutiable goods abroad, and their sale on return to Britain seems to have been widely regarded by their superiors as a harmless perk. At Portsmouth plenty of contraband came ashore from naval ships as the personal property of the crews. East Indiamen docked here too, and their crews bought and sold enthusiastically on their own account. If the cargo wasn't secured they sold that too. East Indiamen were generally escorted to Spithead by naval vessels, and lay at anchor there with a handful of customs officers on board to prevent the cargo from falling into the wrong hands. However, the system wasn't perfect, and there were plenty of opportunities for abuse.

East Indiamen anchoring in the Yarmouth Roads (off the Isle of Wight) openly traded with small boats that rowed out. By the 1780s, the smugglers had become quite brazen, and were ready to unload cargoes within sight of the preventive forces: they even formed convoys of small vessels guarded by a well-armed cutters and luggers (200–300 tons). Frequently 200–300 men met the boats to unload the goods.

The crews of postal packets were also heavily implicated in smuggling. Packet crews were not just entrepreneurs – they were so badly paid that they had little choice but to smuggle, just to live. Much of the smuggling in the Harwich area, for example, involved postal packets, which were based at the mouth of the Stour and Orwell. Though these ships were supposed to carry only the mail, passengers and their luggage, few would complete a journey without taking on a small private adventure. The passengers were as guilty as the crews of the packets: the collector of customs at Harwich complained bitterly in the mid-eighteenth century about the quantity of lace and needlework brought in by ladies of the court … 'enough to supply all the milliners shops in and around London.'

At Falmouth, postal packets provided what amounted to an import/export service:

> … our shopkeepers … send over great quantities of woolen stockings, hatts, pewter and other goods to ye value of some thousand pounds by ye saylors for sale, upon getting a certain price upon ye goods to be paid for when sold (what the saylors make beyond the price set being their own), and if not to be returned. The Saylors on receiving ye money for ye goods at Lisbon lay it out in wines, Sugars, fruit and divers other things which they sell at an advantage when they come home, and so pay the shopkeepers either in money or in such Portugall comodityes as he deals in.

The writer then goes on to explain how the licensed wine dealers and British traders in Portugal (who were, of course, being undercut) were spoiling it for everyone by complaining to the customs authorities, and as a result 'a pacquet on arriving would be rummaged and stripped of whatever goods were found in her …' This in itself was not usually a disaster, because under the former system, the customs men were gentlemen of honour, and the shopkeepers could get back the seized goods by:

> gratifying ye officers who seized them, but this is now refused and severall bales of these goods bro't ashore from ye pacquets of late, are ordered to be condemned ... The commissioners of the Customs are making sad work among our shopkeepers and pacquet people, and seem determined to break ye neck of the trade carryed on in these things, which I apprehend will be an ugly thing for the Falmouth people, this trade being ye best support of our shopkeepers.

Recognising the risk of seizure, the steward of Falmouth manor-office instructed that the twenty-four hams he ordered from Portugal, should be sent in two consignments:

> ... for as they are lyable to the Seizure of ye Custom house officers, a greater number by one ship would be in danger ... the best way to have them safe, I believe, will be to Send a trustey Servant for them, who will consult with the captain on ye safest means of escaping ye officers.[2]

NOTES

1   *Sussex County Magazine* Vol. 4, 1903; *Smuggling in Sussex 100 years ago*, by B.F. Richards. Quoted by Hufton, Geoffrey, and Baird, Elaine, 1983

2   Gay, Susan Elizabeth, 1903

8

REGIONAL VARIATION

Smuggling took many forms around Britain's coasts. Some areas saw huge cargoes landed on open beaches in brazen defiance of the customs authorities; collusion and deceit were the rule in other spots; and small, secretive landings characterised the free trade in a few places.

Many circumstances affected smugglers' practices and procedures. Clearly, the character and intensity of the government's efforts to stop smuggling was a major, and perhaps the most important, influence. The following chapter considers this topic in some detail. But other factors affected how crossings, landings and onward shipment proceeded.

The length of the crossing obviously influenced the intensity of smuggling activity, but also the choice of an appropriate vessel. On the Channel coast, for example, smugglers sometimes rowed across in swift galleys. The crossing from Roscoff to Cornwall, though, demanded a more substantial ship.

The coastal topography dictated the practical details of a landing. On a moderately sloping open beach a crew could bring a vessel to the very edge of the surf, and unload a cargo into the arms of the land party. In an estuary, by contrast, thick mud made this impossible. Where cliffs lined the coast, most smuggling took place at the few, easily policed low gaps.

The proximity and size of major markets substantially dictated the scale of smuggling operations, and, indirectly, their method of financing and the professionalism and commitment of those taking part. In isolated areas smuggling was most often small-scale and low-value, and subsidiary to other occupations such as fishing. Contraband was also more likely to be a staple such as salt or food. But close to towns and cities smuggling efforts were far better organised; those involved were less likely to have any other career; and high-value, low-volume luxuries made up more of the cargoes.

THE SOUTH EAST

A glance at an atlas is all that's needed to see the advantages that the South East of England offered to the enterprising smuggler. To the east, within sight on a clear day, lies Northern France, the source of much of the contraband; and to the north and west lie rich farm land, and the wealthy, wicked capital city – ready markets for the fine laces, wines and brandy that the smuggler obligingly shipped across the Channel.

It's hardly surprising, then, that British smuggling began here – not as an import activity, but with exports. And in a sense, the South East might be regarded as the cradle of big-business smuggling for the whole of the British Isles.

Drive across misty Romney Marsh, and you'll need little further explanation. Contented sheep still chomp the salty grass of the marshes, just as they have done for centuries, and it was the wool from their backs that was carried out of the country by the ton to the waiting weavers on the Continent. Even in the thirteenth century massive taxation on wool exports made the rewards from illegal wool export well worth the risk of capture.

Illegal wool exports from the marsh probably started the very first day that restrictions were imposed: in 1275 the government introduced a tax of £3 a bag on wool leaving England. This was doubled in 1298, and successive administrations tinkered with the laws and duties according to their need for funds. Wool smuggling from Romney Marsh – and elsewhere in Britain – fluctuated in response to the laws, and to market forces; high demand at home meant there was less incentive to smuggle. In the fifteenth century, though, the reverse happened, and as wool prices fell, the producers found it harder to make a living from the home market. The expansion of smuggling was inevitable.

The wool smugglers of Kent generally, and Romney Marsh in particular, were called 'owlers'. There has long been debate about how they acquired this name, and people have advanced various romantic theories, mostly centred around owls – the smugglers hunted at night, so they took the name of the nocturnal bird; or they signalled to each other by hooting like owls.

The most prosaic explanation, and probably the most likely, is that 'owler' is just a corruption of 'wooler', which was a common name for anyone processing wool. Though in linguistic terms the corruption is unlikely, regional usage tends to confirm this idea: most postal addresses containing the word 'owler' are in the traditional wool-producing and manufacturing areas of Britain. The owlers nickname was also used in Lincolnshire – another important area for sheep farming.

The wool smugglers of South East England, and their successors, the import smugglers, developed a reputation for savagery that is often used as a yardstick by other counties claiming a 'gentle' nature for their own smugglers. Certainly the horrific killings of Galley and Chater (see page 148), and the thuggish activities of the Hawkhurst gang lend weight to this opinion, but it's possible to cite evidence of matching barbarity from other counties.

Assuming that the smugglers of the South East really were more violent than their fellows, are there any genuine reasons why this should be the case? Perhaps the long history of smuggling in the area goes some way towards explaining its savage nature. In the heyday of smuggling – the eighteenth and early nineteenth centuries – the trade was carried out by large and highly organised gangs that landed their goods mostly by brute strength. Men with cudgels and firearms lined the beach in such numbers that preventive forces could only stand and watch. This form of smuggling was not unique to Kent and Sussex – certainly the Essex gangs landed goods this way – but it was more prevalent in the South East than elsewhere. In other parts of Britain smugglers seem more often to have favoured the clandestine landing of a smaller cargo, and to have enjoyed the benefits of greater secrecy. By their very nature, open landings demanded greater force.

The size of the cargoes may also have been a factor: Kentish smuggling was on a scale that demanded large amounts of capital. Such sums were often raised not locally but at some distant point, usually London. Outside investors would want to protect their cash, and would have not been averse to hiring hoodlums to do it. By contrast, the finance of smuggling in other parts of Britain was more often on a cooperative basis, with each villager buying a share in the run. This not only ensured total support in the locality (hence less need for violence), but also meant that the capture of a cargo was a loss shared by all, and easier to bear as a result.

Kent became such a centre for smuggling activity that it is hardly surprising to find the earliest preventive efforts concentrated in the South East. In 1690 eight men were stationed in the towns of Lydd, Romney, Hythe and Folkestone in an attempt to prevent wool exports from these areas. These 'Riding Officers' patrolled the area on horseback to detect and deter, but the smugglers would perhaps have outnumbered them a hundred to one.

In 1816 the Kent coast blockade scheme started between North Foreland and South Foreland. In 1824 this was extended north round to Sheerness, and south to Beachy Head, and in 1824 round as far as Chichester. Preventive measures existed in other parts of the country, but were never as strong as in Kent.

SOUTHERN ENGLAND

The South of England was not as close to the sources of smuggled goods as were Kent and Essex, but the coast here had other compensations: the Channel Islands and the Isle of Wight made very favourable staging posts; there were many fine beaches and inlets for landing goods; the winds were favourable; and – at least initially – the coast was less well guarded than that of Kent or Sussex. By comparison with the benign beaches of Hampshire and Dorset, Cornish and Devon coasts were treacherous.

Contraband came in to the South principally from France, though often via Jersey and Guernsey, or the smaller Channel Islands. Some more exotic imports also arrived on ocean-going vessels heading for Southampton; the crews of East Indiamen in particular openly traded with the small boats that clustered around the vast hulls in the Solent.

Oriental luxuries were the exception, though, and in the early years of the eighteenth century the staples of the Hampshire and Dorset smugglers were wine and brandy, along with miscellaneous items wide in variety but small in quantity, such as playing cards and handkerchiefs. During the 1730s there was a shift away from kegs, and the principal contraband became oilskin bags of tea. In the Napoleonic War period a few of the South Coast towns, notably Christchurch, exported gold, but the so-called 'guinea run' was never carried on to anything like the same extent as in Kent and Sussex.

The techniques for landing smuggled goods in the South closely paralleled those in other parts of Britain: until about 1700, bribery of customs officials was regarded almost as a simple business transaction, and was a great deal easier than landing goods at some inconvenient spot in the middle of the night. But as corruption and nepotism began to be ferreted out by diligent government officials (see page 78), this approach became closed to the merchants of the South.

It was replaced initially by open landings at a discrete distance from the official ports, because the government of the day was preoccupied with the wars in Europe, and did not have the will to deal with minor domestic problems. However, when peace returned in 1713, the preventive effort began in earnest, and the smugglers united to protect their cargoes. Defiance was the order of the day, and the free-traders prevailed by sheer force of numbers, often landing goods in full view of the customs authorities. The smugglers wore masks and other disguises to prevent identification by the officials who in small towns might well have been their next-door-neighbours.

Brute force landings like this waxed and waned: they flourished when the stakes were high enough, when the risks of capture were slight, and the punishments meted out not too severe. But when the net tightened, or declining taxation cut profits, subterfuge began: the free-traders' objective was wherever possible to sneak the goods in unobserved. Tubs were sunk from the large smuggling luggers some distance off-shore, then collected inconspicuously by small fishing boats. Where the tides were favourable, barrels could be roped together and rafted in from the open sea to the inland harbours with which the South Coast was so well supplied. This method was used to great effect at Portsmouth, Langstone and Chichester harbours, and to the west at Christchurch and Poole. Dorset and Hampshire smugglers caught in the act of sneaking their goods in would destroy the evidence or simply flee if they ran the risk of the gallows or transportation.

Some of the contraband landed in southern England was consumed locally: tilling the rich soil a little way inland made many a farming fortune, and just as the squire demanded the best brandy, so too his daughters expected the best French lace. However, there is evidence that the smuggled imports often found their way to London: a trail of stories of smugglers' hidden depots points to a cross-country highway that channelled goods from the coast to the markets in the capital.

Amazingly, some contraband made its way to London from as far afield as West Dorset: in 1719 a merchant at Lulworth was importing cocoa beans at a time when there was a taste for drinking chocolate only among the smarter London set. Some contraband travelled long distances inland for different reasons. Cargoes of brandy landed in Dorset in the early nineteenth century were of such poor quality that they were virtually unfit to drink, and the kegs were carted a safe distance from the coast to undergo a further distilling process, before being sold in the town taverns.

London was not the only inland market: sophisticates in Bristol and in the country houses of Gloucester and Worcestershire were also supplied with contraband landed on the South Coast, and moved inland through Dorchester and Sherborne. Though land transport was vastly more expensive than freight over water, the inland route would have proved much less risky as preventive measures were stepped up.

Parts of the Dorset and West Hampshire coasts were flanked by untamed heath and woodland that made concealment easy and pursuit difficult. Some regions of the New Forest were effectively no-go areas, and once a cargo entered the Forest, it was usually safe from the clutches of the revenue men. Even Bourne Heath, where inoffensive Bournemouth now stands, had at one time a fearful reputation, and the dense woodland of Cranborne Chase was felled precisely because it provided a haven for smugglers and other undesirables.

Although the larger and more powerful smuggling gangs from the South East spread their tentacles out as far west as Poole, native Hampshire and Dorset smugglers seem to have preferred persuasion to compulsion in their dealings with the local population (though not the revenue men). One figure in particular, Isaac Gulliver, had such a non-violent reputation that he was nicknamed 'the Gentle Smuggler'. Such gentleness was relative: his gang was reputedly forbidden from carrying firearms, but they probably weren't averse to swinging a weighty club when met by any of the King's men.

THE ISLE OF WIGHT

In Hampshire, the smuggler's job was made especially easy by the proximity of the Isle of Wight. The island had a well-developed trade in wool exports, and until the late eighteenth century, its coasts were only lightly guarded against the attentions of free-traders: any ship's master with sufficient navigational ability would have been able to slip into one of the island's bays or creeks with little risk of losing a cargo to the land-based forces.

A chase at sea was perhaps more of a risk, but in the early eighteenth century, the smugglers relied on their superior seamanship to evade the preventive forces.

The south-east side of the island is fringed with treacherous rock platforms, notably Rocken End, and the risk of a wreck was not something that the master of a revenue cutter contemplated with pleasure. Any smuggler who knew a way through the rocks, and was prepared to ride out the ferocious south-westerly winds that batter this part of the coast was unlikely to be followed too far.

There seem to have been no large gangs on the island, and the free-trade apparently enjoyed the support of many of the inhabitants. To a certain extent this may reflect the fact that many local people despised rule from the mainland – until the end of the thirteenth century Wight had been an independent principality, and even at this early date, export smuggling of wool was already taking place on the island and the mainland. Little wonder that the islanders and were disrespectful of the customs authorities!

SOUTH WEST ENGLAND

As in other parts of the country, the early smugglers from Devon and Cornwall were not importing, but exporting. Here, though, the outgoing contraband was likely to be Cornish tin, rather than bales of wool. Tin was one of the earliest strategic metals, and lined the holds of many vessels apparently loaded with other more innocent cargoes.

The counties of the South West, and Cornwall in particular, are so famous for smuggling that many people today believe this to be the only area of Britain where the activity took place. The traditional stereotype of the Cornishman – taciturn, suspicious of strangers and rather sly – owes a lot to the area's reputation in the free-trade. In reality, the men of Cornwall and Devon probably smuggled much *less* than their contemporaries in the South East of England. The crossing to the Continent was very much farther; the market for smuggled goods was strictly local; and there are fewer suitable landing places on the South West coast.

However, smuggling in Cornwall and Devon was stimulated by a number of local factors, notably the lack of prevention, and extreme poverty. The alluvial tin-miners or streamers in the West Penwith area were especially active, because of the seasonal nature of their work, which caused them to be laid off in the summer when there was a shortage of water: 'A trip to Roscoff or Guernsey formed a pleasant change after a spell on tribute underground or working stamps.'[1] By contrast with this poverty-stricken existence, smuggling brought fantastic wealth into the area. One writer observes that 'When smuggling was in full swing, money became so plentiful that neighbours lent guineas to each other by the handful, not stopping to count, or being so particular as to reckon by ones and twos'.

When increased duty made imports more important than the exported ore, continental supplies for the South West came mainly from Brittany and the Channel Islands. The trade from Guernsey was at least partly stopped when a preventive boat was stationed there in 1767, but this did not deter the French traders who were getting rich by shipping goods through the island. The French responded two years later by making Roscoff a free-port (see page 30): and within months the sleepy port was transformed into a hive of industry, supplying the tubs and bales needed for transport across to Devon and Cornwall. The historic link is still maintained, with a ferry from Plymouth plying the same route. The Channel Islands were soon back in business, though – by 1775 it appears that the government's resolve had weakened, and reputedly many people from the island made fortunes in the latter part of the eighteenth century 'simply by manufacturing casks'.[2]

Financing arrangements in the South West don't seem to have been quite so centralised as elsewhere in Britain. Instead of a 'Mr Big' bankrolling the whole operation, everyone took a share: ' … the farmers, the merchants, and, it is rumoured, the local magistrates, used to find the money with which the business was carried on, investing small sums in each voyage.'[3] At Falmouth, where smuggling by postal packet carriers was rife, local traders organised an extraordinary 'sale-or-return' agreement with ships travelling to Portugal.

THE SOUTH COAST

Beyond the Lizard from Falmouth is the golden curve of Mount's Bay, with St Michael's Mount set like a jewel on the western side. It is the most westerly point in the country protected from the Atlantic storms, and the natural shelter made the area especially suitable as a fishing base, and, of course, for smuggling. The geographical situation lent itself to the free-trade in other ways, too. Mount's Bay was well-placed for trips to France, to the Channel Islands, and the Scillies.

In the eighteenth and nineteenth centuries, the whole region was extremely isolated, and this helped the cause of the free-trade. Overland communication was very difficult, because the roads were little more than cart tracks. Prevention therefore centred on the sea, and Penzance, which looks out over the west side of the bay, was furnished with a revenue cutter at an early stage in the game.

THE SCILLY ISLES

Prior to the development of tourism, the population of the Scillies was hard put to find any legal employment besides fishing, which was in any case seasonal. Smuggling was therefore the mainstay of the islands' economy, and the Scillies were for a long time a valuable staging post for smuggling in the West Country.

This idyllic state of affairs came to an end with the establishment of a preventive boat on the islands in the early part of the nineteenth century. The boat was effective, and the almost immediate result was financial ruin for the inhabitants. In

1818 they petitioned the Prince Regent, and their plight caught the attention of the Magistrates of the Western Division of the Hundred of Penwith. This grand-sounding body sent what would now be called a fact-finding mission to the islands to find out whether the pleas of the islanders had any foundation. The conclusion drawn was that the islands' economy had indeed been destroyed, and that:

> some substitute should be provided ... When this powerful measure was adopted by the present administration, it never could be in their contemplation to crush forever a multitude of families on those islands; who had for generations been brought up in this mode of support, and whose proceedings must at least have been very mildly treated for many years ... the new System in the islands has destroyed almost every comfort of the unhappy sufferers.

The problem was partly solved by a cash injection to stimulate the fishing industry.

THE NORTH COAST

Smuggling boats landed goods from the Continent on the *South* Coast of the peninsula in all seasons, but the North Coast was used for continental traffic principally during the summer, when the Atlantic storms had abated.

The coastline on the North is less favourable for landing smuggled goods: there are fewer sandy beaches, and many of the suitable coves are too exposed to the wind, making approach more hazardous. The heavy surf for which the area is now famous was another problem, breaking up the floating 'rafts' of roped-together tubs. The main advantage of a North Coast landing to the smuggler was that it was inconspicuous: revenue vessels kept an eagle eye on the South Coast, but were less vigilant on the North.

Smuggling activity on the North Coast focused on traffic with the West Indies, and with various off-shore depots, such as Ireland, the Scillies and Lundy Island. Ocean-going vessels heading for Bristol found it a simple matter to keep a clandestine rendezvous with small boats off the Devon coast.

THE JOLLY CORNISH SMUGGLER?

Compared to their companions-in-trade from Kent and Sussex, smugglers from the South West have a benign, rather jolly image. The accuracy of this is open to dispute, and it's possible to call up examples to support both sides of the argument. The pacifists maintain that West Country smugglers were not organised in gangs to anything like the same extent as free-traders in the east, and that this had some bearing on their reluctance to use force against their adversaries. Furthermore, some sources suggest that, whereas the boats used in the east of the country were generally large, purpose-built, and heavily armed, smugglers in the west tended to use fishing vessels and other small craft.

However, the size of ships used, and their complement of arms probably varied according to the degree of vigilance of the preventives and their strength. In the boom years of the free-trade, Cornish and Devon boats were probably every bit as big as those in the South East and East of Britain: according to one authority the vessels used here ranged from 50–250 tons, 'were often heavily armed' and had up to 1,000-square-feet of canvas in the mainsail. As prevention developed though, such a ship would have become too conspicuous to be of any practical use, and the smugglers began to favour smaller boats, masquerading as fishing vessels or coasters. Since these boats are more recent, they obviously figure more frequently in the oral history of the free-trade.

A further factor which must have influenced the necessary degree of violence is the proximity of the sea: only a small part of Cornwall is more than a day's walk from the coast. Eighteenth-century pundits were fond of the generalisation that 'everyone smuggled', but in Cornwall the statements could quite well have been true.

'The coasts here swarm with smugglers from the Land's End to the Lizard' one man wrote in 1753 and with the active support of the local population, these swarms would need to use violence only against the revenue forces – and the King's men didn't count anyway, in the eyes of most otherwise law-abiding citizens.

But perhaps the most convincing argument advanced to support the non-violent reputation of Cornish smugglers was advanced by Frank McLynn in his *Crime and Punishment in Eighteenth-century England*. He suggested that smuggling in Devon and Cornwall was substantially integrated: those who organised the smuggling runs also owned the boats and distributed the contraband. This made it easy for them to keep their activities secret, and informers posed no threat. In the South East distribution and sale were organised separately from import, making informers more of a danger – and their intimidation more ruthless.

When it came to dealing with the preventive forces, there is no evidence to suggest that smugglers from South West Britain were any less violent than their fellows. If anything, accounts point in the opposite direction …

'A rough, reckless and drunken lot were these tinners, and if riots and bloodshed were more scarce in West Cornwall than in some parts, it must have been due to the judicious absence of the Custom House officials, and not to any qualities in the smugglers.'[4]

The story of the Polperro smuggling ship *Lottery* bears this out. The most well-known version has its origins in a nineteenth-century history of the village, and is sympathetic towards the ship's crew: here is a summary …

When Cawsand customs men saw the *Lottery* becalmed half-a-mile from Penlee Point, they thought their luck was in, and put to sea several rowing boats.

The crew of the *Lottery*, seeing that capture was imminent, set to work preparing for battle, and the preventive forces responded by opening fire when they were still some distance away. As the gap closed, a figure on the deck of the *Lottery* took aim and fired, and an oarsman in one of the King's boats fell, dying of his wounds. Seeing this, the boats headed back to port, and the incensed authorities put out orders to seize the crew of the *Lottery*.

The seamen became outlaws in their home town. Some lay concealed in cramped hiding places in their homes; others fled. But eventually one of the *Lottery* crew, Roger Toms, came forward and pointed the finger at Tom Potter as the man who pulled the trigger.

Potter was still free, and Toms became a marked man. As a key witness, he was taken on board a government cutter, and became – effectively – a prisoner himself. However, the Polperro men managed to lure him ashore by arranging a rendezvous with his wife, and Toms was seized at Lantick and spirited away to Guernsey, en route for America.

In Polperro, all eyes were on the patrolling dragoons, and the authorities initially had little success in tracing Potter. However, by raiding the town from the west, they managed to surprise the smuggler in his home, and he was taken to London for trial.

Meanwhile, Toms the informer had been tracked down in the Channel Islands, and was therefore able to give evidence at the trial. He never saw the shot fired, but claimed that Potter had come down from the deck and, swearing, said he had 'done for one of them'. On this evidence alone, Potter was executed.

In Polperro there was fury at the injustice of the conviction. According to one report, the slaughtered oarsman had been killed by a member of his own crew, and the musket ball had entered his body from the side facing away from the *Lottery*. Toms would surely have been murdered had he returned home, and since he was considered a valuable witness in the trial of the other members of the crew (who remained at large) he was kept at Newgate. He was employed there in some menial capacity until his death.

There is, of course, another side to the story. Government records and evidence at Potter's trial assert that the smugglers fired first, and the men in the custom house boat opened fire only when one of their crew members had been shot. The crewman who died was shot in the front of his head, and though some suggest that this is proof that he was shot from the *Lottery*, it's hardly conclusive. Certainly if he was looking at the smugglers' ship when he fell, the ball would have passed through his forehead. But pulling on oars, he would have faced away from the *Lottery*.

However, the most convincing evidence that the shot came from the *Lottery* is to be found in the records of the trial. The Defence never argued that the boatman had been felled by a government bullet, which they would surely have done if there was thus any chance of avoiding the noose.

There are other examples to suggest that West Country smugglers were no exception to a violent rule. The vicar of Morwenstow, who wrote much about local smuggling legends, describes a conversation he had with one of his congregation concerning the hanging of a man who was wrongly convicted of murder. The local wishes to know why it is that grass will not grow on the man's grave, and turf withers on the mound. When the vicar asks what crime the unfortunate man was alleged to have committed, he is told that the deceased ' ... only killed a custom house officer'.

This, of course, is anecdotal, but there is no shortage of historical evidence. In 1735 a gang of armed smugglers attacked excisemen near Fowey, when they tried to repossess some rum. The band had apparently acquired a local reputation for violence. A report on the clash observed that the revenue officers 'go in danger of their lives if they try to seize the goods ... the smugglers having entered into a combination to rescue any person who shall be arrested'.

Even if they were caught, violent Cornish smugglers often got off scot-free. In 1768 smugglers brutally murdered an excise officer at Porthleven, William Odgers. A Gwennap man, Melchisideck Kinsman, was accused of the murder, together with other unknown people. His accomplices were initially thought to have fled the country to Guernsey or Morlaix, but were later reported to be hiding in the tin mines. The principal witness was offered a bribe of £500 to go abroad, and when this didn't work, he was threatened with physical violence, and could not work for fear of his life. He was later paid a state pension of seven shillings a week.

Three of the accomplices eventually surrendered, and agreed to track down Kinsman (presumably in return for leniency). They caught him, and all stood trial at the assizes, but to the astonishment of the judge, none were found guilty. The local collector of customs observed that three of the jury had disappeared after the trial, and suggested that they had been either bribed or 'nobbled'. Little wonder, then, that in the 1750s ' ... nobody can venture to come near [the smugglers] with safety while they are at their work.'[5]

Apologists for Cornish smugglers could perhaps claim in mitigation of their crimes that the preventive forces sometimes offered violence to match that of their opponents: in 1799 two preventives accused fellow travellers between Bodmin and Truro of being smugglers. In the battle that ensued, the innocent travellers were killed, and the preventives absconded. And notwithstanding the *Lottery* case, witnesses and informers sometimes received less brutal treatment than elsewhere. Compared to the torture and murder of Chater and Galley (see page 152), the weapons used in the South West seem positively benevolent. Social ostracism of the informer and his family were the rule, and in at least one instance an informer was simply burned in effigy, but left unharmed.

WRECKING

The treacherous coasts of Devon and Cornwall are notorious for wrecks, and the local people did not hesitate to ransack a ship unfortunate enough to be smashed on the rocks. This is illustrated vividly by a story told of Portlemouth: the vicar of the parish church there was drawing to the end of a particularly dry sermon, and many of the congregation had dropped to sleep. The sound of a man opening the church door woke a few of them – a gale was blowing outside – and they welcomed the diversion as he walked up to the pulpit and whispered in the vicar's ear. The remainder of the congregation were immediately roused from their musings by the vicar bellowing 'There's a ship ashore between Prawle and Pear Tree Point!' He started to tear off his vestments, continuing as he tugged at the encumbering garments ' ... but let us all start fair'. As one, the congregation rose and charged headlong to the beach, with the vicar in the lead.

The legend goes on to relate that the parishioners ignored the cries for help from the drowning crew as they tried to salvage the cargo of the galleon. However, it is difficult to credit this account, just as it's hard to believe tales of ships being deliberately lured onto the rocks, and crewmen cynically drowned, for fear they'd testify about the plundering that took place. Most of the local inhabitants were seafarers themselves, and knew of the inevitable loss of life that followed a wreck. The villagers also had to bury the bodies of drowned crew. It was a highly distasteful task, as this letter from a local vicar to the Lord of Methleigh Manor illustrates:

> Dear Sirs,
> By the enclosed paper you will find that the number of dead bodies and of such parts of bodies as with respect to interment should we think be considered and paid for as such whole bodies, taken up within the precincts of your manor and buried there, after the last wreck amounts to 62. The extraordinary charge of two men attending constantly, one for 12 days, the other for 13 days at 1/6, was thought to be necessary, in order to secure the bodies as soon as they should be cast ashore, from being torn by dogs etc, and to prepare graves for their immediate reception being at that time very offensive.
>
> The circumstance accounts for the great consumption of liquor without which the people would hardly have been prevailed with to touch the broken bodies, and also for the pack and rope by which they were drawn up over the cliff ... [6]

Rather than branding Cornishmen as wreckers it would be fairer to say that the misfortune of the storm could sometimes be turned to advantage, and put a useful bit of jam on what was often a very dry and stale piece of bread for the West Country folk.

Wrecks were the scene of much dispute and argument, not least because dutiable goods washed up should theoretically have been declared at the local custom house. The custom house officers were therefore among the first on the scene, representing the interests of the Crown. Their chance of securing anything would often have been slight though, because they were usually greatly outnumbered by the hundreds of villagers plundering the broken ribs of the beached ship. The searchers and gaugers nevertheless saw wrecking as a form of smuggling, and viewed it as their duty to levy the rightful customs charges.

There were also other interests at odds with the wreckers. The crew of the ship itself – if they had survived – usually looked on helplessly while every item of value was dragged from the hold, or prised free of its mountings. But the biggest disputes were often between the wreckers and the owner of the stretch of coastline where the ship had foundered. These people had 'Royalty of Wrecks' on their land, and were generally entitled to half the value of the goods washed up. The other half went to the rescuer, but both sides were keen to take more than their share.

Often the rights to Royalty of Wrecks were disputed: an example of this occurred in 1743 at Porthleven. Edward Coode, son of the Lord of nearby Methleigh heard of the wreck and went to the beach wearing only a greatcoat and gloves. He was met by a neighbour, Squire Penrose, with a gang of armed men who defied him to touch the cargo. The squire grabbed a musket and cried 'Damn him, shoot him, or by God, I'll shoot him'. Ironically, all they were fighting over was a case of salted pork.

WALES & NORTH WEST ENGLAND

Information about smuggling in Wales and North West England is not easy to find. Many of the official records compiled by the individual custom houses were lost in a fire that destroyed the Thames-side custom house in 1815. What records remain provide a rather scant picture of the activities of the free-traders.

The surviving correspondence between the customs board and the collectors of customs suggests that the level of evasion in this part of the country was fairly typical. However, by comparison with the South and East coasts of England, smuggling here was a comparatively minor problem, and the customs authorities were often more preoccupied with wrecking than with the deliberate running of goods.

The fact that there is so little information to be found certainly doesn't imply that the citizens living on the coast between Bristol to Carlisle were any more willing to pay customs and excise duty than people elsewhere in Britain. In fact, one Victorian writer suggested that wool and corn export began in Wales long before import smuggling began: 'The almost impassable hills and cwms (dingles) were looked upon as protection against discovery'. She added that the people involved in wool export were chiefly landowners, whereas the later importers 'of brandy, Hamburg spirit, tea and silk … were of a lower order, who frequently showed so much brutality that eventually they became a terror to the people.'[7]

It wasn't just luxury goods that import smugglers brought to the eager Welsh and Cumbrian markets: in some parts, grinding poverty and near starvation created a demand for even ordinary foodstuffs, and a resentment of their taxation and control.

This poem, by the eighteenth-century poet and singer Richard Lloyd of Plas Meini, sums up the anger that simmered in Wales against taxation from England:

> They've fixed the tax for the year today
> God would never have done it this way
> A tax when you die
> A tax when you're born
> A tax on the water
> A tax on the dawn
> A tax upon the gallows tree
> Even a tax on being free[8]

A determined and ingenious smuggler can usually succeed in bringing goods ashore practically anywhere, but the geography of Wales, and the character of the Welsh provided the free-trader with some useful benefits: much of Wales was (and is) remote and sparsely populated; the few preventive centres were widely scattered, and under-funded; there are plenty of gently-sloping beaches and sheltered coves, which made landing easy in some areas; and the traditional independence of the Welsh people, and their resentment of interference from England must have also been a considerable aid in concealment of smugglers' activities.

Smuggling in Wales received a boost with the Irish 'troubles' at the end of the seventeenth century. These led to a ban on civil shipping in the West, so honest residents were deprived of much of the cargo that would previously have been legitimately landed. Smugglers were happy to step into the breach, and import the creature comforts that people had become used to.

SOUTH WALES

Smuggling on the South Coast of Wales has a long history: French traders were bringing uncustomed wine into Pembrokeshire ports as early as 1611, according to a contemporary document. This is perhaps unsurprising, for the coast here had two great advantages – proximity to Bristol, which was the main British port for trade with the New World; and relatively high population, eager to buy uncustomed goods. The long, tapering outline of the Bristol Channel was an asset, too:

when the King's men were being unusually diligent at Bristol, the ships' masters simply headed for the South Wales coast, and added only a few hours to their journey time.

Some contraband came ashore from ships unloaded on remote beaches, but this wasn't the only ruse used by South Wales' smugglers. It was a simple matter to transfer to small boats at least part of the cargo from inward-bound ships as they sailed serenely along the Bristol Channel. When docking, the master could attribute the shortfall on arrival to 'spoilage' or 'lost in storms'. More often, bribery secured the silence of Welsh officials. When tobacco smoking came into vogue, many Welsh clay pipes were filled with Virginia leaf imported in this manner.

The Channel Islands were a major source of contraband entering South Wales, and at least one Guernsey smuggler, Richard Robinson, had vessels off the coast of Glamorgan. He commanded the largest of these himself, and a smaller vessel was in the charge of his son Pasco. The pair were operating in the 1730s, principally landing goods on Flat Holm, for later onward shipment to Wales. In 1771, customs inspectors found eighteen kegs of brandy on the sands at Briton Ferry, with ropes attached ready for carrying. They commented that the brandy came from Guernsey, and probably came ashore as a raft, 'as is the practice made use of by smugglers'. If this is true, it is a rare Welsh example of goods being rafted in. Guernsey smugglers continued to land goods in the area, and in November 1787 customs men seized the *Polly* of Guernsey at Neath Abbey. Their searches were interrupted by a mob of colliers and copper men who tried to storm the vessel, stoning the customs men. A second attack, at midnight, was only repelled by firing on the crowd.

NORTH WALES AND THE NORTH WEST

The Irish Sea laps at the coast of North Wales and North West England, and there is evidence to suggest that much of the contraband landed here came from Ireland. Heavy taxation on salt made this a favourite cargo for smuggling ships, and Ireland was a major source of rock-salt. Recognising that there was a problem, the authorities carried out a survey of the Welsh coast in 1740 – a member of the Salt Board trudged wearily from port to port, largely (and often prematurely) reporting 'no smuggling takes place here'.

Irish vessels didn't necessarily take the shortest route and may have avoided mid-Wales because of the risk of running aground on the sandy shallows which abound in the local bays. Instead, many Irish ships made a longer trip through St George's Channel, to land goods on the South Wales coast.

Besides being a major original source of some forms of contraband, Ireland was also used as a depot for goods brought in from the continent. The trip from the Irish coast took only a matter of hours with favourable wind and tide, and an overnight stop in an Irish creek must have seemed an attractive option to exhausted crews who might otherwise face an opposed landing at the end of the long trip from France.

Ireland wasn't the only off-shore depot. North Wales and Northern England are conveniently close to the Isle of Man, and certainly much of the untaxed brandy quaffed on Anglesey and in Cumbria came into Britain via the three-legged isle. Islands to the south was heavily used by smugglers for storage and freight forwarding, and other islands – especially Ramsey, Skomer and Skokholm off the Pembroke coast – were probably used in the same way.

CUMBRIA

As in Wales, the earliest records of smuggling from Cumberland (as the region was then called), deal with the export of wool. It was moved across the border to Scotland, and by sea, to Ireland. Men of the cloth were implicated: in 1423 Abbot Robert of the Cisterian monastery at Furness was accused of smuggling wool out in a 200-ton vessel from Piel (Fowdray) to Zealand. Wool export smuggling in Cumbria continued as late as 1788, when nearly 3 tons were seized and sold at Carlisle.

As in Scotland, Cumbrian use of the word 'smuggling' covers not only illegal import and export, but also illicit stilling of spirits, which lies beyond the scope of this book. Certainly this fraud on the revenue was widespread in the eighteenth century, and the few smuggling yarns that are to be found in books – notably centred on one Lancelot Slee of Langdale – generally fall into this category.

With this notable exception, there is relatively little anecdote and folklore about Cumbrian smuggling, and majority of what we know about the free-trade in the area comes from the Revenue side of the fence. Court records detail sentences, and custom house books methodically note every seizure. So the picture we get of the Cumbrian smugglers is a dry and rather dull official one, rather than the more human folk image that prevails in many other areas.

The archives provide a fairly typical picture: a mixture of success against impossible odds, mundane trivia of custom house life, and tragic battles involving brutality and loss of life. Records of sales of seized goods provide a guide to the level of smuggling activity around the Cumbrian coast, and in some years the quantities are considerable. However, the source of much of this contraband was vessels seized at sea, so it's hard to distinguish between goods that would have been run into England, and those that were headed to Scotland. Few seizures took place on beaches or at ports. This is perhaps surprising, since Cumbria would seem to be ideally situated for smuggling: it is just a short distance from the Isle of Man, a major source of contraband, and borders Scotland. Possible explanations are the low population, or that smugglers found it easier to land goods in

Scotland than on the English side of the Solway, and had a ready market north of the border.

Certainly the latter explanation is confirmed by some of the comments in the local custom house letter books: in 1733 the authorities at Whitehaven reported that they regularly saw small boats from the Isle of Man 'Steering up for the Scottish Border where they generally land without much opposition, then bring the goods on horseback in the night into England'. Nearly two decades later the collector of customs at the same port noted that, although large quantities of goods came in via Scotland, landings on the Cumbrian side of the Solway had declined.

In the early eighteenth century, most of the smuggling activity in Cumbria seems to have been of an amateur nature – the crews of fishing vessels and colliers bringing in the odd barrel as a treat for the family. Persecution (or just prosecution) of those guilty of these minor tax evasions was seen in an extremely bad light by the local populace, and the price of over-zealousness was a transfer for at least one customs officer from Ellenfoot (Maryport).

THE EAST COAST

East Coast smugglers dealt mainly with Holland and Northern France: trade links with Holland in particular had historical connections dating from the time when English wool was systematically smuggled out to Holland to avoid the legal staple in France. In the golden age of import smuggling the most important commodity was over-proof gin: enormous quantities came over from Schiedam, where the stills produced several million gallons of spirits a year. However, the East Coast trade in strong 'Geneva' was not to the exclusion of other contraband – most of the heavily taxed products that made up the smugglers' stock-in-trade elsewhere in Britain were landed here too.

The Dutch applied their legendary business skills and trading acumen to smuggling with as much alacrity as they did to any legal venture: the bulky tobacco took up too much space in the ships' holds, so the companies supplying the contraband found it profitable to invest in tobacco presses for compacting imported leaves into smaller bales. When British ships proved inadequate for the task of ferrying the bales and barrels, the Dutch bought their own ships to move the goods across the North Sea. Trade in the contraband took place either afloat, or at the destination in England.

The pattern of landing and distribution in England along the East Coast changed with the evolving policies of prevention. For example, the Suffolk coastline was well-supplied with good beaches which suited the open landing of contraband – a technique that worked well in the eighteenth century while the preventives dozed in the distance or were open to bribes. As the net tightened in the early nineteenth century though, smuggling intensified among the creeks and estuaries of Essex, where activity was less easily observed, and where tubs could be secretly sunk in the murky waters for later collection.

Although tactics changed with time, the general character of the free-trade in the East of England did not. In the East, the involvement of the local population was most often as haulage contractors, landing goods that were brought to the country by foreign entrepreneurs. This was in marked contrast to the South East, where the whole operation, including financing, was the concern of big smuggling companies.

However, the scale of the smuggling operations was similar. Some indication of the extent of smuggling in this part of Britain may be gleaned from a document which relates to the period 1 May 1745 to 1 January 1746. This details all the runs which came to the attention of the customs officers – the total must have been much more. The area covered was the county of Suffolk. 4,550 horses are mentioned, and based on the assumption that a horse could carry 1.5cwt, the loss of duty would have been over £58,000, and the amount of currency sent overseas to pay for the goods, £43,000. In today's currency, this would have amounted to some £26 million.

Further north, in South Lincolnshire, smuggling was made easy by the comparative isolation of many of the beaches, and by the difficulty of patrolling the long coastline from preventive stations that were frequently undermanned. Perhaps for these reasons smuggling seems to have continued here long after it had been stamped out in southern England.

YORKSHIRE AND THE NORTH EAST

The Yorkshire coast is some 200 miles from Holland across the windswept North Sea, so it is not entirely surprising to find that Yorkshire smugglers crossed to the Continent less often than those who simply had the narrow Channel to negotiate. However, in the late seventeenth century and the early years of the eighteenth there was a brisk export trade in wool and sheep, snatched from contented grazing on the lush Yorkshire Ridings. And certainly as the century wore on, the ships crossing to Holland returned loaded with tea, gin and brandy.

Yorkshire lacked the vast and concentrated market of South East England, and much of the early eighteenth-century smuggling activity was piecemeal, with big, heavily armed luggers hovering off-shore as floating supermarkets, to service demand from the coastal fishing villages and farming hamlets. Hull, though, was the exception. It had the considerable advantage of a large population, eager for contraband goods, and the city was at the root of a vast distribution system formed by the rivers Ouse and Trent. In terms of its importance as a port, Hull ranked behind only London and Bristol. Much of the town's trade was in coal, exported to Holland, and moved coastwise to London, and cargoes of smuggled goods slipped into the town quay in the black holds of ships returning in ballast.

North of Newcastle, the character of the free-trade begins to change, and the influence of Scotland becomes apparent. Much of the contraband activity in the border areas consisted of through transport of scotch, but there was also a thriving trade in gin from Holland, and in salt.

SCOTLAND

In Scotland whisky dominates the story of smuggling, for to a Scot, 'smuggling' meant not just illegal import and export, but also illegal distilling. We are primarily concerned with coastal aspect of the free-trade, and the subject of illegal stilling has been dealt with thoroughly in other books. However, the excise officers charged with stamping out stilling were also concerned with illegal imports, so it would be remiss to ignore the subject completely.

Most of the stilling went on in the glens, where there was a plentiful supply of the clean fresh water needed for the soaking of the grain prior to malting. After several days soaking in a burn, the grain was spread out on a warm floor, and allowed to sprout. Roasting and grinding of the sprouted grain made the malt, which was mixed with hot water to create the wort. After fermentation, the wort was boiled in a copper container, and vapour condensed in a spiralling tube, called the worm, to make the spirit.

All this was legal (though taxable) until 1814, when small stills of less than 500 gallons were prohibited. The response from the highlanders was, needless to say, not very sympathetic, and much of the public fury was vented against the officially approved distillers, which were hugely outnumbered by illicit manufacturers. In 1778 there were eight legal stills in Edinburgh – and an estimated 400 working without payment of duty.

As much of the stilling process as possible was carried out in the heather rather than on the hearth, and the stills were hidden in caves and hollows on the hillsides. Smoke curling up from the peat fires gave away the location of the stills, and it would be these plumes that the exciseman was seeking.

He had an unpopular task, because the trade had wholehearted support from every section of the community, including in some areas even the clergy: for example, the Revd Andrew Burns was the minister of Glen Isla, and was clearly in sympathy with the illegal distillers of whisky. His house overlooked the hotel where the excisemen would stop for refreshment before continuing with their searches further up the glen. The minister would keep his eye on the arriving party, and when the last of the group disappeared inside, the Revd Burns would amble from his garden leading his pony, as if to set it grazing further up the glen. Once out of sight, though, he'd leap on the bare back of the nag, and gallop with all possible haste to the nearest house where he'd borrow a saddle and reins. Then the pair would charge on up the valley, the reverend waving his hat at every bothy that housed an illicit still, shouting 'The Philistines be upon thee, Samson!'[9]

Not all the illegal hooch was consumed locally: much of it was moved south of the border, often in very odd containers. 'Belly canteens' for the transport of spirits held 2 gallons and were made of sheet iron. They gave the female wearer a convincing if somewhat rigid appearance of advanced pregnancy. Another container was made to look like a passenger riding pillion behind the horse-borne smuggler – a leather head made the illusion complete.

IMPORT AND EXPORT

Smuggling in the sense of cross-coast trade certainly went on, but the business was on nothing like the same scale as in southern England. Poverty and the sparseness of the population accounts for this in part – with the exception of the principal towns, the market for costly foreign luxuries in Scotland was very restricted.

Perhaps in response to these circumstances, the smugglers concentrated on the import of staple goods that were heavily taxed. Salt in particular was essential for preserving meat and fish over the harsh dark winter months, and the tax was high: at one stage 15s a bushel. The regulations governing salt imports were enormously complicated, and even a twentieth-century historian of the customs and excise commented that he could not see how the local fishermen managed to cope with the complexity of the laws governing the use of salt.

Great quantities of salt entered the country principally from Ireland, via the West Coast. Salt smuggling was especially important on the Mull of Galloway: the principal source of rock-salt was Carrickfergus in Northern Ireland, just 35 miles away, and ships landed the salt at Float Bay, Ardwell Bay and Clanyard Bay. Farther north, Saltpans Bay was an occasional landing place.

Along with the salt, of course, came other forms of contraband, because import smugglers used Ireland as a warehouse and staging-post on their way from the Continent, especially after control over the Isle of Man returned to the Crown. Tea and tobacco came in this way, and were then transported to the Scottish cities on horseback.

The character of Scottish smuggling was to a certain extent shaped by the Act of Union, merging England and Scotland, which took effect in 1707. Prior to this date, there was a wide discrepancy between duties north and south of the border, and the Scots had taken advantage of this situation to smuggle highly taxed goods into England. When the two countries were united, duties on some products north of the border increased sevenfold. The taxes were seen by the Scots as oppressive, and resistance to them, positively patriotic. Walter Scott commented: 'Smuggling was almost universal in Scotland, for people unaccustomed to imposts and regarding them as an unjust aggression upon their ancient liberties, made no scruple to elude them whenever it was possible to do so.'

The change in tariffs was not all one way: duties on spirits in Scotland were lower than in England until the mid-nineteenth century, so even legitimate imports to places like Dumfries (conveniently close to the border) could then be clandestinely moved into England.

On the West Coast, silting of the harbours around the Solway served the interests of the smugglers: trade could take place legally only through the Royal Burghs, but the routes to them had become too clogged with mud to accommodate ocean-going ships. Cargo was thus transferred to barges for the last stages of the journey, but somehow, not all of the goods unloaded found their way to the official custom house quay. For example, goods travelling to Dumfries on the River Nith were unloaded at the port of Carsethorn, and frequently completed their journey overland – to arrive untaxed via illicit salesmen, instead of properly inspected and recorded at the custom house quay. Tobacco smuggling at Dumfries eventually became so extensive that by 1760 the legal traders in the town had been driven out of business.

Lack of resources also hampered the customs authorities: without military support they were powerless. In the summer of 1761 the collector of customs at Dumfries wrote that:

> If smuggling is not more frequent ... the insolence and audacity of the smugglers is certainly much increased. Since the departure of two companies of Highlanders ... [the smugglers] ride openly thro the country with their goods in troops of 20, 30, 40 and sometimes upwards 50 horses suffering no officer to come near to try to discover who they are, far less to seize their goods.

The clan system, the powerful Scots Church and Jacobite sympathies further united the population behind the smugglers, and made it unlikely that a free-trader would be found guilty in a jury trial. Even when the customs men managed to secure a conviction, the fines were paltry.

FOOD SMUGGLING

Hunger also drove the Scots into the smugglers' camp. Food imports were sometimes banned by law, and in times of famine illegal imports of grain and oatmeal from Ireland won the local people over and united them against the customs authorities. At Greenock there were riots when ships brought in food from Ireland in 1770:

... a most violent and outrageous mob has risen at Greenock and by force
broken open the hatches and carried away the sails of the vessels laying in that
harbour laden with oatmeal ... and taken and carried away all the said meal
despite of whatever could be done to prevent it ...

The complement of twenty dragoons could hardly control the mob of 5,000. A
magistrate who tried to intervene would have been thrown over the quay had he
not been caught and dragged into the custom house.

Similarly, at Campbeltown, periods of hunger led to riots when a ship carrying
dutiable food arrived at the quay. When a boat from Ireland docked at the port
with a cargo of oatmeal, which the customs authorities refused to allow to be
landed:

... a parcell of women headed by one Brown, an old soldier assembled with a
piper playing, went to the quay and boarded the vessell, deforced the tydesman,
unriged her and proceeded to take the meall ... the comptroller who lives a
little distance from the office and is obliged to go through a great part of the
town was attacked by some women who give him very abusive and threatening
language.

Antagonism between the revenue men and the Scottish population turned
to violence elsewhere, too. The most famous example is the Porteous riots in
Edinburgh, which were triggered off by the execution of a smuggler in 1736.
Andrew Wilson, the condemned man, had gained popularity when he helped a
colleague escape from the Tolbooth gaol, and a mob gathered to jeer at the gallows. They insulted Captain John Porteous, the officer in charge of the guard,
and pelted him with mud. The terrified Porteous fired into the crowd, resulting
in several fatal injuries. Although he was sentenced to death for the shooting,
there was a rumour that he would be pardoned, and a party, wearing disguise,
broke into Edinburgh prison and lynched Porteous from a signpost. Prominent
Edinburgh figures were implicated in this barbaric but popular murder, and as a
result, Westminster imposed a £2,000 fine on the city.

After Union, the Scots' customs and excise system was modelled on the prevailing English system, and abuses were imported along with the rest of the
bureaucracy. At Edinburgh, for example, customs officers at the city gates checked
permits of goods arriving from the ports and did not hesitate to seize even the
most mundane objects if they could be expected to make a few pennies from the
sale. One zealous officer even impounded a worn pair of gloves!

The methods used by Scottish smugglers were broadly similar to those in use
elsewhere in the British Isles, with a few small variations. For example, to signal to
ships at sea during the day smugglers sometimes stretched a bed sheet on the roof
of a croft or a peat-stack, a practice that doesn't seem to have occurred elsewhere.

The danger of chance discovery by routine patrols, while low in England, was virtually negligible in Scotland, so open, unopposed landings were the rule, and the tubmen or 'lingtow men' on the beach would be interrupted only if an informer had named the time and place of the landing.

Robert Louis Stevenson described the scene at a typical landing: 'There, against the sun which was then dipping, we saw the free-traders with a great force of men and horses, scouring the beach.'[10]

Sinking of tubs was rare, possibly because it was unnecessary, or perhaps because surf crashing on the rocky Scottish coastline would soon destroy a raft. Surf was a perennial hazard, threatening even ordinary landings of contraband. When the Monarch or Heisker Islands off the coast of North Uist were used as a smuggling depot the swell in 1791 was so heavy that two ships took a fortnight to land 1,500 ankers of brandy and gin. The smugglers stored the goods in houses on the island, but because of bad weather were only able to take goods off piecemeal, as local demand warranted.

NOTES

1   John Cornish, in his introduction to Carter's 1900 autobiography
2   Coxhead, J.R.W.
3   Cornish *op. cit.*
4   Cornish *op. cit.*
5   George Borlase in 1753, reported in the Lanisley Letters (Journal of the Royal Institute of Cornwall vol. XXIII, pp 374-9)
6   *The West Briton*, reprinted in an undated mimeographed information sheet supplied by the present owner of Methleigh
7   Trevelyan, Marie b. 1853
8   Quoted by Thomas and kindly translated by Hugh Denman
9   Grewar, David
10   *Masters of Ballantrae*

9

HOW SMUGGLING DEVELOPED

The description of a smuggling run outlined in the previous chapters draws together elements that might have been separated in time or geography, and gives no sense of how smuggling methods evolved in the course of the eighteenth and nineteenth centuries. So it's worth now turning briefly to look at how changing patterns of taxation and prevention shaped smuggling practice.

Obviously, smuggling as a business proposition requires something to smuggle – contraband that on crossing a border, is taxed, or levied, subject to a duty – or even banned and impounded. Broadly speaking, then, smuggling is the evasion of a levy imposed, or the movement of prohibited goods. English society prior to the twelfth century was substantially self-supporting, and cross-border trade so insignificant that it did not attract the attention of the administrators of the day. Since trade was unregulated, the smuggler as a character really didn't exist.

It was the growth of trade with Europe that brought an end to this situation, and provided smugglers with their first opportunities. There had always been a very small-scale cross-Channel trade, largely in luxuries such as wine that could not be produced satisfactorily in England. However, with a growing rural population, and improved methods of farming, England began to develop an agricultural surplus that could fill the returning French and Dutch boats. The biggest export was wool.

The English climate and topography are particularly well-suited to the sheep, and traditionally the animal had fed and clothed much of the nation. Flax certainly grew in Ireland, and in parts of England and Wales, but common people were clothed in wool and leather. Wool production gathered momentum throughout the 1200s, and by the century's end, legal exports amounted to 30,000 sacks a year. Some large English estates specialized in wool production: abbey flocks at Crowland in Lincolnshire numbered in excess of 4,000 sheep.

English wool was highly valued abroad: it was tough, and the fibres were long, making them easier to spin. English fleeces made for good fabric, and the surpluses found ready buyers among the merchants of Flanders and Italy. Fleeces were transported to the 'staple' – the only place where they could be legitimately traded with foreigners – and there they were taxed and sold. The staple was often moved from place to place, but in 1347 Calais became a British possession and remained the staple for over 160 years; when the port fell to the French, the staple moved to Middelburgh in the Netherlands, and then to Bruges. Though much wool was exported through the staple as fleeces, there was a small but expanding domestic fabric industry: by 1300 there were important wool-manufacturing centres in the South West and South, and in Yorkshire and Cumbria.

Locally produced wool cloth was of a poor standard, and those who were wealthy enough imported foreign wool fabric to make up into fine garments. The best cloth came from the low countries, so in the mid-fourteenth century Edward III encouraged immigration by skilled weavers from these areas, and thus provided a much-needed stimulus for the domestic wool processing industry. The weavers were given considerable protection – both physically, from their xenophobic English neighbours, and just as important, in business, from foreign competition.

The plague of 1349 further stimulated wool production. The Black Death reduced the population of England from about 4 million to 2.5 million in little more than a year, and landowners looked for a form of agriculture less labour-intensive than the manorial system that had prevailed earlier. They found it in sheep-farming: the land that had been open to all was ditched and hedged, and herds of sheep put to graze where serfs had once sweated. Wool production rose dramatically, and with it, the potential tax revenue to the Crown.

This lucrative source of income had been spotted long before the wool trade expanded in fourteenth century England: wool was the first product on which export duties were levied, as far back as 1275. In that year Edward I taxed wool exports to raise revenue for a hard-pressed Crown. The charge amounted to half a mark, or 6s 8d (33p) on a 26-stone sack. The same charge was levied on each 300 wool-fells (wool still on sheep skins) and 13s 4d (67p) on 'each last of 200 hides'.

At the same time as imposing the duty, the King also recruited the first customs staff to collect the dues. This small full-time staff was simply involved in collecting the revenue: they didn't have the time nor the resources to make sure everyone paid up. Within a few years of the imposition of the duty, it was quite clear that considerable evasion going on. This had serious consequences for the King, who needed the income from the duty to finance a succession of wars in Europe.

This connection between duties and wars is a reprise that is played with monotonous frequency down the centuries: when Britain embarked on the Hundred Years War with France in 1337, Edward III taxed imports and exports to pay for the costly campaign. The King imposed a tax on wine – called 'tunnage' – at 3s 4d (16p) per barrel to fund the navy's defence of the trade fleet, since the war with France was partly to protect England's exports of wool to Flanders. Other duties imposed at the same time covered the export of wool cloth. Many goods were taxed by value, at 5 per cent.

Tunnage was not the only tax imposed on wine imports. If a ship brought more than twenty tuns in, the King claimed his 'prise' (a right to buy at cut price) of two tuns, one taken from before the mast, one from behind. Prisage was paid only by English ships; foreign vessels instead paid tax, or 'butlerage' of 2*s* (10p) a barrel.

Though wine imports were the primary target of the King's Customs, late fourteenth/early fifteenth-century officials zealously pursued anyone they suspected of evading even the most trivial duties. In 1394 a Hull merchant was caught smuggling a barrel of honey and 200 oranges! The poundage due was just tuppence-hapenny (1p), which suggests that early smuggling was habit – merchants just didn't want the aggravation of paying duty. Passengers were a target, too: on the Thames, a customs officer boarding incoming vessels at the bustling Gravesend quayside in 1410 discovered a monk carrying a gold ring and a substantial sum of money. A Flanders woman, Petite Gerderoic, searched under similar circumstances at Haarlem, Gravesend, was caught carrying twenty-one gold rings, a block of gold, jewellery and rare books with coral-encrusted bindings.

As the Hundred Years War continued to be a financial burden, taxation spiralled upwards. In the centuries that followed further territorial conflicts with England's continental neighbours would make British monarchs turn to import and export taxes again and again as an easy way of raising revenue. To pay for the wars each administration imposed ever more complex regulations and prohibitions; or they simply increased the level of existing duties.

This happened, for example, in the middle of the sixteenth century, when debasement of the coinage had reduced the revenue generated by import and export duties. Tunnage was increased dramatically in 1558, from 3*s* 4*d* to 53*s* 4*d* (£2.66), and Queen Mary's reign also saw the introduction of a new book of rates, which set out the duties payable on each item. This greatly increased the duty of 1*s* (5p) in the pound on many of the liable goods.

Each escalation or trade embargo provided new opportunities for smugglers. By evading duties they could supply goods well below the legitimate market price, and they could provide items that were hard or impossible to obtain legitimately. Their customers included not only the British public, but even the country's foes abroad. For example, in the sixteenth century, when Britain was at war with Spain, Bristol merchants were shipping out cannon to the enemy. 'Culverin' guns were exported from the port by the shipload, along with ammunition. These guns were made in the Forest of Dean iron-foundries, and fetched a high premium abroad. The Spanish Armada was quite literally armed by the country it was fighting!

But why choose the import or export of goods as the taxable activity? Why not tax the sheep themselves on the hoof at the place they were grazing, for example, or the sale of wine by merchants? The answer is simple: coastal trade is conspicuous, so the coastline was the natural place for the authorities to try and tax the trade, or to stop it altogether. As an island, the borders of Britain are graphically defined and unshifting. Moving goods across England's borders was therefore an obvious business – the flags and sails of a ship signalled its approach on the horizon even before the hull itself was visible.

Other factors also made the movement of shipping easy to see. The ebbing and flowing of the tide regulated sailing times: in these days of deep-water harbours we tend to forget that for millenia shipping had to wait for the tide before sailing, and at low water, boats simply grounded in the mud at the foot of the quay. Wind was a factor, too. The square-rigged sailing ship that dominated until the advent of fore-and-aft rigging was restricted by the wind. To leave a port, such ships needed a breeze blowing them out to sea.

All these factors meant that trade across England's coastline was easy to spot. Taxing such obvious activity therefore must have seemed a natural way to earn revenue for the Crown. Unfortunately, imposing a tax and collecting it are two different matters. When Edward I created the customs service, he did little to ensure that the customs dues were actually paid: he simply provided the apparatus of collection, in the form of a custom house with a small staff at various points around the coast. This *laissez-faire* approach to the gathering of revenue prevailed for some considerable time, but by the early fifteenth century, the rudiments of enforcement were beginning to appear.

At this stage, legal import of goods meant using an official port – there were thirteen of these, each serving one section of the coastline. Goods could be landed elsewhere, but only with the explicit permission of the authorities at the main port. Naturally it was impossible for a handful of officials to control a whole stretch of coast from a single point: the East Anglian coast, for example, was controlled from Yarmouth, but the customs authorities there were expected to keep watch on nearly 90 miles of coastline, up as far as Blakeney and right down to Woodbridge.

At each of these key ports there were two principal officials responsible for the collection of the customs dues. The *collector of customs* was the official who had to actually do the work, but he was overseen by a *controller of customs*. Between them, the two men were supposed to collect the dues payable, and sign and seal the relevant receipts and other export documents. This two-part arrangement was designed to ensure the honesty of the officials, and a further precaution was that the port seal was made in two halves. Each official had half the seal – all documents had to carry both halves to be legal, and each of the two officials was separately accountable for the transactions of the port.

These customs officials were very badly paid, but they benefited from seizures of smuggled goods, and made a charge on every receipt sealed. The temptation for the two men to collude was irresistible, and the sale of blank receipts soon became a problem: signed and sealed, the merchant simply filled in whatever he chose on the piece of parchment. Blank receipts were so commonplace by 1433 that the practice was discussed in Parliament. However, even the stiff penalty – three years in jail plus seizure of all belongings – proved little deterrent.

In an attempt to enforce honesty on controllers and collectors, a third official was appointed: the *surveyor of customs* at each port was supposed to monitor his colleagues as they worked.

Backing up these three officials was a minor army of lesser bureaucrats: the *tide waiter's* task was to board incoming vessels arriving on the high tide and check that they tied up at the appointed place on the quay. The tide waiter joined London-bound boats, for example, at Greenwich, and made sure that the cargo was not unloaded on an isolated jetty out of sight of the waiting triumvirate of controller, collector and surveyor (all eyeing each other suspiciously, no doubt). To ensure the honesty of the tide waiter there was another official, the *tide surveyor*.

When these functionaries had safely guided the boat to dock in the right place, other officials took over: the *coast waiter* supervised the unloading of cargoes from home ports; the *land waiter* watched over loading and unloading of boats from foreign ports; the *land surveyor* similarly kept an eye on both the land and coast waiters. At the bottom of the ladder the *searcher* was responsible for checking that the boat's cargo tallied with what was on the receipt; the *weigher* unpacked the cargo and weighed it; and the *tidesman* stayed with the vessel until the unloading was complete.

This hierarchy of officials had to administer a welter of complex laws that were added to the statute book over the centuries to protect the wool industry. The restoration of the monarchy in 1660 added still more, and additionally jacked up the penalties for illegal foreign sale of wool: all export of wool was forbidden, and soon afterwards further legislation ensured that those who smuggled wool out risked the gallows for their sins. The legislators of the day probably saw this as a major deterrent, but if anything, it simply made the owlers of Romney Marsh more desperate still. If you're to hang for smuggling wool, why hesitate to shoot your pursuer? Other measures, intended to boost demand for wool, seem extraordinary: a 1666 statute even obliged everyone to be buried in a shroud made of pure wool cloth!

These restrictions outraged wool producers, who, faced with low prices in England, naturally turned to the export trade to stave off financial ruin. This was hardly a new situation: as early as 1390 there was a stockpile of unsold fleeces amounting to three years output. However, as the seventeenth century came to a close, export of wool from England's southern counties was getting seriously out of control, as fleeces fled to Flanders by the thousand almost as soon as they had been separated from the sheep's back. According to one estimate, 120,000 packs of wool annually were exported illegally.

Smuggling had become an epidemic, and Romney Marsh was the centre of the infection. Public opinion on the Marsh generally sided with the owlers, but in other circles, there was outrage at the scale of illegal wool exports. The most vocal and aggressive opponent of the thriving free-trade in wool was merchant William Carter, who set himself up as a one-man private preventive force and propaganda machine. In 1671 he published a tract, *England's Interest in Trade Asserted*, in which he alleged that the owlers exported wool not just from the marsh, but from a catchment area some 20 miles in diameter. Carter also documented the armed guards that the smugglers used to protect their cargoes.

In all fairness, William Carter cannot be described as an independent witness. He was a clothier, and was therefore concerned that foreign competition should not affect his own trade. Nevertheless, Carter went to extraordinary lengths to stamp out owling, often risking life and limb in the process. In 1669 he obtained a warrant from the King, and armed with it, arrested the master of a smuggling ship berthed at Dover. Carter planned to take his prisoner to Folkestone for trial, but the mariner's wife rode ahead and mustered a large stone-throwing mob to greet Carter when he arrived. The would-be smuggler catcher fled, releasing his prisoner.

Carter was nothing if not persistent. He was still enthusiastically pursuing the cause nearly twenty years later. With some assistance from his friends, he arrested ten owlers on the marsh, and took them to Romney for trial. However, the trade enjoyed such popular support that the Mayor of Romney hesitated to proceed, and he had the ten men released on bail. The outraged owlers naturally set out to exact revenge, and William Carter and friends were chased to Lydd. There the smugglers attacked by night, and the Mayor of Lydd suggested that these free-lance preventive officers should make haste for Rye to save their skins. Carter and his group were followed by fifty armed men as they headed for Guldeford ferry, planning to get a boat from there to Rye. However, they never reached the ferry: at Camber Point they were so terrified of capture that they abandoned their horses, and climbed into the nearest available boat to make good their escape. A contemporary account says, 'had they not got into the boats, Mr Carter would have received some hurt, for many of the exporters were desperate fellows, not caring what mischief they did.'

But the efforts of Carter and others like him only emboldened the owlers. They pooled their resources, and soon an owling venture involved hundreds of armed men.

Something clearly had to be done to stop the rot. In 1671 Charles II had set up the Board of Customs, and by 1685 there were ten smacks patrolling the coast between Yarmouth and Bristol. On land, a force of mounted customs officers – called riding officers – was established in 1690. However the riding officers could hardly be described as an effective opposition, since there were just eight of them to patrol the whole of the Kent coastline. Their burden of work was made even greater by further restrictive legislation on the wool trade. The 1698 Wool Act obliged all producers with farms within 10 miles of the coast to register their annual production with the local custom house immediately after shearing. The act also controlled movement of wool close to the coast.

Above: 1 Though romantically embellished, this print of a land party waiting for a smuggling ship contains some telling details, such as the sail, the small kegs and ragged clothing

Right: 2 Another romantic view, interesting mainly because it shows clearly how smugglers carried tubs, roped together in pairs, over their shoulders. Tubs were actually substantially larger than the artist has shown them

Above and below: 3, 4 The types of small open vessels favoured by smugglers before increased prevention forced them to use heavily armed ships

5 Smugglers or fishermen? Unfortunately for customs officers, the boats and carts that smugglers used were also the stock in trade of innocent seamen, like these characters relaxing on Dover beach

6 This print of coastguards on a cliff-top shows one of them on crutches. The engraver might have intended this as a tribute to plucky officials injured in the line of duty. It's more likely that he was lampooning the service, and suggesting that only the halt and lame were employed

7 One of the pistols used by the Hawkhurst Gang in their attack on Goudhurst (see page 166). The gun, and two other weapons, are in the collection of the Maidstone Museum

8 Where the tide ebbed far from the shore, as in the Solway, a caravan of ponies carried contraband away from smuggling vessels aground in the mud

JOHN RATTENBURY.
of Beer, Devonshire.
"THE ROB ROY of the WEST".

Right: 9 Portrait of Rattenbury (see page 189), from the frontispiece of his biography

Below: 10 On the South East coast much contraband came ashore through cart gaps like this one at Broadstairs

11 Steps taken in the early eighteenth century to prevent a French invasion also handicapped smugglers in the South East. This print shows a Martello tower (see page 135-6) one of 105 built around the coast

12 Engraved from a watercolour by J.M.W. Turner, this supposedly shows smugglers burying contraband on the cliffs above Folkestone. In fact, this rarely happened

Right: 13 This eighteenth-century print vividly captures the sometimes desperate war that waged between the smugglers and their adversaries in the customs service

Below: 14 Where the water was shallow – as in this illustration of Arched Rock on the Isle of Wight – smugglers shuttled their cargo ashore in small boats

A Representation of ye Smuggler's breaking open ye King's Custom House at **Poole.**

The images that follow depict the notorious murders of 1747-8 carried out by Sussex smugglers, and described on pages 148-154

Above: 15 Raiding the Poole custom house

Left: 16 Torture of Richard Hawkins

John Mills alias *Smoaker,* & *Rich.ᵈ Rowland* alias *Robb,* Whipping Rich.ᵈ Hawkins. to Death. at ye Dog & Partridge on Slendon Common; & Jeremiah Curtis. & Thoˢ. Winter alias Coachman. Standing by Aiding & abetting ye Murder of the said Rich.ᵈ Hawkins.

17 Galley and Chater put on horseback together, their legs tied under the horse's belly

18 Galley and Chater can no longer sit upright, and slide down beneath the horse

William Galley, brought cross a Horse to a Sand Pit where a deep Hole is Dug to Bury him in.

19 The smugglers enlarge a fox-earth to bury Galley

The unfortunate William Galley put by the Smugglers into the Ground & as is generally believed before he was quite DEAD.

20 Galley buried

Chater, Chained in ye. Turff House at Old Mills's
Cobby, kicking him. & Tapner, cutting him Cross ye
Eyes & Nose, while he is saying the Lords Prayer.
Several of ye other Smugglers standing by.

21 Chater tortured in the turf-house

Chater hanging at the Well in LADY HOLT Park.
the Bloody Villains Standing by

22 The unsuccessful attempt to hang Chater at Harris's Well

The Bloody Smugglers flinging down Stones after
they had flung his Dead Body into the Well.

23 The smugglers throw rocks down Harris's Well to silence Chater's screams

The riding officers not only had to contend with the owlers, but with the growing tide of smuggled imports. The most recent war – again with the French – had necessitated a further hoisting of import duties, and the smugglers now found they could make a profit on both legs of their cross-Channel journey. Ships that went out loaded with wool came back groaning with foreign goods.

The inadequacy of the eight brave men of Kent was recognised in 1698, when the scope of the force (now called the Landguard) was expanded and numbers increased to 50 and later to 300. However, the riding officers were hampered by the fact that prevention was largely land-based. Smugglers at sea had the benefit of much greater mobility, and could simply land goods at an unguarded spot. The sea-based preventive effort had been abandoned in 1690 with the appointment of the eight riding officers, and for the next eight years the custom houses had relied on the navy to oppose the smugglers at sea. At the turn of the century, though, the Waterguard was established, with twenty-one vessels stationed all the way around the coast.

These twin forces were to be the principal opponents of the smugglers for the next century or so, and their effectiveness varied according to the calibre of the officers, their pay and conditions, and other factors. When pay was good, and the service was able to hire committed and diligent officers who could call on the military for assistance, the preventive effort could be remarkably effective. Regrettably, this seemed to be the case for only a minority of the time. The job of riding officer in particular was not well paid, and out of their £42 annual salary, the officers also had to buy and maintain a horse. The temptation to turn a blind eye to a smuggling venture in return for payment of a small fee was irresistible for some.

The difficulty was exacerbated by the fact that the riding officers lived in the hearts of the communities they were supposed to be policing. If they were diligent in their efforts to prevent smuggling, they were ostracised and persecuted; the alternative was collaboration with the smugglers, an easy life, and a regular supplement to the meagre pay. The easy option must have seemed attractive indeed.

JACOBITE SMUGGLERS

In the absence of really effective opposition, it was inevitable that wholesale evasion of duty would expand. The process was accelerated in the early years of the eighteenth century by the spread of Jacobitism. Jacobites were supporters of the Catholic King James II of England, who lost his throne to William of Orange in the 'Glorious Revolution' of 1688. When James fled to France, many of his supporters went with him, and they used sympathetic smugglers to keep in touch with those Jacobites who remained in England.

Jacobites argued that England's economic problems stemmed from the Commonwealth – the republican government that ended with the restoration of the monarchy in 1660. They claimed that subsequent administrations were corrupt, and identified custom house officers and the army that assisted them as agents of government tyranny. As opponents of all things bad, smugglers could thus be seen by Jacobites only as forces for good.

When George I replaced Anne as monarch in 1714, the Jacobite cause received a further boost. Many English people were hostile to the new King's German roots, and rallied to the Stuart flag. Open support for Jacobitism became common: in 1718, for example, Ashford labourers held a noisy celebration on the birthday of the Old Pretender – James Stuart, son of James II.

This new climate of support made it easier for Jacobite sympathisers in England to organise themselves, and in smugglers they found willing conspirators. Employing ship-owners to carry passengers and correspondence between England and France, they encouraged them to buy brandy on the Continent as a blind for their seditious trips. Jacobites also used smuggling ships to ferry to France recruits for the French and Spanish armies. As Paul Monod argues in his 1991 paper *Dangerous Merchandise*, Jacobite promotion of smuggling made the contraband trade far more organised, coordinated and commercial.

The sympathies and alliances of the smugglers did not go unnoticed. When Admiral Vernon assessed the threat of invasion from France in 1745, he commented that 'smuggling has converted those employed in it … to dangerous spies on all our proceedings for the enemy's daily information.'

Jacobitism was a particular formative influence on smuggling in the South East. Many major land owners in the region had Jacobite sympathies, and connived with the smugglers who carried goods across their lands, or openly operated from them. This was especially true of the Sussex gangs based in Mayfield, Groombridge and Hawkhurst (see pages 165–170). The gangs openly supported the Jacobites and drank their health – the Oak and Ivy Inn where the Hawkhurst Gang met takes its name from the Jacobite emblem. They acted as propagandists, too, and in 1716 distributed copies of the Pretender's declaration promoting a Jacobite rising.

The landowners who tolerated their activities did so not just out of a shared cause, but for paternalist reasons. They recognised smuggling as a popular cause, and saw its support as a way of enhancing their own prestige and local power. They may also have benefited directly from smuggling revenues. Landowners implicated included Henry Campion, who owned farms at Hawkhurst and Goudhurst; the Hale family, who were the major landowners in the Romney Marsh area; the Ropers, who had estates around Sittingbourne. And it's no coincidence that the customs officer murdered by smugglers in 1748 was buried in a well on Ladyholt Park: the estate was owned by the Caryll family, who were Catholics and Jacobites. The previous year the lake at Parham, home of Jacobite Sir Cecil Bishopp, had become the last resting place of one of the Hawkhurst gang's murder victims.

These powerful figures openly assisted the smugglers when they could. After the Hawkhurst smugglers famously broke into the Poole custom house in 1748, Sir Cecil Bishopp praised the robbery as 'a gallant expedition, for as such it was esteemed by most of this neighbourhood.'

Jacobite smuggling was of course also particularly enthusiastic in the Catholic strongholds of Scotland and Ireland, where there was widespread support for the rebellion of 1715. At Perth in particular there was considerable anti-English feeling. The customs authorities there were never popular, and they frequently had to be supported by the military.

THE HOVERING ACT

The government responded to the widespread evasion of customs duty with a further rash of legislation, clamping down on smuggling in every form. One novel development that posed a growing threat was the smugglers' practice of 'hovering' off the coast in their ships. When their crews sent signals to the shore, fishermen would sail out in their small boats to pick up the contraband goods.

The 1718 Hovering Act made it illegal for vessels smaller than 50 tons to wait within 6 miles of the shore, and brandy imported in smaller ships (under 15 tons) was also liable to seizure. Vessels involved in these offences were impounded and destroyed, usually by being sawn in half, and their ropes unravelled. The divided vessels were useless at sea, but found many on land. Dickens wrote of Pegotty's house that:

> ... the wonderful charm of it was, that it was a real boat which had no doubt been upon the water hundreds of times, and which had never been intended to be lived in, on dry land. That was the captivation of it to me. If it had ever been meant to be lived in, I might have thought it small, or inconvenient, or lonely; but never having been designed for any such use, it became a perfect abode.[1]

Other legislation passed soon afterwards outlawed Kent and Essex boats with four or more oars, in an attempt to prevent contraband from being rowed across the Channel. Transportation to the colonies was simultaneously introduced as a penalty for smuggling, and the scope of the Act was cast to include virtually anyone carrying firearms, or wearing a mask to hinder identification.

If anything, the effect of this legislation was to make smugglers became more brazen: and the ill-equipped preventives were no match for the free-traders, as this complaint from Gower in 1730 illustrates: 'The smugglers are grown very insolent and obstruct our officers in the execution of their duty ... the master and mariners of the ship Galloway ... came up on deck with pistols and drawn cutlasses and refused them to rummage.'

To avoid identification which might lead to conviction, smugglers resorted to kidnapping, and officials were a particular target. One victim was Gabriel Tomkins, a bailiff and reformed smuggler from Mayfield. In 1735 he arrested Thomas Moore, a Rye smuggler. However, Moore was bailed by the magistrate, and he returned to Rye's Mermaid Inn to find Tomkins. With the aid of the landlord, he smashed his way into Tomkins's room, dragged him through the streets and on board a boat, probably with a view to landing him in France and leaving him to fend for himself. However, the local revenue men intervened, searching vessels moored at Rye, and Tomkins thus narrowly avoided involuntary emigration.

Other officials were not so lucky. Seven years later the luckless John Darby found himself enjoying a weekend break in France. He and one other officer had tried to impound some tubs of brandy but – as usual – they were heavily out-numbered. The smugglers kidnapped the two men, and hustled them on board a French boat from which they had just unloaded tea. This story has a surprising ending: with unusual courtesy, the smugglers made sure that when the two men had secured a passage home from the Continent, their horses were waiting for them at the Old George Inn in Rye.

THE ACT OF INDEMNITY

It was legislation of 1736 that perhaps set the scene for the appalling violence that characterised mid-century smuggling in the South East. A parliamentary com-mittee of enquiry investigated the free-trade, and painted a damning picture that demanded immediate action from the government. The result was the introduc-tion of the death penalty for injuring preventive officers in the course of their duty, and heavy fines for bribery. Even an unarmed smuggler resisting arrest faced transportation. The legislation was called the *Act of Indemnity*, and it was indeed the indemnity clauses that perhaps most provoked smuggling violence in the sub-sequent decades. A smuggler who revealed the names of his collaborators was granted a free pardon, making virtually anyone involved in the free-trade who turned King's evidence a mortal threat to his companions.

These new laws had little effect on the level of smuggling, and three years later the outbreak of the War of Jenkins' Ear against Spain pushed the already over-stretched customs services almost to breaking point. Things got worse when the conflict became a mere sideshow to the War of the Austrian Succession, and when, in 1745, Jacobite sympathies exploded into full-scale rebellion.

The customs authorities were still hampered by the incompetence of their staff; around this time an official described the five coast-waiters of Anglesey as 'Two fools, one Rogue, one Bully and one Numbskull'.[2]

By the 1740s smuggling in the South East had reached a climax, with large forces of armed men defying the authorities to act against them as they landed

enormous cargoes on open beaches. Now the government faced two press-
ing issues: not only did the smugglers represent a huge loss of revenue to the
Exchequer; they were also a threat to public order.

Finally, the government realised that smuggling would never be stopped by
force alone, and instead adopted an economic solution, radically reducing the
tax on tea in 1745. This move was only a partial success. Far from being ruined,
the smugglers merely turned to new forms of contraband, notably spirits, and tea
duties were in any case raised again soon afterwards.

The government passed still more draconian legislation the following year
– and once more, failed to back it up with greater resources for the preventive
forces. Like the Act of Indemnity ten years earlier, these laws aimed to undermine
the smugglers' power base in the countryside by providing an inducement to
inform; and again, the smugglers responded with a further escalation of violence
and intimidation of witnesses and jurors.

GAZETTING

The core of the 1746 Act was the publication of the names of known smugglers
in the *London Gazette*. A smuggler thus 'Gazetted' had forty days to turn himself
in, and at the end of that period he was effectively outlawed, with a bounty of
£500 on his head – a fabulous sum when a building labourer earned just 16*d* (7p)
a day. The death penalty was extended to cover not just smuggling, but assembling
in preparation for a run, and even the harbouring of smugglers. The bodies of
smugglers who killed officers were to be hung on gibbets around the coast.

The new laws sparked bestial violence by gangs that aimed to obtain silence
from witnesses either by intimidation or – if necessary – by murder, but if anything, the terrorism that followed was counter-productive. It led to a concerted
attempt by the authorities to capture the most desperate smugglers. By mid-
century the largest smuggling gangs had been broken up.

Smuggling continued, however, and further conflicts abroad over the next three
decades both provided a periodic distraction from the problems posed by the smugglers, and exacerbated the loss of revenue caused by the free-trade. For example, the
cost to the Exchequer of the Seven-Years War which started in 1756 was considerable, because 200,000 troops were being paid. Land Tax had been a shilling in the
pound in the 1740s, but had quadrupled by the end of the war. The government
was forced to borrow £60 million to finance the conflict, but they also used import
duties pay for the war: duties on tea that had been cut in 1745 from 4*s* 9*d* (25p) a
pound to 1*s* (5p), were in 1759 raised again. This of course created a renewed surge
in demand for contraband tea, which the smugglers were only too happy to satisfy.

Smugglers again openly defied the authorities. For example, in 1767 nine
smugglers' vessels, including armed sloops, sailed from Penzance harbour in broad

daylight; a man-of-war looked on, powerless to stop them. Five years later a customs boat from the same port was plundered and sunk by smugglers, and later that year, another smugglers' boat captured the revenue cutter *Brilliant*, which was lying in Penzance harbour with seized goods on board.

The collector of customs at Penzance describes how, eight years later, the smugglers worked in full view of the customs authorities:

> Two Irish wherries full of men and guns (one about 130 tons, and the other less) came to anchor within the limits of this port, and within half a mile of the shore, and lay there three days, in open defiance discharging their contraband goods. We are totally destitute of any force to attack them by sea, and as the whole coast is principally inhabited by a lot of smugglers under the denomination of fishermen, it is next to an impossibility for the officers of the revenue to intercept any of these goods after they are landed … the officers, being on the look-out, saw a boat come off from one of [the wherries] and come ashore near where the officers had secreted themselves, and the crew began to land the goods. The officers interfered, and attempted to make a seizure of said boat and goods; but a blunderbuss was immediately presented to one of their breasts, and the smugglers, with great imprecations, threatened their lives.

On another occasion, a large wherry landed 1,500–2,000 ankers of spirits, 20 tons of tea and other goods on the beach here, and a local officer of the customs wrote the following plaintive letter to his superiors:

> In the western part of this county, smuggling, since the soldiers have been drawn off, has been carried on almost without control. Irish wherries, carrying 14, 16 or more guns, and well manned, frequently land large quantities of goods in defiance of the officers of customs and excise, and their crew, armed with swords and pistols, escort the SS a considerable distance from the sea. In this way, goods are carried from one part of the country to another almost every night … The beach lies near a public road which, whilst the goods were discharging, was filled with armed men, in order to stop every traveller in whom they could not confide, till the goods were safely lodged in the country … A few days after, two officers got information that a very considerable quantity of goods was concealed in the house and premises of a well-known smuggler. They obtained from me a search warrant, but were forcibly hindered from executing it by four men, one armed with a pistol and a large whip, the others with sticks and bludgeons. They were told that if they persisted they would have their brains blown out. As the law now stands, I fear a criminal prosecution would have been useless for the reason, which it shocks me to mention, that a Cornish jury would certainly acquit the smugglers … . These, my lord, are the facts. It would be mere pedantry to describe to your lordship the shocking effects, the moral and political consequences of

smuggling carried to such a daring height, but I cannot help saying that perjury, drunkenness, idleness, poverty, and contempt of the law, and a universal corruption of manners are, in this neighbourhood, too plainly seen to accompany it.[3]

Smugglers resisted the new measures with equal insolence elsewhere. At St David's in 1770:

The *Pelham* cutter, in the service of the customs ... was attacked by two large smuggling cutters and a wherry, and, the officers being obliged to quit it, was boarded by the crew of the wherry. It has since been found at St Davids, with several holes in the bottom, and almost rifled of everything. The Commissioners have offered a reward of 200l for the conviction of any of the offenders.[4]

Occasionally the authorities were more prepared to use overwhelming force against the smugglers, but their efforts were only partially successful. In 1781, 100 mounted soldiers and 900 infantrymen moved in on Deal, one of the most notorious smuggling centres, expecting to find £100,000 worth of contraband concealed there. The troops didn't bother with the formalities:

Some flint and many stones came at the windows and many shots were fired by the soldiers but most miraculously nobody was killed and only one man considerably wounded who, having thrown a mattock-iron [a pick, with an adze blade at one end] from a garden at the officers, a Middlesex militiaman fired at him as he was scrambling over a wall.[5]

The troops left with perhaps a tenth of what they'd expected, probably because an informer had forewarned the Deal men, who had spirited the goods back to their source on the Continent for the duration of the raid. This slap in the face for the authorities evidently made them all the more determined, for three years later, William Pitt sent in troops again. The townspeople were once more forewarned (by carrier pigeon this time), and turned out in considerable numbers to resist the raid. However, the military prevailed by sheer force of numbers, and after resting overnight, they marched down to the beach where the smugglers had pulled their boats well above the high-water mark to secure them from the storms. After a nominal 'anti-invasion drill' a prearranged signal initiated the coordinated destruction and burning of the boats, in front of their outraged but helpless owners.

THE ACT OF OBLIVION

These attacks on the country's most powerful smugglers were an exception. In general, the customs authorities were inadequately supported by the military.

This was partly a consequence of the outbreak of the American War of Independence in 1776 as troops formerly assigned to guarding the coast in peace-time were whisked away to fight abroad.

By the 1780s, the free-trade had once more reached alarming levels. The revenue cutters put up a spirited defence at sea, but the wages of crews had fallen behind that paid on merchant ships, and the quality of seamen attracted to the service was lower as a consequence. Once goods had been landed in England, the run inland took place virtually unhindered, and smuggling gangs had once more sprung up to defy the authorities.

One collector of customs at Whitby summed up the situation succinctly:

> Very great quantities of prohibited goods have been Rum, spirits, tea, etc., are loaded into boats and cobles which are guarded by a great number of armed men who are totally defiant of the [customs] Officers, and the Country People, many of whom follow no employment but this illicit practice, are constantly in waiting, and being armed with Bludgeons, etc., and provided with Horses, immediately convey the Run goods to some distant place. Vessels are generally of the Cutter or Lugger kind, which we have reason to believe are often built in Kent, and are generally between seventy and one hundred and fifty tons, with crews of 15 to 25 men.

The revenue men stood little chance of success when faced with such opposition: eighteen six-pounder carriage guns, each firing iron balls the size of oranges, was not an unusual complement of arms for a smuggling cutter. When the master of one of these ships was asked whether he didn't fear the customs cutters, he simply tapped his pistols in reply.

On land, too, the smugglers were brazen in their defence of their interests: in February 1780 a supervisor of excise set out from Whitstable for Canterbury, with 183 tubs of gin that had been captured earlier. The caravan was guarded by a party of eight troopers and an officer, but fifty smugglers attacked at Borstal Hill, the steep road that crawls up out of Whitstable. In the battle, two soldiers were killed, and Joseph Nicholson, the supervisor, fled with the survivors. A fat reward induced an informant to supply the name of an eighteen-year-old (John Knight) who played a minor role – this man was executed at Penenden Heath, Maidstone and later hung in chains at Borstal Hill.

By 1782, shortage of manpower had induced the government to take a softer line on smugglers in an attempt to woo them into the service of the Crown: the *Act of Oblivion* allowed a smuggler to wipe the slate clean by volunteering for the armed forces. Smugglers' skills as seamen were especially prized, and even their most vigorous opponents in the revenue services occasionally expressed admiration for the men's ability.

The effectiveness of this new law was, however, reduced by a clause that allowed substitution. A smuggler who could find two others willing to take his place would be released from a previously imposed penalty up to £500, and four men were sufficient to repay any smuggling crime except the killing of a revenue officer. Substitution particularly affected rich smugglers such as Isaac Gulliver (see page 181), who could afford to buy the services of others, and people even placed advertisements offering themselves as substitutes on payment of a fee.

PITT SLASHES TEA TAX

In response to this crisis, the government had set up yet another committee of enquiry in the early 1780s, and it came up with the blindingly obvious conclusion that the prevalence of smuggling could be attributed to high duties. William Pitt took note of the committee's report, and in 1784 slashed the duty on tea from 129 per cent to 12.5 per cent, and thus rendered tea an unprofitable cargo. As in the past, though, this simply caused a shift into other forms of contraband, and the trade went on largely unabated. For example, at Goldcliff in South Wales that year customs officers seized not tea but 10,000lbs of tobacco, and 40 gallons of brandy, and a couple of months later a further 130 gallons of brandy. All of this would have been destined for nearby Cardiff and Newport.

The cut in duty did nothing to improve the quality of the personnel in the customs service: around this time the collector of customs at Weymouth, for example, was described in an official report in terms far from glowing. He had 'a debauched life and conversation, seldom sober, and hardly ever goes to bed till three or four a clock [sic] in the morning and many times not all night.' The customs officers of nearby Portland were little better: of one was said he 'never did any service, but rather the contrary'.

Violent resistance continued just as before as an incident in October of 1791 illustrates. A Newport custom house officer tried to board a small vessel (15–20 tons), anchored at the mouth of the Usk River:

> the persons on board her, with horrid imprecations, recited him, swearing that if he presumed to come on board, they would blow his brains out, and at the same time brandishing a cutlass and pointing a pistol, with horrid threats of his life, etc ... There is 6 or 7 desperate ruffians on board ... but we are assured she belongs to Barry Island, and built on purpose for smuggling ...

THE FRENCH REVOLUTIONARY WARS

The turn of the century was marked by yet more conflict with Britain's European neighbours: the French Revolutionary War began in 1793, and went on until 1802. There was then a short peace before fighting started in the Napoleonic War, which continued until 1815. The back-to-back wars once more drew preventive forces away from Britain's coasts, and again proved a financial drain. As in other conflicts, smugglers played a role that was at sometimes ambiguous, and often downright treacherous.

Smuggling ships traded freely with French ports throughout the wars, and took reports of English conditions over to the enemy, returning with letters to spies in Britain. Smuggler 'Saucy Jack' (see page 194), for example, related while in prison awaiting execution that:

> Since the French War, smugglers carry intelligence to many parts of France, what was doing in these kingdoms, and what shipping was fitting out; for which the French amply rewarded them, and they always had free liberty to land in any port they had a mind to, for carrying on their wicked purposes.[6]

In all fairness, though, some of the smugglers probably also acted as double agents, and some certainly remained loyal to the Crown, bringing back to England intelligence about French shipping.

Clearly treasonous, though, was smugglers' transport of gold across the Channel. A flourishing export trade in bullion grew up, as Napoleon struggled to pay his mercenaries while the economy collapsed around him.

The Emperor described in his memoirs how he arranged for gold to be smuggled out of England to support the Franc:

> I got bills upon Vera Cruz ... the bills were discounted by merchants in London, to whom ten percent, and sometimes a premium was paid as their reward. Bills were then given by them upon different bankers in Europe for the greatest part of the amount, and the remainder in gold, which last was brought over to France by the smugglers.

Vast galleys, rowed by dozens of men, propelled the gold across the Channel at speeds that would look respectable to a modern day-tripper. It was at Deal that the 'Guinea boats' were constructed: they were monsters, up to 40ft long, and 7ft wide. A dozen oars each side pulled the boats over to France in less than five hours during calm weather, and even with a head-wind, the Kentish oarsmen were no slouches. On one occasion a rowing boat leaving Dover had difficulty getting out of the harbour because of the wind, and had to hitch a tow from a steamer. Once they had left the cliffs behind, though, the oarsmen overtook the steam ship, and beat it to the French coast.

Pursuit of these galleys in a sailing vessel was futile, as a preventive officer succinctly summed up when he described such a chase as 'sending a cow to catch a hare'. Little wonder that the construction of the galleys was eventually forbidden in England.

Prohibition didn't end the 'Guinea run'. Laughing at the authorities, the smugglers of Deal, Dover and Folkestone simply built their boats across the Channel, under the self-interested protection of the French government. The boats were so cheap that they could almost be considered expendable at the end of a trip: building a twenty-four-oared galley cost £40 or so, a small sum compared to the £30,000 worth of gold that the smugglers might be carrying on a single trip. There's a modern-day parallel here, in the drug smugglers who abandon a light aircraft and speedboats once they've ferried in their valuable cargoes.

Though the scale of gold-smuggling in the French Wars was unprecedented, gold wasn't a new contraband. Two centuries earlier merchants from Lyme Regis were suspected of smuggling bullion out of Britain. In 1576 the suspicions became so strong that one Ralph Lane was despatched to the town to investigate, carrying a warrant to search ships that were alleged to be taking part. The result was a riot – the warrant was destroyed and Lane's deputy was thrown overboard.

Another surprising aspect of smuggling in this period was the trade in people. Smuggling vessels ferried the French in both directions. During the Revolutionary War, aristocrats fleeing the tumbrels sought refuge in England, often choosing a passage on a smuggling ship as the route least open to discovery. In the Napoleonic Wars, the traffic flowed in the opposite direction, with escaped French prisoners fleeing from the North Kent coast. The enormous numbers of POWs had put a considerable strain on the Britain's resources, and led to the construction of new prisons (including Dartmoor). But many French prisoners lived in appalling conditions in prison hulks – filthy, overcrowded and disease-ridden vessels anchored off-shore. Through an elaborate network of contacts and safe havens, prisoners who succeeded in escaping from the hulks would be brought to London, then smuggled on a hoy or an oyster-boat to a timber platform at the low-tide mark near Whitstable.

This platform was a mooring for the oyster-boats and fishing vessels that were prevented from reaching the true shoreline at low-tide by the 2-mile-wide ribbon of mud that fringes the beaches here. Mingling with fishing folk and wildfowlers, the French escapees were able to make their way back to the shore, rest up and hide for a few days, then make a clandestine departure one dark night from Swalecliffe Rock – a shingle spit close to the Herne Bay road. Relatives of the wealthier prisoners would no doubt have paid handsomely for their safe return, and the arrangement no doubt suited the smugglers, who would otherwise have had to pay for their returning cargo of contraband in currency, rather than people. The trade continued between 1793 and 1814.

MARTELLO TOWERS

The smuggling of gold, exiles and POWs provided an isolated boost to smuggling in the French wars. In other respects the fighting made smuggling considerably more difficult, because preparations for the widely anticipated French invasion also handicapped the free-traders. This was most marked in the South East, where the construction of defensive Martello towers provided purpose-made look-outs for the forces of law and order, and a new canal severely restricted access to some of the most important smuggling beaches.

Named after Genovese forts at Mortella Point in Corsica, the Martello Towers were drum-shaped blockhouses. Some twelve metres high, they had a garrison of twenty-five men and an officer. Each had three floors: the ground floor was used as storage; the first as a barracks; and the open top floor was a gun platform with a panoramic view. Construction began in 1805, and within eight years there was a chain of 105 towers stretching from Seaford in the South to Aldeburgh in the North.

The Royal Military Canal was intended not for navigation but as a water obstacle to halt the advance of Napoleon's troops (should they elude the Royal Navy and the Martello Towers). Romney Marsh was considered to be the most likely target of a French invasion, and the canal aimed to cut off the marsh from the land beyond. At 28 miles in length, and typically about 10 metres wide and 150cm deep, it was constructed over about five years, starting in 1804. Earth dug from the wide ditch was thrown up to provide a defensive parapet, and a military road ran alongside.

The canal's construction must have caused some consternation among the marsh smugglers. An obstacle that could stop an invading army was equally effective at stopping the movement of contraband from the marsh coast to the markets inland. Some parts of the canal were shallow enough to ford, but these points weren't always easy to locate: several smugglers drowned at Pett Levels when they were chased into the water by the preventive services – evidently they searched unsuccessfully for a safe crossing point.

THE PREVENTIVE WATERGUARD AND THE BLOCKADE

A reorganisation of the preventive services also made life more difficult for the free-traders. In 1809 the Preventive Waterguard was established. This brought the cutters and small rowing boats of the customs service under more central control, and provided greater coordination. Pay was improved to a level superior to that of comparable posts in the navy.

Smuggling continued nevertheless, and its perpetrators were just as willing to use violence as their predecessors in the previous century. A pathetic gravestone at Minster on the Isle of Sheppey describes the consequences:

O EARTH COVER NOT MY BLOOD
SACRED TO THE MEMORY OF A MAN UNKNOWN, who was found

MURDERED, on the Morning of the 22nd April 1814, near SCRAPS-
GATE in this PARISH, by his Head being nearly Severed from his Body. A
SUBSCRIPTION was immediately entered into, and ONE HUNDRED
GUINEAS REWARD offered on the conviction of the PERPETRATORS
of the HORRIBLE ACT, but they remain at present undiscovered.

According to local legend, the unfortunate man was mistaken by smugglers for
an informer, and dealt summary justice on the spot. That the reward should have
failed to bring the villains to book is hardly surprising: it's said that the smugglers
themselves carried out the collection to conceal their guilt. They also paid for the
memorial stone, which used to stand in the churchyard.

The establishment of the Waterguard improved morale in the service and a
gradual decline in free-trade activity began. However, when the Battle of Waterloo
in 1815 brought the Napoleonic Wars to an end, the drop in smuggling halted as
enormous numbers of military personnel returned to a civilian life that must have
seemed dull by comparison with the excitement of battle. Many of these men
were skilled seamen, and Britain's fishing and merchant fleets couldn't hope to
absorb such an influx of labour. Smuggling again seemed an attractive option.

In response to this new challenge, the preventive effort was stepped up yet again
two years after Waterloo, with the introduction of the 'Coast Blockade' between
North and South Foreland on the east Kent coast. The blockade was a force
of land patrols commanded by Captain 'Flogging' Joe McCulloch. At first the
blockademen had little enthusiasm for their task, and were considered fair game
for bribery in cash or contraband. Nevertheless McCulloch eventually made the
force into a useful deterrent, and blockademen were frequently involved in skirmishes with smugglers. Their bases were the Martello towers, and watch houses a
few miles apart, and the blockade was soon extended to Seaford, and then round
to Chichester.

Almost simultaneously, the 'Coast Guard' was established in regions where the
blockademen did not patrol, and by the end of the 1820s the effectiveness of the
two forces was beginning to bite.

THE COASTGUARD

In 1831 the coastguard service replaced the blockade all the way round the coast,
and thus laid the foundations of the preventive force that we know today.

The coastguards and blockademen drove the smugglers underground, and
smuggling methods began gradually to change: concealment took the place of
force. On the simplest level, smugglers would hide the illegal imports under
a legitimate cargo such as coal, timber or stone. But human ingenuity knows
no bounds, and as the customs men got wise to the smugglers' tricks, so the

hiding places became more difficult to find. Masts and spars were hollowed out and stuffed with contraband; some vessels even had double hulls, with space for contraband between the two skins. The suppliers of contraband also used extraordinary ingenuity in packing their goods in disguised form. For example, tobacco was made up into ropes, and some warehouses supplied as stock items a whole range of such ropes, from thin cord right through to hawsers as thick as your arm. Innocently coiled on the deck, or tossed casually into a locker, these illicit packages aroused little suspicion. Similarly, spirits were stored in barrels with false bottoms – the tub was then topped up with drinking water, or perhaps with wine, on which lower duty was payable. When the English customs men got wise to the trick, and resorted to dipping the barrels to find the true depth, the cunning French coopers constructed the hidden compartments at either end of the barrel, tapering away from the official's stick.

To see how smugglers' methods had changed by the 1830s, it's instructive to look at a couple of examples. A newspaper report for 24 May 1839 provides an interesting insight into the ingenuity of smugglers from Falmouth. A schooner loaded with coals docked at the port, and immediately attracted attention from the onlookers on Customs House Quay. They suspected the ship of being used for illicit activity, but had never been able to gather enough evidence to prosecute. The coals were gradually unloaded, and the crew were so blasé about the operation that the customs authorities began to think their suspicions were misplaced. However, when a customs officer set to work boring holes in the hull with a gimlet, the crew mysteriously melted away – obviously anticipating what was to happen next. Withdrawing the gimlet, the customs officer received a face-full of brandy, from a tub stowed in a cavity between the false interior of the hull and the outside. Altogether there 276 barrels of brandy and gin in the space, but the loss to the smugglers cannot have been too disastrous, since the ship had been operating for three years without detection.

At Newport the 72-ton schooner *Good Intent* was owned by a consortium of five of the city's businessmen, one of whom had strong links with the revenue services. The ship apparently plied a perfectly innocent trade with France, but when passing through Mount's Bay in 1837 a close inspection by a revenue cruiser revealed that the intents of the captain and merchant owners were far from good. The schooner had false bulkheads concealing 1,100 gallons of brandy in 259 small kegs. The ship was cut up, and the master was sentenced to a long spell in Monmouth gaol. Significantly the owners simply lost their ship.

Though subterfuge had largely replaced brute-force in the 1830s, traditional smuggling runs were not completely stamped out. As late as 1832 an early chronicler of Worthing history was recording that in February he was:

> ... aroused by an uproar in the High Street and the sound of firearms. A big
> cargo of spirits had been landed and was being taken up the High Street towards

Broadwater while a number of men armed with stout staves had come down from the country to protect the smugglers and their cargo. The Preventive Force got wind of the affair, and attacked the procession as it made its way up High Street, and there was a running fight all the way up the road. At the top of high street was a footpath leading to Broadwater, closed by a gate which happened to be padlocked, so that only one man could get over at a time. The staff men, as they were called, closed round the smugglers and laid about vigorously with their staves in order to hold off the Preventive men. The latter drew their pistols and fired into the crowd, hitting and killing a young man named William Cowerson.

Cowerson, a stonemason, was buried in the churchyard at Steyning, his home town. His grave can still be seen there, though the inscription on the tombstone is now only partially legible. A local churchwarden[7] recalls that it ran:

Death with his dart did pierce my heart
When I was in my prime,
Weep not for me my dearest friends
For 'twas God's appointed time.

Cowerson wasn't quite the last smuggler to die 'in the line of duty'. That dubious honour must go to Thomas Monk, a fiddler who was shot by the coastguard in the dunes at Camber Sands the following year.

Ironically, perhaps, it was not the newly invigorated preventive services that brought an end to smuggling, but simple economics. In the 1840s Britain adopted a free-trade policy that slashed import duties to realistic levels. A few Dutch vessels continued to land tobacco in Lincolnshire as late as 1846, but by the middle of the century large-scale smuggling had effectively ceased.

NOTES

1 *David Copperfield*
2 Hawkes, 1986, quoting from Lewis Morris
3 Penzance custom-house book
4 Letter from Edward Stanley to Richard Sutton, 12 May 1770, published in the *Pembroke County Guardian*, April 27, 1901
5 *Morning Post*, 31 October 1781 quoted by Douch, John, 1985
6 Skinner, John, 1746
7 John Cox, letter in the parish magazine, January 1988

10

MYTH AND REALITY: DECONSTRUCTING KIPLING

If you wake at midnight, and hear a horse's feet,
Don't go drawing back the blind, or looking in the street.
Them that ask no questions isn't told a lie.
Watch the wall, my darling, while the Gentlemen go by!

Chorus:
Five and twenty ponies, trotting through the dark –
Brandy for the Parson, 'Baccy for the Clerk;
Laces for a lady, letters for a spy,
and watch the wall, my darling, while the Gentlemen go by!

Running round the woodlump if you chance to find
Little barrels, roped and tarred, all full of brandy-wine,
Don't you shout to come and look, nor use 'em for your play.
Put the brushwood back again and they'll be gone next day!

If you see the stable-door setting open wide;
If you see a tired horse lying down inside;
If your mother mends a coat cut about and tore;
If the lining's wet and warm – don't you ask no more!

If you do as you've been told, 'likely there's a chance,
You'll be given a dainty doll, all the way from France,
With a cap of Valenciennes, and a velvet hood –
A present from the Gentlemen, along o' being good!

Rudyard Kipling wrote this verse in 1906. The great era of smuggling was only half a century in the past, but its mythologisation was already substantially complete.

Kipling's poem arguably finished the job, sanitising and romanticising smuggling, and neatly packaging it for consumption by succeeding generations of school-children who learned the rhyme by rote.

Kipling had been living at Bateman's in East Sussex for three or four years when he wrote the poem, and he no doubt based it on local yarns. He skilfully captured many aspects of smugglers' methods, alluding indirectly to the coercion that was part and parcel of every run, and the risk of injury that free-traders faced at the hands of those pursuing them.

Kipling's chorus is rooted in smuggling practice. A Lowestoft writer described in 1730 how:

> We went together aboard one of the small trading ships belonging to that town, and as we were on shipboard we took notice of two of the seamen that were jointly lifting up a vessel out of the hold: when another seaman that stood by, clapped one of them on the shoulder, and asked him why he did not turn his face away? (for he was looking down as he would see what he and his fellow were lifting out of the hold). Upon which he turned his face away. The meaning of which we soon understood to be this: that he would be obliged to swear he saw nothing taken out of the hold; not that he took nothing out of it.[1]

Similarly, near Beaulieu:

> All the farms along the river were more or less concerned in the traffic … At Ginn's Farm … a gentleman rode up and said to the servant girl 'Do you ever see anything of the smugglers about here? If you can give me any information, I will give you a sovereign'. The girl was not likely to betray her friends, and replied 'Smugglers Sir! Why we be always all in bed by nine o'clock'. A few minutes later the handmaiden found her master entertaining the stranger, who was deeply interested in the con-traband trade, and who had only been trying to test the girl's fidelity. He at once gave her the sovereign, not for giving information, but for withholding it[2]

Kipling was far from the first to make shilling or two from the popular appeal of smuggling. As early as 1837 the Revd Richard Barham included in his *Ingoldsby Legends* an epic poem entitled 'The Smuggler's Leap'.

It begins with a smuggling run on the North Kent coast:

> The fire-flash shines from Reculver cliff,
> And the answering light burns blue in the skiff,
> And there they stand, That smuggling band,
> Some in the water and some on the sand,
> Ready those contraband goods to land:
> The night is dark, they are silent and still,

– At the head of the party is Smuggler Bill.
Barham paints an attractive picture of Smuggler Bill:
Smuggler Bill is six feet high,
He has curling locks, and a roving eye,
He has a tongue and he has a smile
Trained the female heart to beguile,
And there is not a farmer's wife in the Isle,
From St. Nicholas quite
To the Foreland Light,
But that eye, and that tongue, and that smile will wheedle her
To have done with the Grocer and make him her Tea-dealer …

The poem continues in similar gothic style for dozens of stanzas. Though the chase ends in death for both Bill and Gill, Barham succeeds in making the exciseman's job sound almost exciting, and never questions the morality, motives or ethics of his adversary.

THE POPULAR SMUGGLER STEREOTYPE

Woven into both poems are the unspoken assumptions that the reader sympathises with the smugglers, and that they enjoy the complete support of the community. Virtually all smuggling legends take the same perspective.

Two centuries after smuggling's inglorious peak, it's impossible to be objective about the level of public support for the free-trade. Certainly there were times when support for smugglers was indisputable. For example in 1737 smuggling around the Ogmore River in Wales was so popular and open that a local landowner wrote to the collector of customs in London, complaining of the activities of the smugglers. He commented that the Bridgend smugglers (most of whom were shoemakers), 'have a bell for a signal, which they have agreed to ring if any of them should be apprehended, that the whole town may rise to rescue the prisoners.' The letter was provoked by a violent incident at Nash Point, where over 300 people, many of them armed, turned out to pillage a vessel that had run aground, laden with tobacco.

Some forty years later the free-traders of Robin Hoods Bay enjoyed equally widespread support, especially among the alum-workers from the nearby quarries. Even itinerant labourers were happy to throw in their lot with the local people and form a temporary, but effective alliance. In 1779 the building of a sea-wall brought hundreds of workers into the area, and these men lived in Redcar, Coatham and Easton, where they joined local smugglers and formed large gangs to ship goods inland virtually unopposed despite the efforts of the local customs officers.

As late as 1820 smugglers could still turn out an armed mob when the need arose. That year a blockade man at Folkestone caught a smuggler red-handed, and marched him and the incriminating evidence – a tub of spirits – to a nearby watchhouse. However, before the blockade man, one John Kelty, had the opportunity to take his prisoner to more secure accommodation in Dover, a crowd armed with clubs, rocks and pistols closed in; they freed the smuggler and injured the blockade man. The incident perhaps came as no surprise to the local customs authorities, who were quite clear about the allegiances of the Folkestone people. One officer commented that, 'As most of the Inhabitants of Folkestone, Sandgate and Hythe are in the confidence of the smugglers, no information can be expected of them.'

The same year the population of Dover turned out in force to free a group of smugglers imprisoned in the town gaol. A revenue officer called Billy 'Hellfire' Lilburn had caught eleven Folkestone and Sandgate smugglers on a run, and had them locked up in Dover gaol. Word soon got around, and the prisoners' fellows raised a huge mob which quickly broke down the door of the gaol. When it was discovered that the captured smugglers had been moved to the most secure cells, the mob started to literally pull the prison apart, pelting the troops that had by now been called in with a hail of stones and tiles. The mayor of Dover arrived, but when he attempted to read the Riot Act, he was set upon, and gave up. By this time, Hellfire Lilburn himself had appeared, and tried unsuccessfully to persuade the commanding officer (reputedly 'Flogging Joe' McCullock, the founder and mentor of the Blockade) to fire on the crowd.

Eventually the smugglers were released, and made good their escape in hired horse-drawn carriages – the forerunners of today's taxis! They stopped at the Red Cow to have the conspicuous and unwieldy chains removed from their hands; meanwhile outside the mob continued to rampage through the town, smashing windows. The gaol was damaged beyond repair and a new one had to be constructed. The whole event was commemorated in a folk-song.

Another incident from Snettisham, set two years later, illustrates that the Norfolk free-traders enjoyed similar support. A smuggling boat landed eighty tubs, and when the preventives impounded them, the local population turned out in a band of over 100 people to rescue the goods 'armed with bludgeons and fowling pieces'. The smugglers escaped along the Old Peddar's Way, at a time when virtually nobody else used the track.

FOLKLORE AND THE BENIGN SMUGGLER

The smuggler of legend isn't just popular: he's harmless, too. Story-book smugglers are not violent criminals, but shrewd cheeky chappies always out to put one over on their customs adversaries. For example, one yarn tells of an 1822 storm that loosened a raft of tubs near Chesil beach. There was a race between the revenue and the tubs' owners, to see who could reach the contraband first.

The revenue boat was in the lead, but the smugglers raised another sail, and surged ahead. As they passed, the helmsman dropped his trousers, 'striking his posterior in derision' at the downcast revenue men.

Stories from North Norfolk portray the customs and excise service as fools or worse. One concerns a farmer from Blakeney who had had several good horses confiscated when he was caught carting smuggled goods up from the coast. The beasts were due to be auctioned, and the astute farmer went along, knowing that at that time, his animals would be starting to moult. Counting on the ignorance of the sea-faring customs men (obviously not riding officers) he pulled at the hair of one of the horses. Naturally it came away in his hand and he told the supervising officer, 'Whoi, the poor brute have gotten t' mange and all t'udderuns'll ketch it ef you int keefful' An examination of the other horses proved that his worst fears had been realised, and he was able to take the horses off the man's hands for £5 before the mange spread.

When smugglers and revenue men actually clash in yarns, the result is generally humiliation rather than physical injury.

Again in Norfolk, the Revd Forbes Phillips described how just a little to the south of his home in Gorleston, smugglers detained a preventive officer whom they caught snooping by pushing his head down a rabbit hole, then hammering a stake into the ground between his legs to prevent his escape.

If yarns acknowledge smugglers' violence, they often describe it in mild terms, or excuse it as mere self-defence, as in this tale from Cranborne: a local man, known as Dan, was cutting turf when his brother-in-law rode up to tell him that the exciseman had searched Dan's house and found eleven tubs hidden in the cellar. Dan then returned to Cranborne, and took up his habitual seat in the bar of the *Flower De Luce*. Eventually the exciseman appeared, bragging that he had seized the tubs, and stored them at his house. At this, Dan slipped unnoticed from the bar, and tore off to rally support. A gang of smugglers returned at midnight, and Dan went into the town and chalked a mark of the exciseman's door (presumably so that he would not have to attend in person):

> Being made sure of their prize the ruffians soon followed, and one of them beat in the door with the sledge hammer, whilst another stood in the street with a loaded horse pistol, threatening to blow out the Exciseman's brains, or of any other person who offered to resist them. Having secured the 'goods' they soon loaded their carts and horses, and with one outrider in front, armed, and another in the rear they galloped away with them; *nor had the incident any unpleasant sequel so far as I ever heard,* and it only afforded a subject of gossip in the Public-houses of Cranborne.[3] (Author's emphasis.)

A famous tale from Scotland tells how a group of smugglers had run some goods from the coast of Troon inland through a valley in the Dundonald Hills, by the

Awt or Aut – a hanging wood. They encountered a detachment of dragoons, and seeing their adversaries, Tam Fullarton, a man renowned for his 'strength, courage and dexterity' volunteered to hold off the soldiers while his comrades escaped. He stood behind a dry-stone wall, and hurled it rock by rock down onto 'the red anes'. Only when the smugglers were well away did Tam melt away into the woodlands, earning himself the accolade 'the man who threw a stane dyke at the sodgers',[4] and this rhyme:

> Tam Fullarton, who hailed from Loans
> A Hector when he took to stones,
> Declared that 'wi' a dry stane dyke
> At hand, he wad ha'e skailed the bike'.
> That night Tam was not slack nor slow,
> But dealt and warded many a blow.

VIOLENT REALITY

All of these rather jocular legends belie the violent reality of smuggling in the eighteenth century. In fact, when the free-trade was at its height, aggression, force and violence were essential parts of almost every smuggling run. Without aggression, smugglers could not have secured the resources and labour they needed to move their cargoes inland. Without brute force, they could not have kept the customs authorities at bay. And without violence, or at least the threat of it, they could not have silenced witnesses to their criminal activities.

It's instructive to compare the Tam Fullarton legend quoted above with an historical account of smuggling in the same area and at the same time. In fact as in legend, clashes between the smugglers of Dundonald and redcoats stationed at Ayr and Irvine were frequent, but in reality the smugglers did more than just throw stones. They armed themselves with loaded whips and 'kents': fearsome oak cudgels, 5ft long and weighted with lead.

This 1764 account from the local custom house is probably more objective than the yarn of Tam's defence of his comrades:

> Between 7 and 8 in the morning, [customs officers] discoverd a boat coming for the *Troon*, which proved to be a small Isle of Man one, and which they believed contained foreign spirits. She was no sooner arrived than about 100 men, mounted on horses, having large sticks in their hands, accompanied by some women, instantaneously came down from the country, and took possession of the *Troon* and although the officers immediately made an attempt to seize said boat and spirits, they could by no means get access to her for the mob, who threatened to put them to death if they offered to touch her or what was

in her. [The officers] at length, however, laid hold of their carts, with six casks
of spirits in each, but had no sooner made a seizure than they were attacked
by one – – – –, servant to – – – – , in Loans of Dundonald, and by three other
men unknown to them, disguised in sailors' habits: all were provided with great
sticks, who deforced them of the seizure, while others drove off the carts and
spirits, swearing every moment to knock them down, and sometimes lifting up
their sticks ready to lay on blows.[5]

Where customs officers lived in the communities they were expected to police,
threats of violence could ensure that they were too terrified to act against the
smugglers. When increased preventive efforts around Dymchurch forced smugglers to move their operations from there to Lydd in the late 1820s and early '30s
they lost no time in making their intentions known to the local riding officers:
'they have drove Mr Darby and his wife and family from their habitation, threatening to murder him if they can catch him.'

Sometimes threats alone were not always enough to discourage unwanted
interest in smugglers' activities. At Montrose in 1789:

between the hours of 12 and 2 the door of His Majesty's Warehouse was broke
open and 107 ankers of brandy … carried away. At 2 O'clock in the morning
when the guard came to relieve the two centrys that were placed at the warehouse door they found the door open, the centrys gone, their muskets lying
near the warehouse and one of the bayonets lying broke before the door … we
went round the town and finding everything quiet … sent some souldiers to
the [golf] Links to patroall where they found the two centrys lying tied neck
and heel. The officer asked them why they had left their posts, they told him
that 14 or 15 men had come upon them with clubs and other weapons and had
knocked them down and tyed them … and afterwards dragged them to the
links.[6]

The foregoing examples all stop short of actual injury, but in countless conflicts
smugglers demonstrated that they were prepared to use mortal force against the
authorities, luring them to their deaths, or simply beating them to a pulp. Fearing
that the patrols of a local customs man would interfere with their landing, the
Alfriston gang moved the lumps of white chalk that the officer used as way-
markers for his moonlight sorties along the Sussex cliff-edge. Instead of leading
him safely along the coast path, the stones led the poor man over the parapet.
Hearing his cries as he tumbled from the precipice, the gang emerged from hiding, only to find the man desperately hanging by his fingertips. Deaf to pleas for
mercy, one of the gang cynically trod on their adversary's fingertips, sending him
tumbling to the rocks below.

A tombstone in Weymouth's Bury Street cemetery records a similar incident:

> Sacred to the memory of Lieut Thos Edward Knight, RN, of Folkestone, Kent,
> Aged 42, who in the execution of his duty as Chief Officer of the Coastguard
> was wantonly attacked by a body of smugglers near Lulworth on the night of
> 28th of June 1832, by whom after being unmercifully beaten he was thrown over
> the cliff near Durdle Door from the effects of which he died the following day.[7]

Clashes at sea were as fierce.

In June 1770 a large run of contraband was expected on the coast near
Weymouth, and the tide-surveyor took a boat out to intercept the smugglers.
According to stories related after the incident, the custom-house boat and its five
crew was run down by a smuggling cutter (allegedly a Folkestone vessel). The
witness to this event claimed that:

> he saw a cutter run down the King's boat … taking her upon the larboard quar-
> ter, and that he particularly saw Mr. John Bishop the tide surveyor take hold
> of the Bowsprit shroud or Jibb jack in order to save himself, and on that, the
> people on board the cutter let go the shroud …

Some of the battles between smugglers and preventives resembled military
engagements. When the revenue cutter *Ranger* spotted a heavily armed smuggling vessel at Robin Hood's Bay a bloody skirmish began which continued to
Yarmouth. The two ships were fairly evenly matched, in arms and crew. The
Ranger fired over the lugger's bows (a signal that they should stop and prepare
for customs inspection) but the lugger instead returned fire. The fight continued for ninety minutes, and the *Ranger* got the upper hand, so the smugglers
abandoned ship. In the course of the battle, two smugglers and three revenue
man were killed, and seven preventives were wounded, three so seriously that
they had to be pensioned off. The bodies of the three officers were taken to *The
Wrestler's Inn*, which can still be seen in Yarmouth market place, and were buried the following Sunday in St Nicholas's churchyard. Despite a £500 reward
the smugglers were never captured. A similar clash took place at Mudeford (see
page 50).

HORRIFIC VIOLENCE

All these examples pit smugglers against their official adversaries; and in all of
them smugglers use force to escape capture, or to protect their cargoes. But
where legend and fact diverge most sharply, the violence is gratuitous and sometimes sickening. For example, in the early 1760s a gang of Hastings smugglers

and privateers, 'Ruxley's crew', were boarding ships in the Channel with the pretence of doing legitimate business (then a common practice). Once on board they would lock up the crew, kill anyone who resisted, then remove the cargo, and scupper the boat with all hands.

Such behaviour was perhaps not all that outrageous at a time when a licence to attack foreign vessels could be bought from the government (this indeed was the essence of privateering). However, the gang stepped over the mark when they killed the master of a Dutch ship by breaking his back with an axe – then later drunkenly bragged about 'How the Dutchman wriggled when they cut him down the backbone'. The act caused public outrage, and the Hastings population persistently demanded to know what was going to be done. When the mayor could not come up with a satisfactory reply, he was attacked violently. In response the government stationed a man-of-war offshore, and sent in 200 dragoons. The gang was arrested and tried in London (the authorities feared that a local jury would not dare convict) and four of the crew were hanged as pirates at Execution Dock.

Smugglers reserved the worst of their aggression for informers and witnesses. Judiciously applied, threats and injury could secure silence or acquittal. Where these tactics failed, smugglers resorted to murder.

The ugliest chapter in Britain's smuggling history is set in Sussex and Hampshire in the mid-eighteenth century. The killings at its heart are recounted here in some detail because the events described arguably played a role in changing the public image of smugglers, and because the brutality of the murders counters so effectively the 'harmless smuggler' myth propagated by Kipling and Barham.

The story begins in the village of Slindon. This was the home of Richard Hawkins, a farm labourer, whose body was found weighted with rocks in the pond at Parham Park, some 12 miles away, in the spring of 1748.

Hawkins made the simple mistake of getting on the wrong side of a group of smugglers. John 'Smoker' Mills, and Jeremiah 'Butler' Curtiss, both members of the Hawkhurst gang, suspected Hawkins of stealing two bags of tea, and went looking for him on the farm in Walberton where he worked. Hawkins denied all knowledge of the tea, but evidently the two men didn't believe him. Hawkins was hoisted into the saddle behind Mills, and taken off to the Dog and Partridge Inn at Slindon. There it appears there was a smugglers' court, with Hawkins on trial, and Mills, Curtiss and two other smugglers as judge and jury.

When Hawkins denied that he had anything to do with the missing tea, Curtiss shouted 'Damn you, you do know, and if you do not confess I shall whip you till you do, for damn you, I have whipped many a rogue, and washed my hands in his blood.' At this point the landlord of the inn appeared, and remarked 'Dick, you had better confess, it will be better for you'.

When Hawkins continued to protest his innocence, he was whipped and beaten, then forced to strip to the waist; and despite his begging for mercy, the smugglers continued to whip, punch and kick him so hard that they had to pause for breath. In the course of the torture, though, Hawkins let slip 'My father and my brother'.

At this, the beating stopped, and two of the torturers rode off in search of further victims. The respite came too late for Hawkins, for he died soon after the men had left.

At this the two smugglers who had stayed at the inn locked the room and rushed after their colleagues, meeting them as they returned to the pub with the dead man's father-in-law and brother. Realising the danger they were in, the four smugglers released their prisoners, swearing them to secrecy; then they returned to the Dog and Partridge, picked up the corpse, and rode to Parham. They weighted the body with rocks, and dumped it in the lake.

The murder hunt started when the body was found, and one of the four – Mills – was cleverly captured by a fellow Hawkhurst gang member who negotiated a pardon in exchange for this service to the Crown. One of the accused smugglers who had not actually taken part in the whipping gave evidence against Mills at the trial, and thus saved his own skin. Curtiss escaped to France before he could be brought to trial.

This violent story was by no means an isolated incident. Indeed, had Hawkins lived, it's unlikely that any of the torturers would have been brought to justice. And for 'Smoker' Mills, it seems, torture and violence were a way of life, for Mills was part of a group that committed two even more grisly murders less than a fortnight later.

However, this second story actually started four months earlier, with a smuggling trip in September 1747. The voyage was organised by two groups acting in concert: the Hawkhurst Gang that we have already met; and a group from West Sussex. The gangs sent a representative to Guernsey on a Rye boat, to buy about 2 tons of tea and thirty casks of spirits. These were duly loaded, and the vessel set off for the planned rendezvous near Lymington in Christchurch Bay.

However, things went badly wrong. The smuggling vessel was seized at sea by a revenue ship, and although the crew escaped, the contraband was taken to a government warehouse in Poole. The principal sponsors of the trip were naturally dismayed by this turn of events, and at a meeting in Charlton Forest they resolved to take back the tea in a raid on the custom house. This they did on the night of 6 October.

The thirty smugglers had met at Rowland's Castle the previous night, then ridden from there to Poole, resting en route. When they arrived at the town, an advance party went forward to assess the risk of capture, and returned with the bad news that there was a naval guard in the harbour, with guns trained on the doors of the custom house. This caused some discussion and argument – the faint-hearted Hawkhurst men wanted to abandon the enterprise, but the West Sussex contingent said they'd go it alone if their co-conspirators backed out. This threat, and the fact that the falling tide had put the custom house out of sight of the battleship, persuaded the party to go on. They left their horses with two of the gang, and broke open the strong-room with crowbars and axes.

This part of the raid went entirely according to plan. The smugglers took virtually all the tea, leaving behind the brandy, perhaps because they had insufficient transport. The heavily laden convoy then set out for Brook in the New Forest, where they planned to weigh the tea and share it out: each man was to get a little over a hundredweight.

At no point had the smugglers been opposed, and it seems likely that they were elated by their success. As they passed through Fordingbridge, a fine crowd turned out to watch the caravan passing, and it was there that one of the gang made a fatal error. John 'Dimer' Diamond spotted a familiar face in the crowd: shoemaker Daniel Chater. The two men had worked to get the harvest in together, and Diamond shook the other man's hand and threw him a small bag of tea.

The convoy then rode on to divide up the spoils, and Chater, perhaps basking in reflected glory, chatted innocently to his neighbours, saying he knew Diamond. This was to be his undoing, for when the authorities started investigating the theft, they soon began to view Chater as a key witness.

Diamond, meanwhile, had been arrested on suspicion of his involvement, and was in Chichester gaol. To prove the case against him, the collector of customs at Chichester had to get the cobbler to positively identify the smuggler.

So it was that on Valentine's Day 1748 William Galley, an ageing minor customs official, set out with the shoemaker on a fateful journey. They left Southampton heading for the home of a JP near Chichester, carrying a letter with instructions that Chater should go to Chichester gaol to identify Diamond.

They soon lost their way, but were guided by a couple of local men as far as the White Hart Inn at Rowland's Castle. This was an unfortunate place for the two men to break their journey, for it was owned and run by a family who were in league with the smugglers. The landlady became suspicious of the intentions of the travellers, and sent for William Jackson and William Carter, who lived close by. Before these two smugglers arrived though, Galley and Chater wanted to press on; an excuse about lost stable keys delayed them just long enough for the other smugglers to arrive.

At this point the danger that the men were in began to become apparent. The reinforcements arrived, innocent witnesses were sent away from the pub, and the smugglers began to drink heavily. Jackson took Chater aside, and asked him what was happening: Chater replied regretfully that he was obliged to give evidence against his friend Diamond. At this point, rightly suspecting that his witness was being intimidated, Galley emerged, only to be hit in the face by Jackson. The three men came indoors together, with Galley protesting, 'I'm a King's officer, I'll not put up with such usage'. 'You a King's officer!' Jackson spat back at the bloodied customs man, 'I'll make a King's officer of you; and for a quatern of gin I'll serve you so again'. Jackson raised his fist, but a bystander sprang forward and grabbed his arm, crying, 'Don't be such a fool, do you know what you are doing?'

This calmed things down a bit, and the smugglers apologised. They persuaded the two men to drink with them, and soon Galley and Chater were drowsy with the drink, and went to sleep in an adjoining room. As they slept, the smugglers crept in and took the letter.

The contents plainly spelt out the intentions of the men, and the smugglers held a council of war. A great deal of drinking went on, and there were various proposals as what they should do with the prisoners. The most humane was to send them to France, but this idea was soon discounted on the grounds that they might return. Someone suggested that they might be kept captive until Diamond's trial, and then be made to suffer the same fate as him.

The conference was inconclusive, and when it ended Jackson put on his spurs, and woke the sleeping men by getting on the bed, spurring their foreheads and whipping them, providing a foretaste of the torture that was to follow. Soon the men were taken outside, and put together on a horse, with their legs tied under the horse's belly. One man led the horse – the road was too rough for all to ride – and the rest of the gang followed.

They hadn't got more than a hundred yards when Jackson shouted 'Whip them, cut them, slash them, damn them!' and for the next mile five of the smugglers attacked Galley and Chater with whips so badly that the two men slid sideways, so they hung beneath the horse; at each step one or other was kicked in the head by the horse's hooves.

By now the captives were so weak that they couldn't sit in a saddle unaided, so they were separated, and each sat behind one of the smugglers: the other four took off their prisoners' jackets and rained blows on the pillion riders. The torment only stopped when the smuggler on the horse carrying Galley complained that many of the whiplashes were striking him, as well as their intended victim.

The company moved on as far as Harris's Well in Lady Holt Park, where they planned to kill both men and throw them down. Here Galley pleaded for a quick death, but this only provoked Jackson further, and he swore 'No, God damn your blood, if that's the case, we must have something more to say to you.'

The party set off again, first with the helpless Galley on his belly across a saddle, then sitting in it, leaning forward on the horse's neck:

> … in this posture Jackson held him on for half a mile, most of the way the poor man cried out 'Barbarous usage! barbarous usage! for God's sake shoot me through the head'; Jackson all the time squeezing his private parts …

Galley eventually fell from the horse, apparently lifeless, but probably only unconscious. His captors slung him across a horse, and the grisly caravan trudged on. They reached the *Red Lion* at Rake in the early hours of Monday morning, after stopping briefly at the house of another reputed smuggler who ' … imagining they were upon some villainous expedition … ' refused to help them.

At the inn Chater was still capable of standing, and he was taken out and chained up in a skilling – a turf store. The smugglers hid Galley's body temporarily in the brew-house attached to the pub, and later that night carried the 'corpse' about three-quarters-of-a-mile to Harting Coombe. There they enlarged a fox-earth, bundled the old man into the hole, and tipped the soil back on top.

When the corpse was found some time later, it was apparent that Galley had recovered consciousness after being interred, for he was standing almost upright, and had raised his hand to cover his eyes and keep out the dirt.

For the smugglers, there was still the problem of Chater. He remained chained in the turf house for three days, too ill to eat. After a secret meeting on Wednesday night, it was resolved that Chater should be murdered and his body dumped in Harris's Well as originally planned. The gang went out to the turf house, and one of the group, Tapner, ordered the shoemaker ' … down on your knees and go to prayers, for with this knife I will be your butcher.' As Chater knelt, Tapner slashed the man's face twice, completely cutting through his nose, and virtually blinding him.

Eventually they set off for the well, with Tapner continuing to whip Chater, and threatening him with all manner of tortures if he spilt his own blood on the horse's saddle! The gruesome party eventually reached the well, and after an unsuccessful attempt to hang Chater with a rope that proved too short, they dumped his body into the well, and threw in rocks and timbers until there was silence.

Though they had disposed of the bodies, there were still two dumb witnesses – the men's horses. One had strayed, but the other was knocked on the head, flayed, and the hide cut into small pieces.

The two victims were soon missed, but the murderers had concealed the bodies carefully, and despite a strenuous investigation months passed with no progress. Eventually, though, an anonymous letter led to the discovery of Galley's body, and a second letter named William Steele as one of the murderers. (Some accounts say that Galley's body was found by a man walking his dogs on the common.) On his arrest, Steele turned King's evidence, and named all the others involved. Another smuggler who had played a minor role in the affair surrendered himself, and also turned King's evidence. Soon virtually the whole gang had been rounded up.

At the Chichester assizes the seven men who had played the greatest part in the murders were sentenced to the gallows, but Jackson cheated the hangman, dying in gaol before sentence could be carried out. (Though he was ill, it's said that the shock of being measured up for gibbet chains hastened his end.) The other six were taken up the Midhurst Road and executed on the Broyle, and the bodies of the five principal murderers were hung in chains – one on the Portsmouth Road near Rake, two on Selsey Bill, one on Rook's Hill near Chichester, and one at Horsemonden.

The violence of the 'Sussex Smugglers' was sensational, but not unique. In 1822 there was a similar orgy of violence in Scarborough, again provoked by the threat that witnesses and informers posed to smugglers' activities.

The story started with a fairly routine seizure: acting on information from an informer, revenue officers seized a boat-load of tubs just north of Scarborough in August 1822, but the smugglers who were rowing them in from the lugger anchored off-shore escaped capture.

In the normal course of events, the story would have ended here: losing just one boat-load of gin was regarded as an acceptable risk. However, the local customs authorities weren't satisfied, and cast around for people who knew a little more about the run. Billy Mead from Burniston came forward, and implicated a wool merchant called James Law. Law was certainly a smuggler, but claimed that on this occasion, he was innocent, and that Billy Mead was lying. The case eventually went to the King's Bench in London, and Law won his case against the informer – Mead was found guilty of perjury.

This caused merriment in Scarborough, but also much bitterness. The Scarborough smugglers were looking for revenge, and the target for their violence was a woodman named James Dobson, who had given evidence against Law the smuggler. Dobson visited Scarborough on market day, 13 February 1823, and was met by a mob baying for blood. He was severely beaten, breaking his ribs, rolled around in a dog kennel, then paraded through the streets tied to a ladder. He would probably have died had he not been rescued by a couple of farmers.

Law was apparently involved in the violence, and a witness at the subsequent trial gave evidence that Law kicked Dobson to the ground at the Old Globe, shouting 'damn him, kill him, he is an informing devil'. Whether this is true or not, Law had certainly been drinking in the town that day, because he and some friends rode drunkenly home on the night of the thirteenth, making a point of stopping outside the Burniston house of Billy Mead, the convicted informer. The drunken group hurled abuse at the dark windows, but it appears that Mead was prepared for trouble. He smashed a window of the house and fired a pistol out into the dark. The shot hit Law, who was taken severely wounded to the Dodsworth Farm in Harewood Vale.

This fanned the flames of public anger. The following day, a mob several hundred strong attacked one of Billy Mead's friends who had given evidence at Law's trial for smuggling, and practically killed him. In a separate incident, a group laid siege to the house of a local customs man.

When Law died, Billy Mead was put on trial for murder. For obvious reasons the trial polarised local opinion, and created a great deal of interest. The jury heard that a Burniston girl had warned Mead that Law was after his blood, and, perhaps swayed by this evidence, they took less than half-an-hour to find the man guilty of manslaughter. Mead served just two years for the crime, and was wise enough to leave the area when released. He subsequently pursued a profitable career as a confidence trickster in Leeds.

CUSTOMS EXCESSES

Of course, smugglers did not have the monopoly on violence. Their foes in the customs service sometimes used excessive force, too. Portrayed in folklore as the friendly rivals of smugglers, customs officers were more often bitterly at odds with the free-traders, and fearful for their lives. It's hardly surprising that they sometimes killed in the course of their duties.

Consider, for example, the case of George England, an exciseman who shot dead fisherman Joseph Swaine at Hastings in 1821. When England tried to search Swaine's fishing boat, there was a struggle, during which the excise officer's gun went off, causing a fatal wound.

The incident was the flash point for seething discontent among the fishermen, in a dispute that was focused on the searching of their boats. The increasing vigilance of the government's anti-smuggling campaign had forced the free-traders to rope together tubs into rafts, which were anchored off-shore and (allegedly) recovered by the local fishermen. Fishing boats were so numerous that a thorough and methodical search of each one was impossible, so the customs men resorted to poking a metal spike through the piles of net to feel for barrels concealed beneath. According to the fishing folk, the prodding damaged the nets, and Swaine was shot while trying to prevent such damage to his tackle.

Swaine became a local martyr, with the Hastings mob baying for blood. The exciseman was convicted of murder, despite desperate and heart-rending pleas from the dock as the sentence was read:

> ... you be taken from hence ... *Consider I was in execution of my duty* ... to the place whence you came ... *Gentlemen of the Jury, pray consider your verdict again* ... and from thence to the place of execution, on Friday next, where you are to be hanged by the neck until you are dead, and may the Lord have mercy upon your soul ... *Oh Gentlemen of the Jury, pray consider your verdict again!*

The sentence was never carried out, for England was reprieved soon afterwards, much to the fury of the residents of Hastings. After the shooting there had been considerable civil disturbance locally, and dragoons were sent in to restore order. The reprieve caused a renewal of rioting, and if England had returned to his former posting, the mob would almost certainly have taken the law into their own hands and carried out what they saw as a just sentence. Instead, England was discharged from his job and spirited out of harm's way.

In other incidents customs men used their pistols to bring down fleeing smugglers. At Binstead, near Ryde on the Isle of Wight, the grave of suspected smuggler Thomas Sivell posthumously accuses his killer of murder. Sivell was a Solent ferryman who was shot by the preventive forces in 1785. According to some stories he was innocent of smuggling, but others relate that he was shot while being chased in his smuggling vessel, and that he tossed nearly seventy barrels of spirits overboard to evade capture, along with a considerable quantity of tea! His epitaph tells the smuggler's side of the story:

> All you that pass pray look and see
> How soon my life was took from me
> By those officers as you hear
> They spilt my blood that was so dear
> But God is good, is just and true
> And will reward to each their due

In Pembrokeshire in 1834, the local 'King of the Smugglers' died in similar circumstances. William Truscott's reign came violently to an end at Pembroke Dock. He had been captured at a cave used for storage at New Quay, 'a sequestered little inlet near St Govan's'. He managed to escape, and fled as far as the Pembroke River, which he tried to cross to Pembroke Dock from Bentlas. Here the customs men shot and wounded him and he drowned.

The case aroused more than the usual amount of interest, because it appeared that the revenue officer who fired at Truscott did so the instant he ran into the water, and that the officers ignored the injured man's cries for help. The jury at the inquest judged that the conduct of the King's men 'was [a] highly reprehensible, cowardly and cruel acte.'

Officers rarely killed smugglers callously and deliberately, but such murders weren't unknown. For example, a gravestone at Slains Kirkyard notes only that the memorial was erected: 'To the memory of Philip Kennedy, in Ward, who died the nineteenth of December, 1798. Aged 38.' It fails to record either the brutal manner of the smuggler's death or the fact that his killer went unpunished. Kennedy had been organising the landing of contraband near Slains Castle, from a ship called the *Crooked Mary*. The cargo had been loaded into a cart for transport inland, and Kennedy and two of his companions had gone on ahead to check that the route was clear. It wasn't. The three men were ambushed by customs officers:

> Kennedy attacked two of them, and actually succeeded for a time in keeping them down in his powerful grasp, while he called to his party to secure the third. They, however, thinking prudence the better part of valor, decamped ignominiously, and the enemy remained master of the brave man's life. Anderson, the third officer, was observed to hold up his sword to the moon, as if to ascertain if he were using the edge, and then to bring it down with accurate aim and tremendous force upon the smuggler's skull. Strange to say, Kennedy, streaming with blood, actually succeeded in reaching Kirkton of Slains, nearly a quarter of a mile away, but expired a few moments after his arrival. His last words were:

'If all had been true as I was, the goods would have been safe, and I should not have been bleeding to death.'[8]

Anderson was tried for murder in Edinburgh, and acquitted.

JURY NOBBLING?

Vicious customs men were not the only ones acquitted when they were charged with crimes. Free-traders were treated lightly as well. Jurors were drawn from the areas where smugglers lived and worked, and were notoriously reluctant to return guilty verdicts on their neighbours. Almost certainly some jurors were threatened; in other cases they knew the accused and had bought contraband from them; even when those in the dock were complete strangers, there is evidence that jurors sympathised with them and did not regard them as criminals deserving of punishment.

The story of an abortive 1835 landing close to Fowey and its court sequel illustrates how difficult it was for the customs authorities to secure convictions from a local jury, even when all the evidence points to guilt.

Two coastguards from Fowey went to Lantick Hill, and hid in bushes near Pencannon Point. After a wait, at least 100 men arrived on the beach – twenty of them batmen. One of the coastguards went to get help, and meanwhile, the activity on the beach continued out of sight of his mate. When reinforcements arrived the party of six plucky preventives challenged the smugglers, and there was a fierce battle; one of the coastguards was knocked unconscious, but five smugglers were eventually arrested. A party from the revenue cutter *Fox* eventually met up with the six coastguards, and captured 484 gallons of brandy.

When the case came to court, the men were charged with 'assisting others in landing and carrying away prohibited goods, some being armed with offensive weapons.' The defence argued that the clubs were just walking sticks – this despite the fact that the group had been caught red-handed. The local vicar was called as a character witness for one of the accused, and local farmers vouched for the good name of the others. The judge pointed out when summing up that if the coastguard had been killed, instead of just being knocked out, the five prisoners would have been on a murder charge. Despite this, the jury acquitted, adding that they did not consider the clubs to be offensive weapons.

A similar example from North Norfolk has a lasting memorial in the graveyard of St Mary's church at Old Hunstanton. Two soldiers who were killed in battles with smugglers are buried there. The epitaphs read:

In memory of William Webb, late of the 15th D'ns, who was shot from his
Horse by a party of Smugglers on the 26 of Sepr. 1784
I am not dead but sleepeth here,

And when the Trumpet Sound I will appear
Four balls thro' me Pearced there way:
Hard it was. I'd no time to pray
This stone that here you Do see
My Comerades Erected for the sake of me.
Here lie the mangled remains of poor William Green, an Honest Officer of the
Government, who in the faithful discharge of his duty was inhumanely mur-
dered by a gang of Smugglers in this Parish, September 27th, 1784.

Two smugglers were caught in the battle that killed Webb, and when brought
to trial there was, according to contemporary accounts, 'no doubt' of their guilt.
Nevertheless, against all the evidence, a jury found them not guilty. The prosecut-
ing counsel demanded and got a new trial, but again the new jury displayed its
sympathy with the smugglers and returned a second not guilty verdict.

VICIOUS PSYCHOPATHS OR HARMLESS FREE-TRADERS?

So to what extent is the Kipling depiction of smuggling an accurate one? At first
glance it would seem to be completely incompatible with the historical record.
How could smugglers simultaneously be vicious bullies and popular purveyors of
tax-free luxuries?

In fact, *both* of these views of smuggling are stereotypes. Looking more closely
at the circumstances surrounding the expansion of smuggling in the first half of
the eighteenth century reveals a situation that is both more complex and more
interesting than either of these two simplistic views might suggest.

ENGLISH SOCIETY IN THE EARLY EIGHTEENTH CENTURY

Change was sweeping through English society in the early eighteenth century.
It was a period of rapid population growth: about 5.5 million people lived in
England and Wales at the beginning of the century, but sixty years later the pop-
ulation was nearer 7 million.

There was a drift from the countryside to the cities. Enclosure, which had
begun in the Middle Ages, had slowed but still continued, and this contributed
to rural poverty. As industrialisation began, traditional loyalties were eroded and
working people had to make the difficult adjustment to a wage economy.

Though *average* prices and wages were substantially static through the century,
this stability hid extreme local peaks and troughs. Crop failures led to steep rises
in the cost of staple foods. Harvests were especially bad in 1710, 1740, 1756 and
1766, leading to very high prices and sometimes starvation. For example, the cost

of flour soared 250 per cent between 1707 and 1710.When prices rose the hungry rioted.

There were new demands on people's purses, too. Roads were paved and toll-booths erected to pay for the improvements.Those who travelled, or even drove their cattle to market, now had to pay for something that had previously been free.

Though unemployment was not a general problem, work was often seasonal – especially in the country. Fluctuations in demand for labour could be cata-strophic for the families affected, causing desperate poverty.

The existence of an impoverished underclass was striking for visitors to the country. Portuguese traveller Don Manoel Gonzales wrote in 1731 that there were not 'many countries where the poor are in a worse condition.' Poverty hit children particularly hard, and infant mortality was the rule, not the exception: fewer than one in ten children born in some parts of London lived beyond the age of five.

The plight of the poor attracted little sympathy from the better-off.Vagrancy acts provided that the homeless and rootless could be 'whipped until bloody' and sent on to their parishes. Alexander Pope wrote that 'God cannot love … the wretch he starves' and a worthy accused of plundering the funds intended for poor relief quipped 'Damn the poor – every man in want is knave or fool.'

Some special social factors were at work in the South East of England where smuggling was at its most intense. Here, industry had contracted.The textile trade had been badly hit by the expansion – and lower costs – of weaving and spin-ning in the Midlands and North. The Weald had formerly been famous for its ironworks – the first iron cannon were cast here. But the growth of the industry had destroyed the forests on which it relied for fuel. By 1720 there remained only ten blast-furnaces in Sussex.When coal began to replace charcoal as a fuel around 1760 the industry would grow again – not in Sussex though, but in regions where coal was more abundant.And ironically, the legal maritime industries in Kent and Sussex were also suffering, because the sea ports had been affected by silting.

All of these factors led to a rise in crime and general unrest that the existing social structures were powerless to contain. In previous centuries social cohesion meant that policing was something undertaken communally, through measure such as the hue and cry. But with increasing urbanisation, and the fracturing of social values, this approach was no longer effective. Laws might be strong and punitive, but the infrastructure to enforce them was non-existent. Without an effective police force, criminal gangs such as the Yorkshire coiners – and the Sussex smugglers – could thrive unhindered.

However, smuggling was not restricted to criminal gangs. As we saw earlier, in some coastal areas it was almost universal. Smuggling provided valuable employ-ment and cheap goods for those who could not afford to pay high taxes and duties. For the rural poor, smuggling and the purchase of contraband had become – like poaching – a way of making ends meet. Ominously for Britain's ruling classes, few outside of Westminster (and even inside) saw anything wrong with smuggling. As the Ordinary of Newgate commented in 1740, 'the common people of England fancy that there is nothing in the crime of smuggling.' A witness to a parliamentary committee echoed this view five years later, adding that 'The generality of the people on the coast are better friends to the smugglers than they are to the custom house officers.'

He was absolutely right. As outlined in Chapter Two, all social classes were involved in smuggling. Comfortably off publicans and merchants retailed the contraband; wealthy members of the establishment financed the trade; and *everyone* bought smuggled goods.

Smuggling may have been universal, but the *crime* of smuggling was the monopoly of the poor. Read again the list on page 23, of prisoners convicted of smuggling at Lyme Regis. Conspicuous by their absence are 'parson', 'squire', 'wine-merchant' or 'tobacconist'. Smuggling may have crossed social boundaries, but its punishment did not. The 'better classes' largely escaped without penalty. And though they may have benefited from the free-trade, they also felt threatened by it. For Britain's establishment, what was perhaps most frightening of all about the smugglers, and their allies in the seething, faceless impoverished mob, was their lack of traditional deference. Smugglers not only failed to doff their caps and tug their forelocks in respect: they openly defied the authorities to challenge them in their illegal business.

SMUGGLERS' VIOLENCE

But it was the smugglers' willingness to use violence that was most alarming, and that perhaps epitomised their notorious insolence. However, smugglers' aggression was sharply focused. Though there is widespread evidence that they used intimidation to secure cooperation, their brutality was largely directed at two specific groups: the preventive forces, and informers or hostile witnesses.

It's clear that smugglers did not consider that these people 'counted': they dismissed violence against them as unimportant. When smugglers killed an exciseman in Dorset in 1723, for example, one of them commented 'they did no more matter to kill him than they would a tode.'[9]

Others who kept the company of smugglers shared this attitude. When the Sussex smugglers were debating the fate of the 'informer' Daniel Chater and customs official William Galley (see page 152), two of their wives urged them on to murder, crying out 'Hang the dogs, for they came here to hang us.'

Though smugglers had always used force, their aggression escalated from the 1720s onwards. This was an unintended consequence of legislation that aimed to stamp out smuggling by the imposition of ever more brutal penalties.

In the early years of the century, the law dealt lightly with the offence. Smugglers had their boats, horses and equipment confiscated, and were fined multiples of the value of the captured contraband. But from 1721 onwards armed or masked smugglers could be transported for seven years.

Fifteen years later the Act of Indemnity made informers a particular target for smugglers' violence. The Act provided that smugglers who revealed the names of their collaborators would themselves be pardoned – for all current and previous offences. Significantly the Act also made smuggling a capital crime if the perpetrators carried arms.

Despite this provision, transportation was the usual punishment for smuggling. This changed in 1746 when hanging instead became the standard penalty; it was also extended to assembling in preparation for a run, 'wearing a wizard mask' wounding a customs officer, and harbouring smugglers.

This, then, was the legal context in which Galley and Chater were so brutally murdered. Their assassins had nothing to lose. Implicated in the robbery of the Poole custom house, they would hang if convicted. Why then hesitate to kill those who sought to give evidence against them?

Other provisions of these acts further stoked smugglers' hatred of informers. There were fabulous incentives to give evidence against smugglers. If informers provided intelligence that led to a conviction, they could earn rewards of up to £500. This was a huge, life-changing sum of money, equivalent to about £55,000 today. As critics commented at the time, such rewards were '... so large that they open a wide door for perjuries, false and malicious informations and give the informer the power to swear away a person's life.'

Though the provisions of these new laws tended to make smugglers more aggressive, their violence should also be seen against the backdrop of a society substantially more brutal than today's. It has become a cliché to point out that these were violent times, but clichés become hackneyed only through constant repetition of sometimes uncomfortable facts. Violence in the eighteenth century truly was endemic. In sport, bare-knuckle prize fights and cock fights drew huge crowds. In the home beating children was hardly a cause for comment, and even beating wives did not merit punishment.

The law itself was violent, too. Smuggling was of course far from the only capital crime; the statute-book bulged with them and further swelled as the century continued. There were just 50 capital crimes in 1688, but by 1765 the number had grown to 160. Called 'The Bloody Code', the roster of capital crimes included such trivia as cutting down a cherry tree or being seen for a month in the company of gypsies! Those who committed lesser crimes faced the pillory, whipping or branding. Naturally, the burden of these brutal laws fell disproportionately on the shoulders of the poor and powerless.

CHANGING PUBLIC OPINION?

The murders of Galley and Chater was certainly a landmark in the fight against smuggling. They led directly to the round-up of many Sussex smugglers, and probably to a reduction – albeit temporary – in the quantities of contraband crossing the South East coast. It's also tempting to regard the case as a turning-point in public opinion. Soon after the trial and execution of the murderers a book was published that chronicled the crimes in graphic detail. It was reprinted four times in 1749 alone. It has appeared in full and abridged forms at least five times since then. The book contains grisly engravings reproduced on pages 120–3 of the men's last moments, which would have impressed even the illiterate. This sensational publicity, so the argument goes, must surely have turned public opinion against the smugglers.

Certainly there is some evidence to bear this out. Around the time of the murders, some communities were taking a stand against lawless smuggling gangs that were intimidating them. The *Goudhurst Militia* (see page 166), for example, routed an attack by the Hawkhurst gang and killed some of its members. A similar vigilante group, the *Cranbrook Associators* (or *Association*), formed in a village closer to Hawkhurst.

Farther afield and very much later, there are other examples of citizens combining to oppose smugglers. When a smuggling run interrupted a race meeting on Wells beach in 1817, watching customs men were heavily outnumbered, and appealed for help to a yeomanry major in the crowd. With mounted friends he formed an improvised cavalry charge, and succeeded in clouting with his riding whip – among others – the local baker. Despite this spirited opposition the smugglers escaped with all but six tubs.

However, it's debatable whether these efforts represented 'grassroots' opposition to the smugglers. They were all initiated by the local gentry, and the purpose of the Cranbrook Associators at least was explicitly the collection of bounties on the heads of known smugglers. Historian Paul Muskett has also recently unearthed evidence that the motives of the Goudhurst Militia may have been similar. In his unpublished thesis, he suggests that the showdown was the result of a falling-out between the Hawkhurst men and a gang based in Goudhurst. The Goudhurst men later tried to claim a £500 bounty for the arrest of Hawkhurst man Thomas Fuller, who was executed at Tyburn in 1747.

If there really *was* a groundswell of opinion opposing the smugglers, then you might expect that their prosecution for the Poole raid, and for Galley and Chater's murders, would have been an easy matter enjoying widespread public support. In fact, this was not the case. The investigation and prosecutions were largely the personal responsibility of the Duke of Richmond, Charles Lennox (1701–1750). Rounding up the culprits was not easy, and Richmond had to resort to paying informers. Cal Wilmslow, in his influential essay *Sussex Smugglers*, expresses bafflement at Richmond's motives: 'His chief interests in Sussex were hunting, cricket, and his garden at Goodwood.' Richmond may have seen the smugglers as a broad, general threat to his authority in the county, and he was also a fanatical anti-Jacobite. The Sussex smugglers made no effort to hide their support for the Jacobite cause.

It is even possible to argue that, far from being in the vanguard of opposition to smuggling, Richmond was waging an unpopular war against the smugglers at a time when their public support was undiminished. In May 1848 officials in Hastings reported that citizens of the town were victimising a local informer called Harrison, adding that nine out of ten Hastings residents 'would as freely murder Harrison as they would eat and drink when hungry or dry.' This hardly sounds like a community that shared with the Duke of Richmond the desire to rid the region of smugglers.

HONEST THIEVES

So is Kipling's view of smuggling romanticised? Certainly. And did smugglers use violence liberally? Of course they did. But are these two facts irreconcilable? No they are not. Smuggling was not just a fraud on the King. It was part of a much larger social movement which saw the poor and unemployed grasping at whatever opportunities they could find to avoid starvation or to raise their living standards. As their popular support grew, Britain's criminal underclass threatened the establishment's grip on power and social control. Many of the measures taken to stamp out smuggling had the unintended consequence of aggravating already-existing violence.

So how should we look back on Britain's smugglers? Certainly not with Kipling's gilded perspective. But nor should we use the distorting mirror that demonises smugglers. Perhaps instead smuggling deserves to be re-evaluated on the margins of Britain's labour history. Maybe those hanged and transported should take their place alongside the Tolpuddle Martyrs and Watt Tyler.

NOTES

1   Whiston, Revd William *Historical memoirs of the life of Dr Samuel Clarke*; London, 1730
2   *Hampshire Notes and Queries* v.IX, p.104–5
3   *Somerset and Dorset Notes and Queries* VIII
4   Hewat, Kirkwood, 1899
5   Mackintosh, Ian M., 1969
6   Custom-house records for October 1789
7   Legg, Rodney, 1972

8   *Lippincott's Magazine of Popular Literature and Science* Vol. XI, No. 27, June, 1873

9   Beattie, J.M., *Crime and the Courts in England, 1660–1800* (Oxford 1968) p.138, quoted by Muskett, Paul, (1996) p.202.

II

FAMOUS AND INFAMOUS SMUGGLERS

Criminals are necessarily secretive about their activities, so what records we have of smuggling are fragmentary. Broadly speaking we know most about the failures, and about the spectacular successes. The former were caught, prosecuted, and ended their (often brief) careers in Australia, or 'dancing the hempen jig'; the latter survived, thrived and wrote their memoirs.

About the broad middle ground, we know little. Over the two centuries or so during which smuggling made up a major part of British commerce, hundreds of thousands of smugglers plied their trade, and inconspicuously slipped away into obscurity. These figures mostly don't appear in the historical record.

Of those we know about, our knowledge varies greatly. Of the failures, we often know little more than a name and a trade (see page 23). Where a crime was particularly sensational – as was as the murder of Galley and Chater – opportunistic publishers produced accounts of the crime and trial. Of the successful smugglers who penned autobiographies (often with the help of ghosts) we know far more, but the reliability of their accounts is frequently questionable. Few could resist the temptation to exaggerate, and some, such as John Carter, turned their books into religious polemics.

Given this patchy coverage, the list that follows cannot possibly be representative. I have tried to include the best-known names, and added few more obscure figures where their stories are of more than local interest.

THE HAWKHURST GANG

This alliance, which dominated Sussex smuggling in the 1740s probably does not hold any special records. Other gangs were longer-lived; a few could probably muster as many tub-carriers and batmen on the beach; and it is likely that individuals in other smuggling gangs were equally violent. However, the Hawkhurst gang had the questionable benefit of especially good (or bad) public relations. The account of the trial of gang members for the torture and murder of two men in 1748 makes grisly reading, and some argued that it turned the tide of public opinion against smugglers gangs in general, and the Hawkhurst men in particular.

Some 10 miles from the coast, Hawkhurst perhaps seems a strange base for a smuggling gang. However, the village was on a main route from the coast to London. Much of the contraband entering the country across the sand and shingle coasts of Romney Marsh soon passed through the sleepy hamlet.

The Hawkhurst gang formed as a separate entity in the mid-1730s. An isolated reference to the gang appeared in 1735, and within five years the company had been consolidated into the powerful fighting force that was to dominate Kentish smuggling for the next decade.

In 1740 the gang ambushed a group of customs officers at Robertsbridge, and recovered a cargo of contraband tea that had been seized in a barn at Etchingham. The gang soon escalated their operations, and perhaps because of the sheer scale of the landings, they cooperated with other local smugglers. However, these joint ventures were somewhat unequal partnerships, and it was always clear who was in command. When the Hawkhurst and Wingham gangs joined forces in 1746 to unload 11½ tons of tea, an uneasy alliance evidently turned to open warfare. The Wingham men tried to leave the landing site at Sandwich Bay prematurely, and were set upon by their collaborators. After a sword-fight in which seven of the Wingham men were injured, the Hawkhurst gang left the scene taking with them forty horses belonging to the other gang.

By the late 1840s, the Hawkhurst gang had developed unprecedented power, and boasted that it could assemble 500 men in the space of a couple of hours. In the absence of any effective policing, this disreputable group soon became a county-wide menace, taking without payment whatever they wished from the local farmers and merchants, and answering tolerance and patience with aggression and insult. The gang's activities did not go entirely unresisted, though. The most spectacular instance of rebellion by the much-abused Men of Kent came in 1747, with a showdown at Goudhurst.

The gang had extended their sphere of influence to include Goudhurst, where they used 'Spyways' on the main street, and the Star and Eagle Inn near the church. The unfortunate citizens of Goudhurst were able to do little but comply when the Hawkhurst gang demanded horses, help or just money. Eventually, though, the villagers rebelled, and organised a vigilante group to defend themselves from their unpopular neighbours. In April they formed the Goudhurst Band of Militia, an armed self-defence group led by a recently discharged soldier. Despite attempts to conceal these plans, news of the Goudhurst group reached Hawkhurst, and the leader of the gang vowed to sack the village of Goudhurst and murder all the inhabitants. With extraordinary arrogance, the gang leader Thomas Kingsmill even made an appointment – 20 April.

When the Hawkhurst men appeared, stripped to the waist and armed to the teeth, Goudhurst was ready. G.P.R. James gives a dramatised account of the battle in his novel *The Smuggler*. He describes how the villagers united, and prepared to defend themselves with ancient (and inaccurate) fowling pieces. On the day of the battle the women and children were sent to the next village, while the men gathered in the porch of the church, and cast bullets in the churchyard. The Hawkhurst men kept their appointment, and were met with a barrage of lead on the road approaching the village from Hawkhurst. The battle was short-lived: it's clear that the smugglers expected little resistance from the village, and turned tail when they suffered just a few casualties.

Hawkhurst men continued to operate in the area albeit with a lower profile. The final break-up came only with the capture, trial and execution of the gang's leaders, Arthur Gray (1748) and Thomas Kingsmill (1749).

You can still find landmarks associated with the gang. In Goudhurst the Star and Eagle still stands next to the church, and Spyways is a short distance down the hill on the same side of the road – a stout oak door up a few steps reminds the visitor that the house once served as the village jail.

In Hawkhurst village, the gang operated from the Oak and Ivy Inn, but various prominent members owned property in the area that was extensively used – or even purpose-built – for smuggling activity. Highgate House used to be a hiding place for contraband; Hawkhurst Place was said to have had a tunnel linking it to Island Pond; and Tudor Hall was supposedly linked by another tunnel to the Home Farm on the Tonges Estate. Tubs Lake and Smuggley were staging posts for contraband coming up from the coast. The most imposing monument to the profits to be made from smuggling was a huge mansion that gang's financier Arthur Gray built at Seacox Heath (the smugglers were known locally as 'Seacocks'). Nicknamed 'Gray's Folly', it incorporated various hiding holes for smuggled goods and even a bonded store. Though the house has gone, Seacox Heath is still marked on maps.

THE GROOMBRIDGE GANG

This Kentish gang rose to prominence in the 1730s, landing contraband at Lydd, Fairlight, Bulverhythe and Pevensey. Like other gangs, this team revelled in nicknames; Flushing Jack, Bulverhythe Tom, Towzer, Old Joll, Toll, The Miller, Yorkshire George, and Nasty Face all humped kegs and bales off the beaches or stood guard. These names weren't just familiarities – they served the valuable role of hiding the true identities of the people involved.

Official records first feature the Groombridge men in 1733. Thirty of them were ferrying tea inland from Romney Marsh via Iden in a convoy of fifty horses when three preventive men, two dragoons and a foot soldier made the mistake of challenging the convoy at Stonecrouch. For their interest the customs men were disarmed, and their guns made useless; they were then marched at gun-point for four hours to Groombridge, and on to Lamberhurst, where their weapons were returned to them after they had promised not to renew the pursuit.

By 1737 the gang were said to be terrorising the area, and the military were sent to Groombridge to restore order. In the same year an informer who signed himself simply 'Goring' provided a detailed insight into the gang's activities, referring directly to an armed clash at Bulverhythe:

> This is the seventh time Morten's people have workt this winter, and have not lost anything but one half-hundred [weight] of tea they gave to a Dragoon and one officer they met with the first [run] of this winter.
>
> … When once the Smuglers are drove from home they will soonall be taken. Note, that some say it was [Thomas] Gurr that fired first. You must well secure Cat or else your Honours will lose the man; the best way will be to send for him up to London [for trial] for he knows the whole Company, and hath been Moreton's servant two years. There were several young Chaps with the smuglers who, when taken, will soon discover [identify] the whole Company. The number was twenty-six men. Mack's horses, Moreton's and Hoak's were killed, and they lost not half their goods. They have sent for more goods, and twenty-nine horses set out from Groombridge this day … all the men well-armed with long guns.
>
> … I will send your Honours the Places where [you] will intercept the Smuglers as they go to Market with their goods, but it must be done by soldiers, for they go stronger now than ever.
>
> … The first [run] of this winter, the Groombridge Smuglers were forced to carry their goods allmost all up to Rushmore Hill and Cester [Keston] Mark … but tea sells quick in London now, and Chaps from London come down to Groombridge almost everyday, as they used to last Winter. When once [the smugglers] come to be drove from home, they will be put to great inconveniences, when they are from their friends and will lose more Goods than they do now … Do but take up some of the servants, and they will rout the masters, for the servants are all poor …
>
> Young [John] Bowra's house cost £500 building, and he will pay for looking up. Moreton and Bowra sold, last winter, some-ways, about 3,000 lb weight a week.

In 1740 the Groombridge gang was implicated in an attack at Robertsbridge on the customs men carrying seized tea to Hastings, and they continued to operate up to the end of the decade, when an informer provided information that led to the round-up and subsequent trial of the majority of the gang's leading lights.

THE MAYFIELD GANG

The village of Mayfield in East Sussex was the base for a powerful company that flourished for a few years in the early part of the eighteenth century. The group was led by Gabriel Tomkins (who later turned from poacher to gamekeeper, see page 128). They landed contraband along the length of the Sussex coastline, and into Kent. Favourite haunts included Lydd, Fairlight, Hastings, Eastbourne, Seaford and Goring.

Tomkins was suspected of the murder of a riding officer in 1717, and his fellow gang members were scarcely less desperate. When two of their number were captured at Dungeness and imprisoned at Lydd, the Mayfield smugglers charged up the stairs firing their pistols and released the pair. Tomkins himself was wounded in this affray.

Such extreme measures weren't always needed. Faced with opposition on the beaches where they landed goods, the Mayfield gang preferred simply to restrain the customs men, rather than beating them senseless. Gabriel Tomkins' half-brother was at one point wanted for tying up a customs officer on Seaford beach during a run, and on another occasion the gang did the same to a preventive on Goring beach, throwing him into a ditch for good measure.

Members of the gang were slippery customers, and narrowly evaded conviction several times. Sensibly they'd resist arrest when possible, and if detained the group were ingenious about avoiding prosecution. Frequently they won the sympathy of the local magistrate, who dismissed the case and sometimes even ordered the imprisonment or flogging of the arresting officer. Few prisons could hold them: Mayfield men bribed the gaolers, or were rescued from the prison cells by their contemporaries.

Gabriel Tomkins was first brought to justice in 1721, when he was captured at Nutley after a chase from Burwash. Though he bribed his gaoler and escaped he was caught again and stood trial in London. On conviction he was sentenced to transportation, but provided the authorities with so much useful information that they freed him – only to re-arrest him three years later, and again in 1729. This time, he gave evidence to an inquiry into corruption in the customs service, and clearly made a great impression on his captors. Far for being punished for his claims to have smuggled 11 tons of tea and coffee in a year, Tomkins was rewarded with the post of riding officer, and within six years had risen to a high rank in the customs service.

However, old habits die hard, and Tomkins slipped quietly out of his job in 1741 to resume activities on the wrong side of the law. In 1746 he robbed the Chester Mail, and the following year helped the Hawkhurst gang in a robbery at Selbourne. It was the mail robbery that proved to be his undoing – Tomkins' long and chequered career ended on the gallows in 1750.

There are still a few reminders of smuggling days in Mayfield, though none that can definitely be connected with the gang. A little way down Fletching Street on the left there is a curious tall house built like a layer cake – masonry at the bottom, then half-timber and brick, then clapper-board, and tiles on up to the roof. This building was cleverly equipped with two cellars in order to fool the excisemen. Smugglers' Lane, an overgrown footpath leading out of the village, was a regular trade route for taking goods inland.

THE ALDINGTON GANG

The story of smuggling in East Kent in the 1820s is largely dominated by the activities of a gang based in Aldington, who worked the stretch of coast between Deal and Rye. They were nicknamed 'the Blues' – supposedly because they wore blue smocks to work – though the customs authorities simply named them after the parish in which some members lived.

However, it would be wrong to suggest that every member of the Blues was from Aldington. The gang could with ease turn out hundreds of workers to unload a cargo, and to supply this amount of labour would probably have meant enlisting the help of half the parish. Rather the nucleus of the group came from Aldington, and – like other gangs – they picked up help from a much broader area of the county.

Early reports of the gang's activities find them rowing from Boulogne to Sandgate, with a cargo of tobacco, spirits and salt. On arrival, the waiting land party of 250 or so formed the customary corridor of armed men running about 40 yards inland from the galley; protected by this cordon, the contraband was moved quickly and relatively safely away. This operation was noted in detail by the preventive forces who sustained several casualties, so it's fair to assume that the group had been operating on a smaller scale, or undetected, for some time prior to the 1820 report.

This run took place in late autumn, and the company didn't come to the attention of the authorities again until the following February. When they did, it was in a dramatic and especially violent way. A blockade patrol spotted the gang at Camber Sands, and within a short time a running battle had started, as the smugglers retreated across Walland Marsh towards Brookland, firing repeatedly at the blockademen. The confrontation was bloody and bitter, leaving four smugglers and one blockademan dead, and many injured.

Two of the Blues were arrested in the 'Battle of Brookland', as it came to be known. According to some accounts the smugglers' leader, Cephas Quested, was found after the battle lying dead drunk on his back in the marsh. When his case came to court, one piece of evidence against him was particularly damning, and probably sealed his fate on the gallows: in the thick of the battle, he mistook a blockademan for a smuggler, and handed him a pistol, suggesting that the man should 'blow an officer's brains out'. The other man arrested claimed to have been an innocent bystander, and attributed the gunpowder stains on his skin to a rook-shooting trip. The gullible (or sympathetic) jury believed this alibi and acquitted him.

The trial was a setback for the gang, and further reports of their activities don't appear for another five years. By this time, George Ransley had assumed the mantle of leadership. The Ransley family hailed from Ruckinge, and were originally farmers, though George Ransley apparently gave up the plough for smuggling when he accidentally stumbled on a hidden cargo of spirits. The proceeds from the sale paid for his house at Aldington, the Bourne Tap, and capitalised his ventures into smuggling. Other legends that surround the family and the activities of the gang contain the usual mixture of truth, exaggeration and simple fiction, but what doesn't seem to have been exaggerated is the violent nature of the gang's activities, and the viciousness of some of the batmen that protected the cargo. George Ransley's second-in-command was his father-in-law, who was reputedly always armed with a threshing flail – a vicious instrument when used to crush skulls instead of corn husks. Circumstantial evidence suggests that the Blues forced cooperation from the more unwilling of the local farmers.

Ransley organised his business methodically and professionally. He retained a surgeon, Dr Ralph Papworth Hougham, to attend to wounded smugglers; his solicitors in Ashford, Langham and Platt (no relation to the author), defended him in court just as they would the most respectable banker; and because Ransley took care of the families of those unfortunate to die on active duty, he seemed able to command considerable commitment from those he led.

At Aldington, the gang used the Walnut Tree as their headquarters, but George Ransley also made a considerable profit by selling smuggled liquor from the Bourne Tap. The house was notorious not only for drunkenness, but also for the scenes of unbridled sexual license that took place on the premises. Local legend has it that George Ransley did not himself take part, but sat sober outside the house during these orgies.

The Aldington gang might have dominated Kentish smuggling for longer but for an 1826 incident on Dover beach that left a blockademan dead. It started as a routine landing of contraband. Two blockademen were on patrol among the bathing machines which then lined Dover beach when they spotted the attempted run. One of the pair, Richard Morgan, fired a shot to summon help. The smugglers returned fire, killing Morgan and injuring his colleague.

The killers escaped, and the dead blockademan was buried in St Martin's churchyard. The incident led to a concerted attempt to round up the gang and bring them to justice. A £500 reward was offered for the arrest of George Ransley and the gang he led.

Ransley's long and distinguished career in the service of free-trade finally at the Bourne Tap one stormy night. A party of blockade men aided by a couple of Bow Street runners encircled the house, cutting the throats of the guard-dogs.

George Ransley was in bed when the doors were smashed down, and was taken to Newgate prison to await trial, the local gaols being considered too insecure for such a big fish in the smuggling world. Seven more of Ransley's gang were taken in a simultaneous swoop, and another eleven were arrested soon afterwards.

At their trial one smuggler turned King's evidence, and the whole group were tried for a variety of offences: Richard Wire was accused of actually firing the gun that killed Morgan. A form of plea-bargaining seems to have secured the lives of the gang; though all were sentenced to death, the punishment was reduced to transportation.

The Ransley family graveboard can be seen in the graveyard behind the church of St Mary Magdalene at Ruckinge. Walk round the back of the church – the board is on the south-west side. William and James Ransley, who were hanged in August 1800 for highway robbery, are buried here, and some believe that George Ransley sneaked back from Tasmania as an old man to die in England, and is also buried here.

THE NORTH KENT GANG

This smuggling gang had its roots in the smaller companies operating in the North Kent area in the eighteenth century. By the early years of the nineteenth century though, these independent operators were faced with a concerted official attempt to strangle their business – and perhaps they drew together to counter the threat. The group was initially based on Burntwick Island, a patch of land that stands just a few feet above the mud of the Medway estuary.

The North Kent gang landed goods at Egypt Bay on the Thames estuary, and used Shade House, a small brick building nearby, driving the many marsh sheep along the trails they had followed inland so that there would be no tell-tale footprints. Shade House was built specifically to aid the landing of contraband on the southern shores of the Thames: significantly, all the windows of this peculiar box-like building face inland, to provide a good view of anyone approaching within a mile or so.

As an organised force, rather than as individuals, the gang seems to have attracted little attention until 1820. In the spring of that year they clashed with two blockademen at Stansgate Creek, which flows sluggishly between the gang's island base and Chetney Marshes on the mainland. The gang, who were unloading a cargo in the creek, escaped by attacking one of the blockademen, wounding him seriously.

This escapade possibly emboldened the gang, for just a year later, in March 1821, they landed a cargo directly opposite Herne Bay blockade station. With extraordinary cheek, the fifty-strong force of smugglers tied up the two duty blockademen while they unloaded their goods from a French boat.

The following month another run on the same beach set in motion a chain of events that eventually led to the destruction of the gang and the execution or transportation of its members.

In the small hours of Easter Monday morning 1821, members of the gang were unloading a boat on the beach at Herne Bay, when they were disturbed by a patrol of blockademen. The leader, Sydenham Snow, challenged the smugglers, who outnumbered the preventive men some twenty to one. The smugglers fired on Snow, but he was unable to return their shots, because his gun misfired. Bravely, he drew a knife and charged on the gang. Pistol balls in the thigh and shoulder soon brought Snow down, and the smugglers then reloaded their weapons, and used them to keep the other three members of the patrol at bay until the run was complete.

Snow wasn't dead, and his colleagues carried him to The Ship nearby, where a naval surgeon made a vain attempt to help him. Snow died the next day, but on his deathbed he was able to provide information that led to the arrest of six gang members.

The trial for Snow's murder seemed set to break the back of the gang – and this was exactly what the authorities wanted. Five of the gang had been accused of the killing, including the leader, James West, and three had turned King's evidence to save their necks. Having as witnesses not only three of the gang but also Snow's comrades on the patrol, the Crown was confident of a prosecution. In the end six were tried at the Old Bailey not for murder, but for smuggling. Unfortunately for the Crown, a defence solicitor expertly cross-examined one of the smugglers, George Griffiths, and discredited his testimony. The jury returned a not guilty verdict on all charges.

This coup made James West a local champion, and just a week or two after the trial, it was business as usual. In mid-June a run at Reculver was interrupted by blockademen, and in the battle both sides sustained casualties. The contraband got through, and none of the gang was captured, but their luck didn't hold: soon afterwards two were taken prisoner during a run at Whitstable. The prisoners were taken to Faversham gaol, but their stay was to be brief. They were sprung just eleven days after their arrest, when their colleagues arrived with pickaxes and clubs, and broke open the gaol to release the captives.

Next time they were caught, the gang was not so lucky. Several weeks after Snow's death, the North Kent gang was landing contraband at Marsh Bay near Margate. A blockademan recognised one of the gang, and called out his name. At this, the smugglers fled. A Margate solicitor, John Boys, took up the case. This earned him the enmity of his neighbours, and the unfortunate solicitor:

> … was the object of general hatred in the town of Margate; he was placarded on the walls as an informer and a hunter after blood-money, his house was frequently assailed, his windows broken, his person assaulted in the dark, the fruit trees in his garden destroyed[1]

Boys refused to be intimidated, though, and eventually Bow Street Runners arrested eighteen of the gang. At a trial in Spring 1822 a Maidstone jury convicted all eighteen for armed assembly. Three were executed, and the remainder transported.

The gang's most famous victim, valiant Sydenham Snow, was buried in the churchyard at Herne. You can still see his grave there, and other places in the village have smuggling associations, too: about 200 yards further up the hill is a house called the box iron, on account of its pointed shape. Excavations there early last century uncovered a network of cellars which were admirably suited to the needs of a smuggler. Windmills in the Herne area – there's still one on the hill above the village – were used by smugglers for signalling purposes.

THE HADLEIGH GANG

In Suffolk, as in Kent, the headquarters of the most important gang was not on the coast, but some distance inland. At full strength, the Hadleigh gang numbered 100 men, each turning out with two horses. Such a force would have been almost unstoppable, even when the customs authorities had military support. Certainly, the precise descriptions of the gang's activities recorded in the custom house letters suggests that the authorities could do little more than watch and count the horses:

20 May	70 horses with dry goods landed at Sizewell
27 May	27 horses with wet goods and 36 loaded with tea landed at Sizewell
11 June	60 horses most with brandy, 53 with tea
2 July	83 horses with tea, 9 waggon loads wet goods
12 July	50 horses tea
17 Sept	120 horses – 100 smugglers
10 Nov	50 horses dry goods, 1 cart w/wet goods
23 Nov	at least 40 horses, mostly dry goods

Bear in mind that this list is far from comprehensive – it's likely that an equal amount of contraband was landed unobserved.

The focal point for the gang's activities was Leiston. Many of the traditional anecdotes and yarns feature the village, and in verifiable accounts of smuggling incidents some of the action takes place in the area. Leiston's principal advantage to the Hadleigh gang was the proximity of Sizewell. Today, Sizewell's only claim to fame is the nuclear power station sited on the low coastline, but two centuries ago, the landscape looked quite different. The sea was flanked by spectacular cliffs, and the most convenient route through them was via Sizewell Gap, just a couple of miles from Leiston. From the cliffs, the gang carried goods inland along an ancient trackway crossing Westleton heathlands, or hid contraband in Minsmere levels.

The document quoted above, detailing the runs by the Hadleigh gang, makes frequent references to Sizewell. This entry is typical:[2]

> June 15th – 80 horses mostly with tea landed out of Cobby's cutter at Old Chapel about 2 miles from Sizewell: at the same time 34 horses all loaded with Tea landed out of the *May Flower* cutter and 20 next morning out of the same at Sizewell.

(There is a suggestion that Cobby, who owned one of the boats involved, was one of the smugglers who broke into the Poole custom house, and was ultimately hanged and his body displayed on a gibbet at Selsey Bill.)

The Hadleigh gang frequently clashed with the preventive forces, but the biggest battle took place in 1735. The gang's store-house at Seymor (Semer) had been discovered, and the customs authorities, backed up by the military, took the cache to the George Inn in Hadleigh, for overnight storage. This outraged the gang, and twenty or so smugglers soon presented themselves at the inn to demand the return of their goods. In the battle that followed a dragoon was shot dead, and others injured; the gang rode off into the night with their prize.

The authorities recognised seventeen of the smugglers, and two were hanged for firing pistols in the battle. This did not deter the rest, though, and twelve years on the leader of the gang, John Harvey, was committed to Newgate prison, and eventually transported for seven years. Even this setback was temporary – the following year the gang broke open the King's Warehouse in Ipswich to rescue their goods.

Some of the places associated with the Hadleigh gang are still in existence. You can visit the George Inn, on the main road through Hadleigh, and Pond Hall, on the Hadleigh to Duke Street Road, was home of gang leader John Harvey.

FAMILIES AND INDIVIDUALS

John Banks

In 1871 Hastings schoolteacher John Banks recorded some of the smuggling stories associated with the town in a book, *Smuggling and Smugglers*. He had plenty to choose from: one native of the town[3] commented that:

> No business carried on in Hastings was more popular and extensive as that of smuggling. Defrauding the revenue, so far from being considered a crime, was looked upon as a laudable pursuit, and the most successful 'runners' were heroes. Nearly the whole of the inhabitants, old and young and of every station in life, were, to some extent, engaged in it.

Banks is careful to tell all his stories in the third person, but he is so knowledge-able about the free-trade that it's hard to avoid the conclusion that he took part in at least some of the escapades he describes. He paints a vivid picture of smug-gling in an era when prevention was at its height, but he also reminisces about earlier times when most of the smuggling activity at Hastings and St Leonards took place on the beach. In these colourful tales the smugglers rely for their safety and that of their cargoes on their traditional allies of darkness, brute force, and the incompetence or corruptibility of the revenue services. The custom house officers could usually be expected to make themselves scarce at the prearranged time of landing, but things didn't always go according to the prearranged time-table. Banks describes one embarrassing encounter and the final resolution, with characteristic humour.

> The boat landing the goods near the centre of St Leonards was owned by one Jemmy Roper, and he made the mistake of beaching the boat before his recep-tion committee had arrived. Worse, a custom-house officer appeared. The two men exchanged curses, and the officer told Jemmy he was a fool for arriving early, and that he would now be obliged to seize the cargo. Jemmy replied 'If you be a man, act like one'. In the meantime, the owner of the cargo had arrived, and negotiations began. The custom-house officer agreed that in exchange for seizing ten tubs of spirits, he would allow the crew to ship the rest inland. The boat was quickly unloaded, and when the 'gentlemen' had melted away into the darkness, the officer fired his pistol into the air to summon help in carrying the seized goods back to the custom house.

William Blyth

One of the most colourful smugglers of Essex was oysterman William Blyth (1753–1830) of Paglesham. Blyth was far from the only smuggler in the village: most of the population was alleged to have been involved with the free-trade in one way or another. Several locals were ship-owners, and used oyster-fishing or legitimate cross-Channel transport as a cover for smuggling. In 1783 the Maldon custom house reported that William Dowsett of the village owned two vessels which he used for illegal trade, and that his brother-in-law, Emberson, also oper-ated a small ship. Another member of the Dowsett family traded from the *Big Jane*, a heavily armed lugger that was frequently in skirmishes with the King's men. But William Blyth – alias King of the Smugglers or Hard Apple – was more notorious than all of them.

When Blyth wasn't at sea, he worked as village grocer and churchwarden. Evidently he found it difficult to separate the two roles, since he often wrapped groceries in pages torn from the parish record books.

Other stories about Blyth are more exotic: in one he drank two glasses of wine in the local pub, the Punch Bowl, then calmly ate the glasses. Another has Blyth playing cricket on the local green with Emberson and Dowsett. Though the men took off their coats for the matches, they took the sensible precaution of laying out their guns and swords ready for interruptions from the excisemen. In the course of one of these matches, there was an unscheduled break of another sort: a bull charged the team. Blyth grabbed it by the tail, and set about the animal with a cudgel. The terrified animal fled, with Blyth clinging on, vaulted over a hedge and ditch, then collapsed and died.

Blyth's capacity for alcohol was legendary: when his boat was captured during a run, and the cargo transferred to a revenue cutter Blyth started drinking with the crew. Before very long, the officers and men were fuddled by drink, and Blyth recovered his cargo.

Another story has the smuggler in irons, captive on board a revenue cutter. The ship grounded on the Dogger Bank, and the captain appealed for help from Blyth. He replied 'might as well be drowned as hanged' but was eventually prevailed upon to get the boat off.

Many of the yarns and legends about Blyth's life can be traced back to the memoirs of John Harriott (1745–1817) from Great Stambridge, who went on to become a magistrate, and establish the Thames police force. See page 19 for Harriott's description of how the Paglesham smugglers provided a taxi service from France.

The Carters of Prussia Cove

The most famous smugglers of the Mount's Bay area, and perhaps of all Cornwall, hailed from Prussia Cove, which is just east of Cudden Point. The place actually takes its name from the soubriquet of one of the family who lived and worked here. John Carter was the self-styled 'King of Prussia', and together with two brothers, Harry and Charles, he ran an efficient and profitable smuggling operation from 1770 to 1807.

John Carter is said to have got his nickname from boyhood games in which he regularly claimed to be the King of Prussia. The cove was formerly called Porthleah, but gradually became known as 'the King of Prussia's Cove', and later just Prussia Cove or King's Cove on account of the Carter family's association with the area. The family used three small inlets for their business: Pisky's Cove on the west side, Bessie's Cove (named after the brewess who kept a beer shop on the cliff above) and King's Cove.

The spot has considerable natural advantages. It is:

> ... so sheltered and secluded that it is impossible to see what boats are in the little harbour until one literally leans over the edge of the cliff above; a harbour cut out of the solid rock and a roadway with wheel-tracks, partly cut and partly worn, climbing up the face of the cliff on either side of the cove, caves and the remains of caves everywhere, some of them with their mouths built up which

are reputed to be connected with the house above by secret passages – these are still existing trademarks left by one of the most enterprising smuggling gangs that Cornwall has ever known.[4]

Certainly some of the fame of the family can be attributed to the autobiography written by Harry Carter. This was penned after he had seen The Light, given up smuggling and retired as a preacher. The book is short, but still makes for heavy reading, rambling on for pages in the best traditions of Wesleyanism. Nevertheless, Carter describes in the course of the narrative some hair-raising scenes.

The most spectacular was probably an incident in which the smugglers fired a fusillade of shots at a revenue cutter, from a battery of guns impudently stationed between Bessie's and the King's Cove. No damage was done, though the cutter returned fire.

One ill-fated smuggling trip took Carter to Cawsand – and almost to his death. As he guided the boat into the harbour, he assumed that the two small boats that came alongside were preparing to unload the contraband. Too late he realised they were from a man-of-war, and a fierce battle ensued. He was struck down, severely wounded, and left for dead, but after several hours his body was still warm although 'his head is all to atoms' as one of the guards observed. Despite his injuries, he was able to crawl across the deck and drop into the water. Once in, he found – not surprisingly – that his stout swimming skill had deserted him, and he was forced to pull himself along ropes at the ship's side, until he could touch the bottom and crawl out of the water. On land, he was picked up, half dead, by local men: 'My strength was allmoste exhausted; my breath, nay, my life, was allmoste gone … . The bone of my nose cut right in two, and two very large cuts in my head, that two or three pieces of my skull worked out afterwards.'

There was a bounty on Carter's head by now, and he fled from one safe house to the next, eventually taking refuge at Marazion and the farmhouse at Acton Castle. He lit fires only by night, so frightened was he of discovery, but recovered from his wounds in three months. That he even lived – let alone recovered – seems extraordinary when you remember that the incident took place in 1788.

Even before he took up the cause of Methodism, Harry Carter was an upright, honest and godly man, and the rest of the family appear to have been from a similar mould. Swearing and unseemly conversation were banned on their ships, and when living in exile in Roscoff, Harry Carter held church services every Sunday for the group of English smugglers in town.

John Carter cherished his reputation for honesty. A favourite story tells how he broke into the Penzance custom house to rescue some confiscated tea stored there. His comrades were reluctant to help in such a risky venture, but John explained that he really had no choice. He had promised to deliver the tea by a certain date, and if he failed to fulfil his side of the contract, his honesty would be called into question. The excisemen, returning next morning to find the place ransacked, are said to have commented 'John Carter has been here, and we know it because he is an upright man, and has taken away nothing which was not his own.'

Smuggling continued for some years after the King of Prussia had quit the throne. One later story tells of two men from the cove who were rowing home their small boat – the wind having dropped. They put in at Mullion, only to encounter a couple of excisemen on the beach. Offers of bribes were fruitless, so the rowing continued to Prussia Cove itself. Here, hidden from the preventives by a headland, they traded cargo with a fisherman hauling in his pots, and when met by the excisemen, were able to show a clean hand.

Cruel Coppinger

> Will you hear of Cruel Coppinger?
> He came from a foreign kind:
> He was brought to us by the salt water,
> He was carried away by the wind.

'Cruel' Coppinger was the most notorious of Cornwall's many smugglers, and the Revd R.S. Hawker paints a vivid picture of Coppinger's arrival in a furious storm. The population turned out in the hope of a wreck, and spied:

> a strange vessel of foreign rig … in fierce struggle with the waves of Harty Race. She was deeply lade or waterlogged, and rolled heavily in the trough of the sea, nearing the shore as she felt the tide. Gradually the pale and dismayed faces of the crew became visible, and among them one man of Herculean height and mould, who stood near the wheel with a speaking-trumpet in his hands. The sails were blown to rags, and the rudder was apparently lashed for running ashore … the tall seaman, who was manifestly the skipper of the boat, had cast off his garments, and stood prepared upon the deck to encounter a battle with the surges for life and rescue. He plunged over the bulwarks, and arose to sight buffeting the seas. With stalwart arm and powerful chest he made his way through the surf, rode manfully from billow to billow until, with a bound, he stood at last upright upon the sand, a fine stately semblance of one of the old Vikings of the northern seas.

The story continues in this vein, with baroque, if exaggerated flourishes by the reverend. Coppinger grabbed the cloak from one of the old women on the beach (note the cruel streak), leapt onto a horse behind Miss Dinah Hamlyn, and rode off to her home, where he introduced himself to the girl's father as Coppinger the Dane. The ship, meanwhile, sank from sight.

Coppinger threw himself on the family's charity, wooed the girl, and appeared grateful for all they did for him. The father though, sickened and died, and Coppinger took over as head of the household. He married Dinah, and immediately 'his evil nature, so long smouldering, break [sic] out like a wild beast uncaged ... '

Coppinger, it emerges, was head of a large and terrifying gang, half-smuggler, half-pirate. After the wedding 'all kinds of wild uproar and reckless revelry appalled the neighbourhood day and night'.

Coppinger indulged in many daring exploits – but the Revd Hawker mentions only a few specifically. One was to lure a revenue cutter into a channel near Gull Rock. Coppinger piloted his ship, the *Black Prince*, safely ashore, but the revenue cutter went aground, and all perished. To deter the excisemen on another occasion, the crew cut the head off a gauger, and carried the body to sea.

Coppinger terrorised the locality, capturing men who had offended him, and forcing them into working on his boat. This story finds confirmation in other sources: a ninety-seven-year-old man told a Penzance woman that he was witness to a murder perpetrated by an associate of Coppinger's, and that to prevent him from telling anyone he was abducted. He was released only when some friends ransomed him two years later.

Coppinger amassed such a fortune that he bought a farm for cash – in gold coin: 'Dollars and ducats, doubloons and pistoles, guineas – the coinage of every foreign country with a seabord'. The astonished lawyer reluctantly agreed to the payment by weight.

Coppinger even controlled land transport, forbidding anyone to move on 'Coppinger's tracks' at night. The paths converged at a headland called Steeple Brink, hundreds of feet below which was Coppinger's Cave, where secret revelry went on 'that would be utterly inconceivable to the educated mind of the nineteenth century.'

Coppinger extorted money from his mother-in-law by tying his beautiful wife to the bedstead, and threatening to whip her with a sea-cat unless the old woman paid up. He also whipped the vicar, and tormented a half-witted tailor, threatening to sell him to the devil. His union with Dinah produced a son, who, though deaf and dumb, was as mischievous and cruel as his father, and who joyfully murdered a playmate when aged six.

Coppinger's luck ran out, and he disappeared as he had arrived, in a violent storm. Standing atop Gull Rock, he waved his sword to the approaching craft and was eventually met by a boat in Harty Race 'with two hands at every oar; for the tide runs with double violence through Harty Race'. The boat picked him up at Gull Creek, and the crew struggled through the waves to the pirate vessel. A crew-man who flagged was cut down with a cutlass. The tale ends:

Thunder, lightning and hail ensued. Trees were rent up by the roots around the pirate's abode. Poor Dinah watched, and held in her shuddering arms her idiot boy, and, strange to say, a meteoric stone, called in that country a storm-bolt, fell through the roof into the room, at the very feet of Cruel Coppinger's vacant chair.

It's hard to sieve the facts from this baroque story, but the Coppinger legend may have been based on the exploits of naval surgeon Daniel Coppinger who was shipwrecked in 1792, and later operated a smuggling business from his home in Hartland.

Myles Crowe

Thanks to an account of his life by Solway customs officer Joseph Train, the best known of all Manx smugglers is Myles Crowe (1749–1828.) Crowe was almost comically incompetent. Originally a schoolteacher, he was persuaded to put what little capital he had accrued into a smuggling enterprise. Since Man was at that time a centre for the contraband trade, this must have seemed like a fairly safe investment. Crowe was successful for a while in his trade with the Solway, but when an informer revealed his 'cog-hole' to the customs authorities, he lost his cargo, capital and livelihood.

After this setback, Crowe moved to Kirkcudbright and worked as an agent for some of the more fortunate free-traders. He returned annually to the Man, to collect the rent from some small property he owned there, investing the income in contraband.

These enterprises were successful as long as he was smuggling spirits, but he had trouble with other forms of contraband. On one occasion his breeches, stuffed with tea, burst as he was boarding a ship in Douglas harbour. On another trip, he 'rolled his person up like an Egyptian mummy, from neck to heel, in spun tobacco.' Though this was a common stratagem, experienced smugglers wrapped the tobacco on top of their underwear. Miles wound it next to the skin, and by absorbing nicotine from it he 'was thrown into a hectic fever' and almost passed out. When the cause of his discomfort was discovered, the captain of the ship on which he was travelling handed him over to the custom's authorities, who unwound him from his narcotic coating.

In old age the smuggler manqué became an assistant ferryman, plying from Kirkcudbright to Castelsod. When he died suddenly after a heavy drinking session, everyone assumed that smuggled overproof spirits had killed him. Investigations later showed that he was the victim of a poisoner who sold his corpse for dissection.

Isaac Gulliver

If the many legends surrounding his life are to be believed, this Bournemouth smuggler was a lovable rogue. Though the real Gulliver could hardly live up to his legendary persona, in one respect at least, he was different from other partners in the free-trade: he claimed never to have killed a man in the course of a long career.

Unlike some other smuggling heroes (such as Sam Hookey, who was created in the 1950s to advertise a holiday camp,) Gulliver really did exist, and carried out some extraordinary exploits. While on the one hand there is ample documentary evidence surrounding his life, on the other it's certain that many of the tales about Gulliver have been embroidered to a greater or lesser extent. So in the account that follows, I've tried to differentiate between the facts and the legends.

Though Gulliver spent much of his life in Dorset and Hampshire, he wasn't born in either of these counties. His family were from Wiltshire, and Isaac was born in Semington, near Melksham, on 5 September 1745.

We know little about his youth, though one Isaac Gulliver does occur in the custom house records 1757: in March, four customs officers found a cargo of spirits and tea at the foot of Canford Cliffs Chine in Bournemouth (it was then called Bitman's Chine). The contraband was guarded by a handful of smugglers, and three of the revenue men seized the goods while their colleague went for a cart to transport the cargo. Before he returned, the smugglers were reinforced, rescued the cargo and beat off the customs officers. An informant later alleged that 'Isaac Gulliver, very often at … the *New Inn* within the Parish of Downton' was one of those responsible.

Our Isaac Gulliver was then only twelve, so it seems likely that the man accused (he was never convicted) was the boy's father.

As he grew older, young Gulliver developed attributes that were to stand him in good stead in his smuggling enterprises: he was described as strong in physique and with great determination of character. In adulthood, he was credited with a genius at speculation, and certainly, he grew to be a very wealthy man.

Of his early smuggling enterprises we know little but it seems likely that he was already established by the time he married Elizabeth Beale in 1768. The union doesn't seem to have been entirely domestic, for his wife's father, William, was later suspected, along with Isaac, of 'running great quantities of goods on [the] shore between Poole and Christchurch.'

This stretch of coast, in fact, was Gulliver's favourite landing place: he used Branksome Chine, Canford Cliffs and Bourne Heath.

While he developed his smuggling skills, Gulliver had to have an alibi. His ostensible profession was as an inn-keeper, and the year he married he took over the tenancy of the Blacksmith's Arms, the pub run by his father-in-law at Thorney Down, in the parish of Handley, on the Salisbury to Blandford road. The location of the pub may itself be significant, for Tidpit, some 6 miles away, has a reputation as a clearing house and distribution centre for contraband.

Gulliver changed the name of the pub to the (possibly ironic) King's Arms, and remained the tenant for ten years. Over this period, he seems to have prospered to an extent that could hardly be explained by the turnover of the small pub, and the farming of the little land around it. In 1777, he had enough money to lend £300 as a mortgage to a farmer near Shaftesbury.

And though there is no direct evidence to connect Gulliver with particular incidents in the area, smugglers were certainly active around Thorney Down: the excisemen seized three-quarters of a ton of tea and nine casks of spirits there in 1778, and stored the haul in the house of the supervisor of excise at Thorney Down. Their glee at the seizure must have been short-lived, for:

> About seven o'clock the same evening a large body of smugglers came with pistols etc, on horseback, forced their way into the house, and carried the whole off in great triumph, shouting along the street, and firing their pistols into the air. While they were loading, they gave two casks of liquor to the mob to amuse them.

From Thorney Down, Gulliver moved to Longham, close to Kinson, and bought the White Hart Inn. Bournemouth now occupies the shore-line to the south of Kinson, but when Gulliver lived there in the late 1770s, the area was desolate. He landed goods all along the coast, but favoured Branksome Chine in particular, moving goods inland along a track that passed through Pug's Hole in Talbot Woods.

Exactly when Gulliver began to organise his 'gang' on methodical lines is not entirely clear, but according to one nineteenth-century description Gulliver 'kept forty or fifty men constantly employed who wore a kind of livery, powdered hair, and smock frocks, from which they attained the name 'White Wigs'. These men kept together, and would not allow a few officers to take what they were carrying.'[5]

Gulliver may have used Kinson church for the storage of contraband – certainly the tower was used by other smugglers for that purpose.

When Gulliver sold the White Hart to move into Kinson itself, he significantly also auctioned off 'Twenty Good Hack Horses' – hardly a necessity for a publican. With the proceeds, he set up a regular alcohol emporium – a wine merchants, a malt-house and wine-cellars. From this base he traded quite legally for three years.

He bought Eggardon Hill, a prehistoric earthwork near Dorchester, in 1776 as a sea-marker for his ships. To make it more prominent 'The small enclosure [on top] was prepared for a plantation to serve as a local mark for vessels engaged in the contraband trade.'[6] The revenue men later cut them down.

In 1782 the government offered a pardon to smugglers who would join the navy, or who could find substitutes to perform military service on their behalf. For a man of Gulliver's means, buying a substitute was no problem (the going rate was £15), and he thus wiped the slate clean as far as his smuggling record was concerned.

At this point Gulliver expanded his interests, setting up another wine and spirits business in Teignmouth, and, it appears, simultaneously increasing his smuggling operations. However, he maintained his links with Kinson, and continued to land goods on the coast south of Bourne Heath. Apparently he moved from the spirits business into wine, which was considered a far less reprehensible form of contraband. The Poole custom house reported in 1788 that:

but a few years ago the said Gulliver was considered one of the greatest and notorious smugglers in the West of England and particularly in the spirits and tea trades but in the year 1782 ... [he] dropped that branch of smuggling and after that year confined himself chiefly to the wine trade ... having vaults ... situated in remote places and we are well informed that he constantly offers old wines considerable under the fair dealer's price from which circumstances there is no doubt that he illicitly imported that article.

The report went on to add that Gulliver had retired from smuggling, but there is a possibility that the author was in collusion with the subject of his letter: the Poole official who dealt with this sort of correspondence was soon after sacked for passing information to smugglers.

The reference to vaults in the report has fuelled speculation that Gulliver built a network of tunnels. One was supposed to run from Kinson to Poole, though this stretches the credulity to the limits.

In 'retirement', Gulliver seems to have constantly bought and sold property, frequently moving round the Kinson district. He had a farm at West Moors that can still be seen, had land at Handley, and at one time lived in Long Crichel, close to Thorney Down. Towards the end of his life he moved to Wimborne.

According to an 1867 magazine report, Isaac Gulliver ran his last cargo of contraband at the turn of the century.

His crowning achievement took place on the beach where the pier is now situated, when three large luggers, manned by determined crews and deeply laden with silks, tobacco and other valuables successively ran their respective cargoes; and it is in the recollection of an old inhabitant of the place, that the cortège conveying the smuggled goods inland extended two miles in length, at the head of which rode the old chief mounted on a spirited charger. Thus ended Old Gulliver's smuggling career; he 'coiled up his ropes' and anchored on shore in the enjoyment of a large fortune.

Though some are dubious, the legends that have sprung up around Gulliver are too persistent to ignore. One tells how, when his house at Kinson was searched, he dusted his face with chalk and lay in a coffin feigning death. Another story tells that the pardon he received was in gratitude for saving the King's (George III) life, by revealing an assassination plot; yet another that Gulliver was pardoned for passing on to Nelson intelligence regarding the French fleet.

Gulliver lived until 1822, and was interred in Wimborne Minster.

Many places associated with Gulliver's story are still worth a visit: one of his farms is on the B3072 just north of West Moors. At Kinson the tower of the church of St Andrew was used for storing contraband, and grooves cut by smugglers' ropes could at one time be seen. Ledges on the tower have also been damaged by the hauling of kegs. The table tomb at the foot of the tower was supposedly purpose-made for the storage of contraband. At Wimborne Minster Gulliver's house is in West Borough, and his tomb stone can be seen in the Minster Church. Eggardon Hill remains impressive: it rises suddenly at the end of a long, flat plain, and a series of concentric trenches and embankments spiral around its circumference. From the top, it is possible on a clear day to look out over the sea some 5 miles away, and the hill gives a good view over all the surrounding countryside.

Tom Johnson

This Lymington smuggler (whose name was spelled in several other ways) was born in 1722 into a seafaring family. His father was a fisherman and smuggler, so it's hardly surprising that by twelve years of age Tom had already developed formidable skills of seamanship, and knew the South Coast of England well enough to act as a pilot virtually anywhere. By fifteen he was a smuggler himself.

Descriptions of him are tinged with romanticism: he was said to be over 6ft tall, with handsome, clear-cut features, dark curly hair and vivid blue eyes. 'Women, children, dogs and horses adored him'.[7] Whatever the facts of his personal appearance, he undoubtedly had a great deal of charisma, backed with some low cunning. His life story is a long saga of dramatic escapes and successes, interspersed with spells in prison, injuries and personal disasters. He turned his coat several times, working both for the French and English governments when they were at each other's throats, playing alternately the role of smuggler and revenue man. He had an easy manner that gained him the loyalty of the roughest seamen, yet apparently enabled him to mix on equal terms with the wealthy and titled in England, France and Holland.

When he was twenty-one Johnson joined the crew of a Gosport privateer to fight the French, and this led to one of his first spells in prison: he was taken prisoner by the French, and briefly languished in a French gaol. He soon negotiated release, agreeing to carry messages on board a smuggling cutter to a spy in England. However, his jubilation at being released was short-lived, for the cutter was intercepted by a naval vessel during the crossing. Though Johnson managed to avoid arrest by handing over the package of letters, he was grabbed by the press gang as soon as the ship docked at Southampton.

In true *Boy's Own* style, our hero fought free of the press gang and escaped – but was effectively an outlaw. Having nothing to lose, he returned to smuggling, initially with some success. He ran a succession of cargoes, including the export of a French double agent released from prison in England, but in 1798 was captured by a riding officer at Winchelsea along with another smuggler. Imprisoned in the New Gaol, the two of them conspired to bribe the turnkey and Tom escaped to Flushing where he lay low for a while.

Returning to England despite the price on his head, he volunteered a year later as a navy pilot in the campaign to drive the French out of Holland. His skill as a navigator to the expedition won him a cheque for £1,000 – a staggering sum in those days – a free pardon, and a personal letter of gratitude from the commanding officer.

With these advantages, Tom was able to set up a fashionable household in London, and he began to lead a profligate lifestyle, running up debts of £11,000. In 1802 his creditors caught up with him, and Johnson was thrown into the Fleet prison. No prison could hold him for long, though. This report soon appeared in a newspaper:

> Johnstone, the notorious smuggler, this morning effected his escape, notwith-standing he was confined in a strongroom with a double door. At the top of each door was a pannel instead of glass, By forcing out these and creeping through them, Johnstone was able to reach the gallery, and from thence the high wall that surrounds the prison. There he found a rope ladder which his friends outside had provided for him. In the evening he arrived in a chaise and four on the coast near Brighton where a lugger was in waiting for him, in which he embarked for Calais, on his way to Flushing. He had a severe wound in the thigh, which he received in the following manner. He had got on top of the last wall that separated him from the street 70 feet from the ground. A lamp was set in the wall, some distance beneath the place where he was. He let himself down, so as to fall astride the bracket supporting the lamp. In so doing, a piece of iron caught his thigh above the knee, and ripped it up almost to the top. At this moment he heard the watchman crying the hour; and had so much fortitude as to remain where he was, bleeding abundantly, till the watchman had gone his round, without perceiving him. Immediately after, he let himself down and crawled to where the post chaise was waiting in expectation of his escape.[8]

Johnson recovered from his wounds in France, and was persuaded to take up the guinea run (see page 134), smuggling gold from England to pay Napoleon's armies. Significantly, Johnson does not seem to have regarded this activity as unpatriotic – despite the fact that England and France were then at war. However, the Hampshire Smuggler evidently had some scruples, because he soon afterwards turned down the Emperor Napoleon himself when asked to lead the French invasion fleet to the shores of England. Johnson's genius as a navigator had evidently reached the ears of the Emperor, who clearly believed he was in a position to make him 'an offer he couldn't refuse'. The plan was for Johnson to have a free pardon in an England under French rule (plus a substantial fee, of course).

Declining the offer led to another spell in a French gaol, and this time it was nine months before he escaped. He managed to hitch a ride to New Orleans on an American ship, but by 1806 had secured yet another pardon from the English, and was working for the admiralty once more, with the American inventor Robert Fulton. The project was the development of limpet mines, and an attempt in 1806 to blow up the French fleet in Brest using these devices was a failure in spite of Johnson's leadership. However, three years later a successful attack on Flushing harbour earned the smuggler a pension of £100 a year.

The final phase of Johnson's career was a surprising one: he became the commander of the revenue cutter HMS *Fox*, pursuing his former comrades with all the vigilance of a poacher turned gamekeeper. He eventually retired with a navy pension at the age of forty-four, but even his retirement was not entirely without incident. He dabbled with submarines (another Fulton invention) and almost drowned during a demonstration of the first practical model, the *Nautilus*. He was also approached by the French to rescue Napoleon from St Helena, again using the submarine. Johnson died – remarkably peacefully, after such an active life – at the age of sixty-seven.

John Key

Mid-eighteenth-century Suffolk smuggler John Key was a publican before he took up the free-trade. He moved to Beccles from Blyford, where he had been the landlord of the *Queen's Head*. In Beccles, Key lived at Swines Green on Smuggler's Lane near St Anne's Road, 'Where five crossways meet'. His house was adjacent to a large barn, and both buildings had numerous places for hiding contraband. Smugglers' Lane was an artery along which contraband moved into the town from the coast and from landing points at Barnby and Worlingham on the River – and perhaps Key took a fancy to the house when helping to move cargoes landed at Dunwich.

Key played a prominent part in Beccles smuggling, and left behind a number of anecdotes. In one of them, revenue officers met up with him at Brampton Church 6 miles from his home, as he was returning from a run. Key spurred his horse onward, but near the Duke of Malborough Inn, Weston, one of the officers shot John's horse (which he had borrowed for the occasion) from under him. Key completed the journey on foot, arriving just before the King's men. To his delight, he found a horse very similar to the one he'd been riding grazing contentedly near his home, so he hurriedly locked it into the stable, and donned his nightclothes on top of his working garments. When he heard the inevitable knock on the door, he was able to lean out the window and shout innocently enough 'Wha' d' ye want?' When the revenue men replied 'Where's your horse … didn't we shoot him less than half an hour ago?' John directed them to the stable, thus providing himself with an apparently watertight alibi.

Despite his ingenuity (or perhaps because of it) Key's life in Beccles ended badly: in 1745, smugglers dragged him from his bed, believing that he had informed on them. They stripped and beat him, then tied him naked to a horse and rode off. A reward of £50 for information elicited no response, and the man was never seen again.

Watt Neilson

'Wild' Watt Neilson was one of the Solway smuggling's most fêted figures. His base was the vast but well-hidden Black Cave, which was part of the Barlocco cave complex. The mouth of the cave is vast – a hundred feet wide and fifty high – and though constantly filled by the sea even at low tide, sailing into it is a simple matter only on a calm day.

Watt was renowned for his ability to enter the cave in any weather, but one night even he found his seamanship tested to the limits. Worse than the weather, a revenue cutter was bearing down on the Watt's boat, the *Merry Lass*. As it drew closer, the smuggling crew saw that the revenue ship was in the charge of Captain Skinner; though Watt had never met Skinner, the captain was the 'maist feared man' in the service of the King.

Wild Watt hatched a plan. He stayed in the small boat, posing as an informer, and sent the *Merry Lass* around the coast to the Waterfit (Waterfoot) at Annan, where the confederates of the smugglers would be waiting to unload the cargo at double-quick pace.

Watt's plan worked. He claimed to be the brother of the gauger at Boggle's Creek (the gauger himself was being 'entertained' for the duration of the run by the landlord of Fell Croft) and offered to pilot the ship up the Solway in hot pursuit of the *Merry Lass*. A deal was struck, and the real Watt took the helm. With the sails full, the lugger sped along into an area of the Solway that was unfamiliar to the King's men; nevertheless, they had the *Merry Lass* in good sight until a cloud crossed the moon. At that very instant, the smuggling boat rounded the headland, and 'wi' a' sails brailled she wa cuddlin intae the shadows amang a cluster o' ither boats in the Annan.'

When the *Merry Lass* disappeared, Captain Skinner began to get impatient with his informer. But known only to Wild Watt, things were happening in the shadows of the Annan. Two small boats appeared in the river mouth, and when Skinner hailed them, threatening to pepper them with grapeshot, they quickly surrendered. In the commotion, none of the revenue men noticed the *Merry Lass* (now unloaded) slipping out to sea, 'ready tae tack and rin wi' the turn o' the tide'. The revenue men had their eyes fixed on the two small boats, apparently laden with rolls of tobacco, sacks of salt, and barrels of brandy.

The situation began to change, though, as the outraged boatmen were hauled aboard, hurling abuse at Skinner for interrupting an honest night's work. Far from ferrying contraband, they were simply out rowing provisions to the farms at the head of the Solway: 'As ye kenna reach them when the tide is oot, can ye think o' onything mair sensible than tae gaun when the tide is in, and the folk stervin' for their meal?' Sure enough, the tubs contained only herrings, the sacks innocent oatmeal, and the 'tobacco' turned out to be dried fish. Watt chuckled at the captain's discomfort as he surreptitiously swung himself over the side and into one of the small boats. The 'wronged' boatmen returned to the oars, and they made haste back to the *Merry Lass*. The duped revenue men watched helplessly as the smuggling ship hauled an empty half-anker to the mast-head, and swept out of the channel on the tide.

Jack Rattenbury

'The Rob Roy of the West' Jack Rattenbury led a gang of smugglers based in Beer, at the extreme east of Devon. Like the Carter family of Prussia Cove, Rattenbury probably owes his fame not so much to his actual exploits as to the diary and journal he wrote. This is essentially an autobiography, and starts with his birth in Beer in 1778. As a child he intended to go into fishing, but found this rather a dull activity, and his real adventures began when he turned fifteen: he set out on a privateer, was taken prisoner by the French, and thrown into gaol in France ... 'Instead of returning to our native country laden with riches and adorned with trophies, we were become ... unwilling sojourners in a strange land.'

Rattenbury became a trusty inmate, though, and eventually managed to sneak away. Escapes of one sort or another soon became his forte: he described how a smuggling brig in which he was travelling was captured by a French privateer, and he was left at the helm to steer for a French port while the crew got drunk below: 'I began to conceive a hope not only of escaping, but also of being revenged on the enemy. A fog too came on, which befriended the design I had in view ... '

Rattenbury steered for the English coast, and when they came in sight of Portland Bill, he convinced the crew that this was Alderney; similarly, St Alban's Heath became Cape La Hogue. When they got closer to the shore, Jack persuaded them to lower a boat so he could go and get a pilot – he eventually completed his escape by diving overboard and swimming into Swanage harbour. He hurried to the local customs authorities, who sent a cutter to recapture the brig from the French.

Rattenbury followed this with a series of daring escapes – from the navy, the press gang, from privateers, from customs men. He hid up chimneys, in cellars, on board small boats, and in bushes.

Jack catalogued this series of adventures, most of them carefully drawn to show him in a heroic light. A typical story has him stripped to the waist, with a knife in one hand and a reaping-hook (hand-scythe) in the other, facing nine or ten soldiers who were determined to arrest him as a deserter. He took up position at the stable door to the cellar, closing the lower half:

I declared I would kill the first man who came near me, and that I would not be taken from the spot alive. At this, the sergeant was evidently terrified, but he said to his men 'Soldiers, do your duty, advance and seize him;' to which they replied, 'Sergeant, you proposed it: take the lead' ... no one, however, offered to advance.

The deadlock continued for four hours, and eventually a distraction gave Rattenbury the opportunity to dash through the crowd and make good his escape – by removing his shirt, he prevented the soldiers from taking a firm hold of him.

Reading through the short book, Jack's increasing wealth is abundantly clear. In the early days he hasn't two pennies to rub together, but by the age of thirty, he had amassed sufficient money to trade in boats much as people today buy and sell second-hand cars: even in the face of adversity he has no trouble in setting up in business once again. He buys a leaky old tub, the *Lively*, and carries out several hazardous smuggling missions in her. Fearing drowning on further forays, Rattenbury beaches the boat for repairs, and buys the *Neptune*. With the wreck of the *Neptune*, the *Lively* comes back into use, but is in turn seized at Brixham, and Rattenbury forfeits a £160 bond. He comments that, on top of the loss of two boats the loss of the bond 'was a great shock to my circumstances' but continues in the next line … 'Not long after this disaster, I bought part of a 12-oared boat, which was 53 feet keel and 60 feet aloft'. Clearly he wasn't short of cash.

Rattenbury's principal smuggling method in the early years seems to have been to buy tubs in the Channel Islands, and sink them off the English coast for later collection. As the nineteenth century proceeded, Rattenbury began to make trips direct to France – usually to Cherbourg. This in good weather took a day or less.

He didn't confine himself to smuggling conventional cargoes, and also considered other enterprises, some successful, some not so profitable. He was caught smuggling out French prisoners, but excused himself by saying he thought they came from Jersey. The magistrates ticked him off and sent him home.

Rattenbury's book also reveals much of the ups and downs of smuggling. He tries to give up the trade and run a pub, but this proves far from lucrative and in 1813 he shuts up the pub, commenting 'there was scarcely anything to be done in smuggling'. And in early 1814 … 'in consequence of the fluctuating nature of our public affairs, smuggling was also at a stand'. (At this time there was a temporary lull in the Napoleonic War – Napoleon was in exile on Elba.)

Rattenbury's shipping transactions cast an interesting perspective on the values of the day. Piloting proved very lucrative for him – sometimes paying £100 in a storm … he buys a boat for £200 … his bail is set at £200 … he pays a fine of £200. His fortunes seem to vary wildly: at times he must have lived hand-to-mouth, because a two-month attack of gout is a considerable set-back.

All in all, though, Jack paints a swashbuckling picture of himself, and probably forms the model for many a fictional smuggler to this day.

Rattenbury mentions many places by name in the text, but few that are specifically identifiable today: Beer, Brixham, Seaton Beach, Loden Bay, Axmouth Harbour, Charmouth, Bridport harbour, Swanage Bay, Christchurch, Kingswear all feature. In 1820 one of his boats ran aground at Stapen Sands and was dashed to pieces … 'the greater part of her goods became the prey of the inhabitants.' One of his escapes was from a pub called *The Indian Queens*, a few miles from Bodmin. Though the pub has now been demolished, a village still bears its name. And at Beer itself, Rattenbury was reputed to have used a cave in the face of Beer Head.

Roger Ridout

Not all of the famous smugglers were seafaring men: Dorset land smuggler Roger Ridout ran a haulage company moving goods inland from the coast. He lived at Okeford Fitzpaine, a small village near Blandford Forum. In an 1895 account of his activities, a local writer commented:

> [my] father stated that when a boy, in or about 1794, he had, when riding … late at night seen the string of horses in the narrow road between Okeford Fitzpaine and Fiddleford with the kegs and other contraband goods on the horses. One or two men, armed, generally were in front and then ten or twelve horses connected by ropes or halters followed at a hard trot, and two or three men brought up the rear. This cavalcade did not stop for any person, and it was very difficult to get out of their way, as the roads, until the turnpikes were made in 1724, would only allow for one carriage, except in certain places. The contraband goods were principally brought from Lulworth and the coast through Whiteparish and Okeford Fitzpaine, through the paths in the woods to Fiddleford, and thus distributed.[9]

The author of this piece was the grandson of a Sturminster Newton JP who was reportedly bribed by Ridout.

From baptism registers, it appears that Roger Ridout was born in Shroton (the parish of Iwerne Courtney) in 1736. He inherited a house in Fiddleford when he was ten, and married when he was twenty. He earned a living as a miller, died in 1811, and was buried in Okeford Fitzpaine graveyard.

But behind these bald facts lie numerous legends. The Ridout of the oral tradition was a bold smuggler who brought contraband – notably brandy – from the coast, and stored it at the mill. Most of the tales tell the usual story of the exciseman outwitted, but their charm lies in the West Country flavour. For example, Ridout owned a horse called locally Ridout's Ratted (or stumped) Tail, for reasons that probably need no explanation, and as he arrived in Sturminster Bridge Street a mob of rival smugglers gathered round the horse and rider, and tried to pull Roger to the ground. Ridout leaned forward and whispered to his nag 'What'd 'ee do fer thy king?' On hearing this, the horse reared up and kicked in the door of a nearby house.

Other stories have Ridout being lowered from the back-window of his house in a bed-sheet to escape the revenue men, and tricking them in other ways. Returning from Fiddleford brewery with a jar of balm, Ridout was met by a curious exciseman. Roger shook the bottle as the exciseman approached, and as

the wily smuggler had expected, the officer asked about the contents of the bottle. Ridout led him on: 'Would 'ee like t'smell 'un?' and handed it over. When the
officer pulled the cork he got a face-full of balm, and the smuggler pushed him
into the ditch and went on his way.

Ridout is reputed to have been employed by Isaac Gulliver, and it is certain
that he spent some time in Dorchester gaol, languishing there until he could pay
the fine. The local stories tell that he was fortified behind bars by his wife, who
would walk a 40-mile round trip to the gaol with a concealed bladder of brandy,
equipped with a tube that she passed through the bars so that her husband could
have a drop of the right stuff.

Saucy Jack

The most notorious of the Colchester smugglers (if only because a tract was
published describing his life and crimes) was probably John Skinner, alias Saucy
Jack or Colchester Jack. As the tract explains: 'Skinner was accounted as great a
smuggler as any in the county of Essex; tho' the better to difguife his Way of Life
he rented two Farms, known by the Names of the Tan Office and Cox's Farm …
at Colchester.'

Skinner's nickname 'Saucy' was well-earned. He was by all accounts quite a
rake, and on one occasion ' … had been at a Bawdy House for ten Days successively, and had spent 60 or 70l, when he should have been at home minding his
Business.'

Skinner spent money wildly, working his way through his wife's substantial fortune, then casting her on the parish, where she went to work in the poor-house.
She was 'brought to ruin and misery by the extravagance of one who in duty, and
the solemn tie of matrimony, ought to have comforted and supported her.'

When he'd squandered his wife's money, he bought the King's Head Inn
at Romford 'and had a very pretty trade, particularly among smugglers.
Understanding what large Profits were gain'd in the Smuggling Way he left his
Inn and commenc'd smuggler.'

This trade apparently went well for Saucy Jack, but in the end, his violent tem-
per was his undoing. He had smuggled some goods in May 1744 in partnership
with his servant, one Daniell Brett, and it appears that Brett had cheated Skinner
by betraying where the contraband was hidden. When Skinner discovered this,
he flew into a rage, and swore he would kill Brett. One witness testified … 'he
answered this Examinant in a great passion, and swore bitterly that let him find
(Brett) where he would he would shoot him dead that night.'

Saucy Jack returned home to Old Heath just before midnight in a confused
state, then rode off to Colchester to fetch a surgeon. While he was gone, Brett
appeared with a stomach wound: from the description, he appeared to have been
shot at point-blank range. However, the loyal servant would not reveal who had
shot him. Despite medical attention, the man died the following day, and Saucy

Jack was tried and convicted of murder. It was his philandering ways that sealed his fate, for one of the principal witnesses against him was a man he had cuckolded … 'He had deluded a great many women, as well married as single, for being a personable man he had seldom (as he often said) found much difficulty in making conquest of the Fair Sex.'

In jail, Skinner made a vain attempt to cheat the gallows, and stabbed himself in a rather inexpert way with a small knife. He was nevertheless hanged, but was too weak to utter any Last Words, which must have come as a blow to the printer of the tract, since the cover page (perhaps printed in advance of the contents) clearly promises the reader a gallows confession.

Joss Snelling

If the mark of a successful smuggler is their ability to avoid capture and prosecution, then Thanet smuggler Joss Snelling was among the best. Born in 1741, he lived to the extraordinary age of ninety-six. Though it's clear that he ran a remarkably profitable smuggling operation, he was only in trouble with the law twice, and was never imprisoned. On the second occasion he was aged eighty-nine and was fined £100 for smuggling.

Snelling's ability to elude the customs authorities is hard to fathom. One explanation might be that he avoided the armed confrontations that left other smugglers mortally wounded or behind bars. However, an incident in 1769 rules out such an hypothesis.

That spring Snelling's company, the Callis Court gang, was unloading a cargo at Botany Bay when they were surprised by a preventive patrol. Five members of the gang fled from the beach, either up Kemp's stairs or by scrambling up the chalk. Unfortunately, their troubles had only just begun, for they were challenged on the cliff-top by a riding officer. To effect an escape, they shot him, and the dying man was taken to the nearby Captain Digby Inn. To locate the killers, the authorities mounted a search of the area, concentrating on nearby Reading Street. In Rosemary Cottage there they found two dead smugglers, and one mortally wounded. In all, the Battle of Botany Bay, as it came to be known, claimed the lives of fifteen of Joss's gang. Nine died of their wounds, and six were later hanged in Sandwich, at Gallows Field.

Joss himself lived another sixty-eight years, and became a cherished local institution: he was even been presented to the future Queen Victoria as 'the famous Broadstairs smuggler' when she stayed at Pierremont Hall in 1829.

Joss Snelling died in Broadstairs in October 1837. Part of the legend that grew after his death was that a local cove and a gap in the cliffs were named after him. In fact Joss Bay had been known by this name for nearly a century before the smuggler's birth, and the Joss Gap was named after a farming family that owned the adjacent farmland.

Thomas Knight and William Arthur

Today Barry Island in South Wales has a benign appearance. It is not even a proper island any more, since in the 1880s the construction of Barry docks closed the narrow waters that separated it from the mainland.

A century earlier Barry was very different. A true island, it was a smugglers' fortified domain. Two different smugglers were the kings of this offshore castle before the Crown dislodged them.

It was Thomas Knight who put the fortifications around the shoreline. He ran a fleet of heavily armed smuggling ships from Barry, importing spirits and tobacco from the Channel Islands, and soap from Ireland. Knight probably arrived in Barry in 1783, in a twenty-four-gun brig called the *John O'Combe*. Opposition from the customs authorities was at first nominal, and with support from local people, Knight quickly made the island his stronghold. The customs men may well have exaggerated the problem, but Knight was reputed to have a force of sixty to seventy men defending the island from uninvited interest.

Knight's influence grew rapidly, and within a year or so, the customs authorities had difficulty recruiting members, since the local population evidently had more respect for Barry's smuggling king than for the legitimate Crown.

Knight's men did not hesitate to fire on preventive vessels, and their crews went in fear of their lives. On occasions the custom house boats refused to give chase, the sailors claiming justifiably that there was no pension scheme for customs men injured in the line of duty. To counter this, a £10 payment was introduced for mariners who lost a hand or foot, and free medical treatment for any injury. Knight was implicated in a huge seizure of tobacco at Goldcliff in 1784, and some indication of the importance attached to his influence in the area can be gained from the fact that the seized goods were taken to Cardiff under armed guard, at considerable expense. The local people refused to help with the transport, because they were terrified of how Knight would exact his revenge.

Knight's reign was brief, and in 1785 a concerted effort by the authorities dislodged him. He retreated to Lundy and his place was taken William Arthur, 'the most daring smuggler in Glamorgan during the eighteenth century.' Arthur proved as tough a nut to crack as his predecessor, and the local collector of customs estimated that it would require the efforts of sixty dragoons to once more make the island safe. Other than this fact, Arthur's connection to the island is obscure, for the centre of his smuggling empire was 60km to the west, on the Gower peninsula.

Arthur operated from Great Highway Farm: nearby Little Highway was the headquarters of another smuggler, John Griffiths. Central on the south coast of Gower, the two farms overlooked Pwlldu headland, a vast 300ft high bluff that guided smuggling boats to the bay at its foot. 'Pwlldu' is Welsh for black pool: a shingle bar blocks the river flowing into Pwlldu Bay, forming a small lake.

The bay was a smuggler's haven: one local writer claims that more contraband was landed here than anywhere else in the Bristol Channel. The reasons for the bay's notoriety are obvious even today. It's very sheltered; the beach slopes gently; and transport inland was virtually invisible, the wooded Bishopston Valley providing plenty of cover. The valley led uphill to the two farms, which were used as staging posts and store-houses.

Arthur's position at Highway at times seemed unassailable. When twelve revenue men raided the farm in 1786 Arthur was waiting for them, put up a stout defence with help from a '… Body of desperate fellows … amounted to One hundred'. The King's men retreated with bruised pride. Two subsequent expeditions to capture Arthur failed in 1788.

A local tale relates how a customs officer arrived at one of the farms with a search warrant, and discovered a half-anker of brandy concealed in the attic. The officer sent for reinforcements, and kept a close watch on the barrel. Meanwhile, the smugglers created a terrific row in the room below to conceal the noise as one of them bored a hole through the floor of the attic and the base of the tub, draining the contents of the barrel into a tub waiting below.

The farms at Highway still exist, some 400 yards west of the crossroads at Pennard. The present occupiers – one of who is descended from smuggler Griffiths – know nothing of the cellars that once concealed hundreds of tubs, and the buildings have been considerably changed over the last two centuries. The former occupant didn't entirely escape the attentions of the law: he paid a fine of £5 5s for concealing prohibited goods in 1789. However, in 1802, the Swansea Guide referred to him as 'a proprietor of considerable stone-coal and culm collieries on the Swansea canal', so he had clearly retired from the free-trade by the turn of the century.

The Warnes of Burley

A windswept hilltop near Burley in the New Forest was the home of the pre-eminent smuggling family of the area, the Warnes. John, Peter and their sister Lovey lived at Knave's Ash at Crow Hill Top. The most picturesque yarns about the family concern Lovey Warne. According to legend, she would visit ships in Christchurch harbour, undress in the privacy of the captain's cabin, and wind herself with valuable silks before getting back into her clothes – somewhat fatter. Evidently the sudden gain in weight passed unnoticed, since Lovey would walk straight past the revenue men without arousing suspicion, and return home to be unwound and relieved of her burden. This clever ruse apparently had to stop when one of the revenue men invited Lovey for a glass at the Eight Bells in Christchurch. Emboldened by drink, he became amorous and started to explore Lovey's fine thighs with his hand. A swift jab in the eye deterred his amorous advances, but this close shave made the family aware of the terrible risks Lovey was taking, and she took a safer job – as a living signal to smugglers on the coast. When revenue men were abroad in the forest, she would parade across Vereley Hill wearing a red cloak, as a warning to free-traders on the coast to avoid the area.

At night smugglers Charles and Murphy Bromfield living at a cottage on Vereley Hill would hoist a lantern up a nearby oak tree to give the warning signal.

John Warne died young after he was wounded by a customs man's pistol during a run at Chewton Bunny, but his brother and sister lived to old age. When Peter Warne died he specified that his beloved grey pony, veteran of many a smuggling run, should be buried with him. However, the vicar of Burley objected to the graveside despatch of the animal since it smacked of paganism. When the pony later died the Warne family made another attempt to get it interred with its master. This was also vetoed by the church, and the beast was buried just outside the graveyard gate.

Owen Williams

This Welsh smuggler carved his niche in history not by the extremity of his exploits, but by the fact that he wrote them down. He thus joins Jack Rattenbury and 'The King of Prussia' in that select band of smuggler/autobiographers. The National Library of Wales purchased the manuscript of William's story in 1982, and a brief summary of it appeared in the Library's Journal in 1985.

Owen was born in Nevern, Pembrokeshire, in 1717, the son of a wealthy farmer. His wayward nature was evident from an early age: his father wanted him to go into the Church, or into law, but he rejected both these plans, and made his distaste for farming abundantly clear, too. When he was fourteen or fifteen he ran away to Haverfordwest to join the crew of a ship trading with Bristol. The novelty of the sailor's life soon wore off; tired of being a skivvy and whipped when he stepped out of line, Williams returned to the farm, but found this suited him even less. On his father's land he was just a labourer, and clearly aimed for something better.

After a second false start on a Bideford ship, his father bought Owen a ship of his own. The sixteen-year-old sea captain soon began to exhibit another side to his character – as a philanderer. He began a debauched affair with a maid, which prompted his father to take back the vessel. Williams retaliated by marrying the girl, and at this his long-suffering father returned the ship, together with cash to set Owen up in business.

Williams traded legally for a while, but was clearly seduced by the rags-to-riches stories of the smugglers he mixed with on the dock-side. He tried his hand at smuggling goods in from the Isle of Man – and got caught on the first trip. He lost his ship and everything he owned, and fled to the West Indies, where he joined a smuggling ship called the *Terrible*.

From this point on, the narrative adopts a tone that shows Williams in a heroic light that is perhaps not entirely true to the facts. The *Terrible* engaged a Spanish ship in battle, and Owen dispatched twenty-five of the crew by rolling a powder keg, fuse fizzing, onto the deck of the Spanish coaster. Despite a wound to his head, Williams was soon back in Barbados, indulging in various licentiousness with the local ladies, and then later we find him on smuggling trips in the area.

On one of these he was captured by a British man-of-war, but was judged such a brave fellow that he was appointed midshipman, and stayed with the vessel for twenty months. Homesickness eventually set in, though, and Williams returned home, to set up a legitimate business with his own boat. He dallied with various local women, and fell out with his wife, who turned to drink.

As the years went by, Williams' catalogue of adventures grew: he returned to smuggling, with considerable success; aiding an Aberystwyth friend, he led a large party who laid siege to a local mansion. Owen secured the surrender in heroic manner by loading a wagon with gunpowder, setting light to the wagon, then rolling it under the balcony of the building. Later we see him masquerading as a baronet off the Isle of Man, and playing double-agent as a customs officer with a lucrative side-line in smuggled goods. He fell in love with a young Manx girl, but was prevented from marrying her by his own reluctance to get a divorce, and by the fact that she was a minor.

Williams, like so many smugglers, had a remarkable ability to smile through adversity. Losing his boat and virtually everything he owned through the treachery of a crew member, he raffled a cow and raised £30.

His fortunes soon changed, and with help from the Manx girl (whom he was now passing off as his wife) Williams bought a new yacht, and resumed smuggling. In 1744, though, the authorities were on his tail, and Owen's ship was attacked in Cardigan. Despite overwhelming odds, the ship's crew escaped, but killed four men, including a customs officer, in the show-down.

By this time, Owen Williams was notorious. Even the Isle of Man authorities, who were noted for their leniency, joined in the search, and Williams and his young sweetheart had to escape from the island on an Irish oyster boat. On the run in Ireland, they posed as peddlers until the heat died down, and then travelled back to Wales, to Ireland again, and eventually back to the Isle of Man. Here, his luck ran out, and he was captured, and brought to trial in Hereford.

Owen Williams must have been a remarkable character, because he defended himself in the trial against 'a very severe prosecution' and was acquitted, largely because of his eloquent defence.

A free man again, Williams resumed a career which interleaved legitimate trading with smuggling and privateering. He became a castaway, wracked by fever on the Barbary Coast, and lost his wife in a shipwreck. He went back to Cardigan to recuperate from the recurring effects of the tropical disease, and eventually fell in with James Lilly, a Cardigan fencing master.

Owen Williams lived such a full and colourful life that the end of the story seems sordid and depressing. Though the details are unclear, it seems that Lilly and Williams had burgled a house in Nevern, and had been spotted in Cardiff. Running from the hue and cry, Williams shot the leading pursuer – the Cardigan post boy – then turned his gun on his companion, Lilly. He was hanged in 1747, aged just thirty.

Captain Yawkins/Dirk Hatteraick

Various colourful figures crop up in the many smuggling legends of the Solway area, but Captain Yawkins stand head and shoulders above the rest. His exploits read like fiction, and indeed Walter Scott used him as the model for his character Dirk Hatteraick in the book *Guy Mannering*. Some of the stories about Yawkins are verifiable fact but others – such as the allegation that he had traded his own soul and a tenth of his crew with the devil – are more dubious.

All are entertaining, though. A typical tale has Yawkins and his crew buying a bullock at Drummore Bay on the Mull of Galloway watched by an outgunned and outmanned revenue cutter. The officer on the cutter declines a roast-beef supper on board Yawkins' *Black Prince*, but they arrange a picnic ashore. When the customs officer admires the smuggler's gun, he is presented with it as a gift, followed rapidly by a decanter and glasses. Yawkins wryly comments that, since the officer had the only thing he values, he may as well take everything else.

There are many other stories: the tale that Yawkins kidnapped a revenue man and sailed him over to Amsterdam echoes other verified accounts from elsewhere on the coast. In another he was landing a cargo at Drummore (some accounts place the incident at Manxman's Lake near Kirkcudbright) when two revenue cruisers appeared, one from the north and one from the south. Yawkins cast off, replaced his pennant with a mast-head cask to identify his chosen trade, and sailed directly between the two ships, close enough to toss his hat onto one, and his wig onto the other. While this may be an exaggeration, it's worth remembering that carriage guns were useless unless the target was broadside on to the ship, so there may well be a germ of truth in the yarn.

Yawkins was such a larger-than-life figure that when he had brushes with the law, the official accounts of them rather pale in comparison with the images perpetuated in myth and legend. Often Yawkins appears off-stage: In 1787 a run by Yawkins was interrupted by an 'Admiralty cruizer'. The local customs authorities heard gunfire off the Abbey Burn at around 10p.m., and discovered that the Admiralty ship had indeed intercepted a smuggling lugger – but not before seventeen boxes of tea had been unloaded and spirited away on the backs of waiting horses. The captured lugger had on board 80–90 boxes of tea, 400 ankers of spirits, and 'a quantity of silks and tobacco' A postscript adds that the lugger 'was commanded by the noted Yawkins and that she was loaded at Ostend.' Yawkins' lugger, the *Hawke*, was delivered to the Liverpool authorities, but was found to be so leaky as to be of no use, and the ship was broken up.

Dirk Hatteraick's cave, reputedly used by Yawkins, overlooks Wigtown Bay. There is no trace remaining of the sleeping platform smugglers built at one end, or of the special pigeon holes that once existed for the storage of the oddly shaped Dutch flagons in which the smuggler traded.

NOTES

1   Douch, 1985, quoting the Crown Solicitor
2   *East Anglian Magazine* 1969 vol XIX (Jan & March). Article by Brown, A. Stuart: 'Smuggling in Suffolk'
3   Alfred Bryant of Enfield, quoted by Cousins, Henry, 1911
4   *Cornish Magazine*
5   Roberts, George, 1823
6   Warne, Charles, 1856
7   *Hampshire*, the County Magazine v8
8   *The Gentleman's Magazine*, for Monday 29 November
9   'Dorset Natural History and Antiquarian Field Club', vXVI (1895), pp 55–8, quoted in *The Greenwood Tree*

APPENDIX:
THE SMUGGLING DIASPORA

Smugglers convicted of the most serious offences were executed by hanging; often their bodies were displayed on gibbets in 'chains' (a made-to-measure cage designed to hold the corpse together and prevent its removal and burial).

However, the death penalty was often commuted to transportation, and this sentence was widely prescribed for lesser smuggling offences from 1718. At first, smugglers were transported to the American colonies, but this practice ended with the American Revolution in 1776. Smugglers and other prisoners who would previously have been transported soon filled Britain's prisons to bursting point. To ease the overcrowding, the government turned to floating prisons called hulks. These were derelict men-of-war: their sails, masts and most other sea-going fittings were removed, and the wooden shells moored either at Portsmouth or on the south coast of the Thames estuary. Hulks were stinking and pestilent, and every prisoner dreaded incarceration in one.

Transportation began again when a penal colony was established in Australia. The First Fleet set sail for Port Jackson in May 1787. On board the six transport ships were 717 convicts. Transportation continued until 1867, by which time nearly 160,000 convicts had been involuntarily relocated.

Transportation did not immediately follow conviction for a smuggling offence. Convicts still faced several months on board a prison hulk. Those who survived their stay must then have welcomed the prospect of the ocean voyage. Their journey to Australia took some seventeen weeks. The convict ships carried some 200 prisoners, who were fed at least as well as naval seamen, and who received medical attention and a set of new clothes. For those who behaved themselves boredom was the principal hardship of the voyage.

In Australia, convicted smugglers faced many years' hard labour in conditions that were sometimes appalling and brutalising. But those who survived were free to start their lives anew.

This system of punishment was regarded as enlightened and humane at the time. It led to the scattering of smuggling families, mostly across mainland Australia and Van Diemen's Land (now Tasmania).

Descendants of these convicts, and their relatives in Britain, frequently contact me for advice about tracing their ancestors. I cannot provide any specific information, but the following guide is a useful starting point for research. Web references may change: check on www.smuggling.co.uk for an up-to-date listing and to avoid typing in long URLs.

SOURCES

National Archives
Based at Kew in West London, Britain's national archives has 9.5 million accessible documents, including the conviction and sentencing records of many transported smugglers. Most are held in paper or microfilm form, and access is time-consuming: you can order only three documents at a time, and may have to wait forty minutes for them to be delivered.

These two web pages introduce the topic of transportation, and provide useful pointers to tracing convicts through the National Archives:

http://www.nationalarchives.gov.uk/catalogue/Leaflets/ri2235.htm

http://www.nationalarchives.gov.uk/familyhistory/guide/ancestorslaw/prisoners.htm

You'll also find here details of published sources on transported convicts.

Internet resources
The following pages are specific to convicts transported from the British mainland.

Convicts to Australia:
This comprehensive 'guide to researching your convict ancestors' is probably the best place to start. It has a useful list of online resources:
http://members.iinet.net.au/~perthdps/convicts/list.html

The Old Bailey:
This site from Britain's central and historic criminal court has a brief introduction to transportation:
http://www.oldbaileyonline.org/history/crime/punishment.html#transportation

Of more interest to those seeking their smuggling ancestors is a searchable database of 100,000 criminal trials:
http://www.oldbaileyonline.org/search/

Smuggling is not listed as a specific offence (it instead appears under 'tax offences') but a keyword search details 225 trials in which smuggling is mentioned.

Convicts and British Colonies in Australia:
Focusing on convict life and the penal colonies, this site from the Australian government's culture and recreation portal also has a list of useful links:
http://www.cultureandrecreation.gov.au/articles/convicts/

Australian Convict Index 1788–1868:
This searchable database from Ancestry.com lists 48,000 names – nearly a third of all those transported. Registration required, though searching is free:
http://www.ancestry.com/search/db.aspx?dbid=5517

Ticket of Leave Index:
Convicts who behaved themselves qualified for a 'ticket of leave' which enabled them to buy land and to work freely before their sentence had expired.
   The Society of Australian Genealogists provides free searches of ticket of leave butts from 1810–1875. There is a charge for a copy of the original butt, which in addition to a prisoner's name, trade, date and place of birth, sometimes also lists trial and conviction details, transport ship and date of arrival, and physical features.
http://svc199.wic003v.server-web.com/collections/tol.htm

Tasmanian Name Indexes:
The Archives office of Tasmania maintains indexes of all convicts transported to Van Diemen's Land, and their applications to marry.
http://www.archives.tas.gov.au/nameindexes

New South Wales Convicts:
Indexes from the NSW Archives and Records Management Authority list Certificates of Freedom; convicts' bank accounts; pardons; exemptions from labours and other documents.
http://www.records.nsw.gov.au/archives/convicts_3689.asp

Australian Mailing Lists:
A long list of lists from Rootsweb.com. Search for 'convicts'.
http://www.rootsweb.com/%7Ejfuller/gen_mail_country-aus.html

BIBLIOGRAPHY

GENERAL

Atton, Henry & Holland, Henry Hurst *The King's Customs, an account of maritime revenue and contraband traffic in England, Scotland and Ireland* (Murray, 1908)

Chatterton, E. Keble *King's Cutters and Smugglers 1700–1855* (George Allen & Co., 1912)

Cleugh, James *Captain Thomas Johnstone, 1772–1839* (Andrew Melrose, 1955)

Cole, W.A. *Trends in Eighteenth-Century Smuggling* (Economic History Review, Volume 10, Issue 3, 1958)

Cross, Arthur Lyon *Eighteenth Century Documents relating to the Royal Forests, the Sheriffs and Smuggling* (Macmillan, New York, 1928)

Duncan, Jonathan *The history of Guernsey: with occasional notices of Jersey, Alderney, and Sark and biographical sketches* (Longman, Brown, Green, and Longmans, 1841)

Jones, Evan T. *Illicit business: accounting for smuggling in mid-sixteenth-century Bristol* (Economic History Review, Volume 54, Issue 1, 2001)

Farjeon, Joseph Jefferson *The Compleat Smuggler* (G.G. Harrap & Co., 1938)

Forbes, Athol *The Romance of Smuggling* (Pearson, 1909)

Fraser, Duncan *The Smugglers* (Standard Press, 1971)

Graham, Frank Moore *Smuggling Inns* (published by the author, 1966)

Graham, Frank Moore *More Smugglers Inns* (published by the author, 1969)

Harper, Charles G. & Shore, Henry Noel *The Smugglers: Picturesque Chapters in the History of Contraband* (Cecil Palmer, 1923)

James, G.P.R. *The smuggle: a tale* (Bernh. Tauchnitz, 1845)

McLynn, Frank *Crime and Punishment in Eighteenth-century England* (Routledge, 1989)

Monod, Paul *Dangerous Merchandise: Smuggling, Jacobitism and Commercial Culture in Southeast England, 1690-1760* In the *Journal of British Studies 30* (April 1991) pages 150–182

Mui, Hoh-Cheung & Lorna H. *Smuggling and the British Tea Trade before 1784* (American Historical Review vol. 74i, 1968)

Muskett, Paul *English smuggling in the Eighteenth Century* (unpublished Open University Phd. thesis, 1996)

Nicholls, F.F. *Honest Thieves* (Heinemann, 1973)

Phillipson, David *Smuggling: a History, 1700–1970* (David and Charles, 1973)

Pringle, Patrick *Honest thieves: the Story of the Smugglers* (1938)

Ruskin, John *The Harbours of England. Engraved by T. Lupton, from … drawings … by J.M.W. Turner.* (Gambart & Co., 1856)

Scott, James Maurice *The Tea Story* (Heinemann, 1964)

Scott, Richard *A topographical and historical account of Hayling Island, Hants* (I. Skelton, 1826)

Shore, Henry Noel *Smuggling Days and Smuggling Ways* (Cassell & Co., 1892)

Smith, Graham *King's Cutters* (Conway Maritime Press, 1983)

Stanfield, Clarkson *Coastal Scenery of the British Channel* (Smith, Elder, 1836)

Thompson, Edward Palmer *The Making of the English Working Class* (Victor Gollancz, 1963)

Trevelyan, George Macaulay *English Social History: a Survey of Six Centuries Chaucer to Queen Victoria* (Longmans Green and Co., 1944)

A Shortened History of England (Penguin, 1959)

Williams, Neville John *Contraband cargoes–Seven Centuries of Smuggling* (Longmans, Green & Co., 1959)

Winslow, Cal *Sussex Smugglers*, in *Albion's Fatal Tree, Crime and Society in Eighteenth-Century England* (Allen Lane, 1975)

Wood, George Bernard *Smuggler's Britain* (Cassell, 1966)

THE SOUTH EAST

Allen, Edward Heron *Nature and History at Selsea Bill* (Elizabeth Gardner, 1911)

Banks, John *Reminiscences of smugglers and smuggling* (John Camden Hotten, 1873)

Barham, Richard *The Ingoldsby Legends* (Grant Richards, 1901)

Brent, Colin E. *Smuggling Through Sussex* (Lewes County Records Office, 1977)

Bullen, Mark *Sussex Coast Blockade for the Prevention of Smuggling* (1982)

Bullen, Mark *Ill-gotten gains: the romance and tragedy of Sussex smuggling 1700–1850* (1978)

Cheal, Henry *The Story of Shoreham* (Combridges, 1921)

Cheal, Henry *The Ships and Mariners of Shoreham* (Bysh, 1981)

Clark, Kenneth Michael *Smuggling in Rye and district* (Rye Museum Association, 1977)

Cousins, Henry *Hastings of Bygone Days – and the Present* (F.J. Parsons, 1911)

Daly, Gavin *English Smugglers, the Channel and the Napoleonic Wars, 1800–1814* from the *Journal of British Studies* 46 (January 2007) pages 30–46

Douch, John *Smuggling: The Wicked Trade* (Crabwell, 1980)

Douch, John *Smuggling; Rough Rude Men* (Crabwell, 1985)

English, John *English's Reminiscences of Old Folkestone Smugglers and Smuggling Days* (Folkestone, 1889)

Finn, Ralph *The Kent Coast Blockade* (W.E. White, 1971)

Finch, William Coles *The Medway, River and Valley* (C.W. Daniel Co., 1929)

Fleet, Charles *Glimpses of our ancestors in Sussex* (W.J. Smith, 1878)

Gentleman of Chichester *Smuggling & Smugglers in Sussex: The Genuine History of the inhuman and Unparalleled Murders of Mr. William Galley, A Custom-House Officer, and Mr. Daniel Chater,* (W.J. Smith, 1749)

Harvey, Wallace *The Seasalter Company – a Smuggling Fraternity, (1740–1854)* (Emprint, 1983)

Harvey, Wallace *Whitstable and the French Prisoners of War.* (Whitstable, 1971)

Hufton, Geoffrey, and Baird, Elaine *Scarecrow's Legion* (Rochester Press, 1983)

Kent County Library *Smuggling in Deal* (Kent County Library, 1984)

Lapthorne William H. *Smugglers' Broadstairs* (Thanet Antiquarian Book Club, 1970)

Martin, Frank *Rogues River* (Ian Henry Publications, 1983)

Middleton, Judy *A History of Hove* (Phillimore, 1979)

Musgrave, Clifford *Life in Brighton: from the earliest times to the present* (Hallewell, 1981)

Muskett, Paul *Smuggling in the Cinque Ports in the 16th century* (Cantium 2, 1970)

Pagden, Florence *A History of Alfriston* (Combridges, 1948)

Parry, John Docrwa *An historical and descriptive account of the coast of Sussex … Forming also a guide to all the watering places* (London, 1833)

Philip, Alexander John *History of Gravesend and its surroundings, from prehistoric times to the opening of the twentieth century …* (Stanley Paul & Co., 1914)

Piper, Alfred Cecil *Alfriston: the story of a Sussex downland village* (Muller, 1970)

Sayer, C.L. *The Sayer Manuscripts: a transcription of extracts from The Collier Papers* (unpublished: Customs & Excise Board Library)

Snewin, Edward *Glimpses of Old Worthing* (Aldridge Bros, 1945)

Warter, John Wood *The Sea-board and the Down; or, my Parish in the South* (London, 1860)

Waugh, Mary *Smuggling in Kent and Sussex 1700–1840* (Countryside Books, 1985)

THE SOUTH

Bettey, Joseph Harold *Dorset* (David & Charles, 1974)

Carson Edward A *Smugglers and Revenue Officers in the Portsmouth area in the Eighteenth Century* (Portsmouth City Council, 1974)

Chacksfield, K. Merle *Smuggling heritage – around Bournemouth: the romantic history of 'The gentlemen of the night'* (Bournemouth Tourist Information Centre, 1978)

Chackfield, Kathleen Merle *Smuggling Days* (Christchurch Times, 1969)

Coe, A. Farquharson *Hants and Dorset's smugglers* (James Pike, 1975)

Dowling, R.F.W. *Smuggling on Wight Island* (Smuggling Museum, Ventnor, Isle of Wight, 1978)

Forster, D. Arnold *At war with the smugglers* (Ward Lock & Co. Ltd, 1936)

Guttridge, Roger *Dorset Smugglers* (Dorset Publishing Company, 1984)

Hardy, Thomas *Thomas Hardy's notebooks with notes by Evelyn Hardy.* (Hogarth Press, 1955)

Hardy, William Masters *Smuggling days in Purbeck: the haunts, methods and adventures of Purbeck smugglers* (Purbeck Press, 1978)

Hutchings, Richard J. *Smugglers of the Isle of Wight* (Isle of Wight County Press, 1985)

Legg, Rodney *Purbeck Island. The industrial, social and natural history of a corner of England* (Dorset Publishing Co., 1972)

Lloyd, Rachel *Dorset Elizabethans. At home and abroad* (John Murray, 1967)

Macgregor, Robert *The Life ... of Rob Roy Macgregor ... To which is annexed ... original and authentic sketches of the Life ... of Capt. T. Johnstone, commonly called Johnstone the Smuggler* (Manchester, 1823)

Mew, Fred *Back of the Wight* (The County Press, Newport, 1951)

Morley, Geoffrey *Smuggling in Hampshire and Dorset 1700–1850* (Countryside Books, 1983)

Oakley, Russell *A Guide to Christchurch Priory and Castle, with notes on the harbour and fishing, and an account of the Christchurch smugglers* (R. Hulton & Co., 1920)

Oakley, E. Russell *The Smugglers of Christchurch Bourne Heath and the New Forest* (Hutchinson & Co. Ltd, 1942.)

Omand, William Donald *Chideock: its church, its saints, its martyrs and its sinners* (British Publishing Co., 1966)

Roberts, George *The History and Antiquities of the Borough of Lyme Regis and Charmouth* (London, 1834)

Short, Bernard Charles *Smugglers of Poole and Bournemouth* (Dorset Publishing Co., 1969)

Sydenham, John *The history of the town and county of Poole, etc.* (Poole, 1839)

Treves, Frederick *Highways and byways in Dorset* (Wildwood House, 1981)

Warne, Charles *Ancient Dorset: the celtic, roman, saxon and danish antiquities of the county including the early coinage* (D. Sydenham, 1872)

White, Allen *Eighteenth century smuggling in Christchurch* (Allen White, 1973)

Young, David S. *The Story of Bournemouth* (Robert Hale, 1957)

THE SOUTH WEST

Bottrell, William *Traditions and Hearthside Stories of West Cornwall, etc.* (Penzance, 1870–80)

Carter Harry *The autobiography of a Cornish smuggler ... With an introduction and notes by John B. Cornish* (Gibbings & Co., 1900)

Farquharson-Coe, A. *Devon's smugglers* (James Pike Ltd, 1975)

Couch, Jonathan *The History of Polperro, a fishing town on the south coast of Cornwall* (W. Lake, 1871)

Coxhead John Ralph Winter *Smuggling Days in Devon* (Raleigh Press, 1956)

Delderfield, Eric R. *Exmouth milestones* (The Raleigh Press, 1948)

Devonshire Association, *Transactions* v.67

Gay, Susan Elizabeth *Old Falmouth: The story of the town from the days of the Killigrews to the earliest part of the nineteenth century* (1903)

Gould, Sabine Baring *A Book of the West. Being an introduction to Devon and Cornwall* (Methuen & Co., 1899)

Gould, Sabine Baring, *Devonshire Characters and Strange Events* (John Lane, 1908)

Graham, Frank Moore *Smuggling in Cornwall* (Newcastle upon Tyne, 1964)

Graham, Frank Moore *Smuggling in Devon* (Newcastle upon Tyne, 1965)

Graham, Frank Moore *Cornish Smuggler's Tales* (Newcastle upon Tyne, 1967)

Harper, Charles George *Haunted Houses: tales of the Supernatural. With some account of hereditary curses and family legends* (Chapman & Hall, 1907)

Harvey, E.G. *Mullyon: its history, scenery and antiquities* (Lake, 1875)

Hawker, Robert Stephen *Footprints of Former Men in Far Cornwall* (London, 1870)

Hippisley Coxe, Anthony D. *A Book About Smuggling in the West Country* (Tabb House, 1984)

Jenkin, Alfred Kenneth Hamilton *The Cornish seafarers: the smuggling, wrecking and fishing life of Cornwall* (1932)

Jenkin, Alfred Kenneth Hamilton *Cornwall and its people* (David & Charles, 1988)

Jones, Evan T. *Illicit business: accounting for smuggling in mid-sixteenth-century Bristol in Economic History Review* LIV, 1 pp 17–38 (2001)

Jones, Penny *Smugglers' Tales: a Brief History of Smuggling In East Devon and West Dorset* (Nigel J. Clarke Publications, 1983)

Knight, Francis A. *The sea-board of Mendip* (Woodspring, 1988)

Matthews, John Hobson *A history of the parishes of St. Ives: Lelant, Towednack and Zennor: in the county of Cornwall* (Elliot Stock, 1892)

Newcombe, Lisa *Smuggling in Cornwall & Devon* (Jarrold & Sons, 1975)

Noall, Cyril *Smuggling in Cornwall* (D. Bradford Barton Ltd, 1971)

Page, William *The Victoria History of the County of Cornwall* (James Street, 1906)

Page, John Lloyd Warden *The coasts of Devon and Lundy Island* (Horace Cox, 1895)

Rattenbury, John *Memoirs of a Smuggler, compiled from his diary and journal: containing the principal events in the life of John Rattenbury* (J. Harvey, 1837)

Vivian, John *Tales of the Cornish smugglers* (Tor Mark Press, 1969)

WALES AND THE WEST

Aberystwyth and Cardiganshire Arch Society *Ceredigion* vol.VII (1972)

Awberry, Stanley Stephen *Let us talk of Barry* (Barry, 1954)

Bailey, Francis Arthur *A History of Southport* (Angus Downie, 1955)

Chappell, Edgar L. *History of the port of Cardiff* (Priory Press, 1939)

Country Quest (Wrexham) Aug 1976

East, Robert *Choice chips of revenue lore. Being papers relating to the establishment
    of the Excise, exsise duties … Also cullings from Excise general letters of the last
    century.* (Hampshire Telegraph Printing Works, 1877)

Dawson, James William *Commerce and Customs. A history of the ports of Newport
    and Caerleon* (R.H. Johns, 1932)

Eames, Aled *Ships and seamen of Anglesey 1558–1918: studies in maritime and local
    history* (National Maritime Museum, 1981)

Edmunds, George *The Gower Coast: Shipwrecks, lifeboats & rescues, history, mystery &
    legend, smuggling, beaches, castles & caves …* (Publications, 1986)

Ellis, Hugh Rees *Rhwng môr a mynydd* (cyhoeddwyd gan Gyngor Gwlad
    Môn, 1961)

Gibbon, Ronald T. *'To the King's deceit'* (Friends of Whitehaven Museum, 1983)

Gower Journal Vol. XXIV (Swansea, 1973)

Hawkes, G.I. *Illicit trading in Wales in the Eighteenth Century* (in Maritime Wales,
    Gwynedd Archive Service vol. 10, 1986)

Historic Society of Lancashire & Cheshire Transactions 1927

Irving, Gordon *The Solway Smugglers* (Robert Dinwiddie, 1972)

Jarvis, Rupert Charles *Customs Letter-Books of the Port of Liverpool, 1711–1813* (Chetham
    Society, 1954)

John, Brian Stephen *Pembrokeshire* (David & Charles, 1976)

Lancashire and Cheshire Antiquarian Soceity *Transactions vol. 58* (Manchester, 1945)

Laws, Edward *The History of Little England Beyond Wales and the Non-Kymric Colony
    Settled in Pembrokeshire* (George Bell & Sons, 1888)

Manx Museum *Myles Crowe the Smuggler* (Journal of the Manx Museum Vol.VII No. 88,
    1976)

National Library of Wales *Cylchgrawn Llyfrgell Genedlaethol Cymru*, 1985,Vol. 24 No. 1

Owen, Hugh John *The Treasures of Mawddach* (Robert Evans & Sons, 1950)

Phillips, David Rhys *The History of the Vale of Neath, a Romantic Valley in Wales*
    (Swansea, 1925)

Qualtrough, John Karran *'That Island'* (Victoria Press, 1965)

Rees, David (ed.) *Gower Anthology* (C. Davies, Swansea, 1977)

Roberts, B. Dew *Mr. Bulkeley and the Pirate. A Welsh diarist of the eighteenth century*
    (Oxford University Press, 1936)

Spencer, Marianne Robertson *Annals of South Glamorgan: historical, legendary and
    descriptive chapters on some leading places of interest* (W. Spurrel & Son, 1913)

Stonehouse, James *Recollections of old Liverpool, by a Nonagenarian* (Reprinted from the *Liverpool Compass*; J.F. Hughes, 186.)

Thomas, David *Hen longau Sir Gaernarfon* (Cymdeithas Hanes Sir Gaernarfon, 1952)

Trevelyan, Marie *Glimpses of Welsh Life and Character* (J. Hogg, 1894)

Tucker, Horatio Middleton *Gower Gleanings* (Gower Society, 1951)

Vale, Edmund *The World of Wales* (J.M. Dent & Sons Ltd, 1935)

Waters, Ivor *The port of Chepstow* (The Chepstow Society, 1977)

Watkins, K.C. *Welsh smugglers* (James Pike Ltd, 1975)

Wilkins, Charles of Merthyr Tydfil *Tales and Sketches of Wales* (Cardiff, 1879)

Williams, Stewart (ed.) *South Glamorgan – A County History* (Stewart Williams, Publishers, 1975)

Wood, John Maxwell *Smuggling in the Solway and around the Galloway Sea-board* (J. Maxwell & Son, 1908)

EAST AND NORTH EAST

Baring-Gould, Sabine *Mehalah: a story of the salt marshes* (Bernhard Tauchnitz, 1881)

Benham, Hervey *The Smugglers' Century* (Essex Record Office, 1986)

Benton, Philip *The History of Rochford Hundred* (A. Harrington, 1867–88.)

Brown, Herbert *History of Bradwell-on-Sea, Essex* (J.H. Clarke & Co., 1929)

Chadwick, Esther Alice *Mrs. Gaskell: haunts, homes, and stories* (Pitman & Sons, 1913)

Chandler, Lewis *Smuggling at Sizewell Gap* (Leiston Abbey Press, 1960)

Dutt, William Alfred *The Norfolk and Suffolk Coast* (Unwin, 1909)

Dykes, Jack *Smuggling on the Yorkshire coast* (Dalesman, 1978)

Harriott, John *Struggles through Life, exemplified in the various travels and adventures in Europe, Asia, Africa and America* (London, 1815)

Jarvis, Stan *Smuggling in East Anglia, 1700–1840* (Countryside Books, 1987)

Kime, Winston *Skeggy! The story of an East Coast town* (Seashell Books, 1969)

Knights, Edward S. *Essex folk: tales from village, farm and marsh* (Heath Cranton, 1935)

Morgan, Glyn Howis *The Romance of Essex Inns* (Essex Countryside, 1963)

Robinson, David N. *The book of the Lincolnshire seaside: the story of the coastline from the Humber to the Wash* (Barracuda, 1981)

Roe, Fred *Essex Survivals, with special attention to Essex smugglers* (Methuen & Co., 1929)

Ruscoe E.H. *Ruscoe's Illustrated Guide to Mablethorpe, Sutton, Louth, Alford ...* (Louth, 1889)

Skinner, John *The Life and behaviour of John Skinner, who was executed Aug. 29, 1746, at Chelmsford in Essex, for the murder of D. Brett ...* (London, 1746)

Thompson, Leonard P. *Smugglers of the Suffolk coast* (Brett Valley Publications, 1968)

Weaver, Leonard Thomas *The Harwich story* (Dovercourt, 1975)

SCOTLAND

Allardyce, John *Bygone Days in Aberdeenshire Being a History of the County from a Standpoint Different from That of Previously Published Works* (Central Press, 1913)

Anderson, George *Kingston-on-Spey* (Oliver & Boyd, 1957)

Anon *Dundee and Dundonians Seventy Years ago: being personal reminiscences of an old Dundonian* (J.P. Mathew & Co.: Dundee, 1892)

Clark, Victoria Elizabeth *The Port of Aberdeen. A history of its trade and shipping from the 12th century* (D. Wyllie & Son, 1921)

Cullen, L.M. *Anglo-Irish trade 1660–1800* (Manchester University Press, 1968)

Cuthbertson, David *The Smugglers of Troon. Including the authentic adventures of Matthew Hay, of the Holms Farm, Dundonald, Ayrshire ...* (J. Menzies & Co., 1927)

Dixon, David Dippie *Upper Coquetdale, Northumberland: its history, traditions, folk-lore nd scenery* (Sandhill, c.1987)

Douglas, George Brisbane Scott *A History of the Border Counties, Roxburgh, Selkirk, Peebles* (Transactions of the Dumfries & Galloway Nat Hist & Antiquarian, 1926)

Dunbar, Edward *Social Life in former days: chiefly in the province of Moray* (Edmonston & Douglas, 1865)

Eunston, George *The ancient and present state of Orkney, particularly the capital borough of Kirkwall. To which are added, the Petty Tyrants or grinders of the poor* (Newcastle-upon-Tyne, 1788)

Grant, James (compiler) *Records of the county of Banff, 1660–1760* (New Spalding club, 1922)

Grewar, David *Story of Glenisla* (1926)

Hall, James *Travels in Scotland, by an unusual route: with a trip to the Orkneys and Hebrides* (J. Johnson, 1807)

Hewat, Kirkwood *In the Olden Times: being papers on places and people of the past* (A. Gardner, 1898)

Imlach, James *History of Banff and familiar account of its inhabitants and belongings; to which are added, chronicles of the old churchyard of Banff* (Banff, 1868)

Leask, J.T. Smith *A Peculiar People, and other Orkney tales* (W.R. Mackintosh, 1931)

Maciver, Daniel *An Old-Time Fishing Town: Eyemouth. Its history, romance, and tragedy* (James M'Kelvie & Sons, 1906)

Mackintosh, Ian M. *Old Troon and district* (George Outram & Co., 1969)

McDowall, William *History of the burgh of Dumfries: With notices of Nithsdale, Annandale and the western border* (A. & C. Black, 1873)

MacLean, Charles *The fringe of gold: the fishing villages of Scotland's East Coast, Orkney & Shetland* (Canongate, 1985)

Neville, Hastings M. *A corner in the North: yesterday and to-day with border folk* (F. Graham, 1980)

Pratt, Rev. John B. *Buchan* (Heritage Press, 1978)

Sillett, Stephen W. *Illicit Scotch* (Impulse Books, 1970)

Simmons, Jean *Scottish smugglers* (James Pike Ltd, 1975)
Smith, Hance D. *Shetland life and trade, 1550–1914* (Donald, 1984)
Thomson, William *The Smuggling Era in Scotland.* (1910)

INDEX